His Dear Time's Waste

A 1950s Literary and Love Life Memoir

STUART HOLROYD

His Dear Time's Waste

Published by Obscuriosity Press

2nd Edition

Copyright © Stuart Holroyd
All rights reserved. No part of this publication may be reproduced, stored in a retrieval system, or transmitted in any form or by any means, electronic, mechanical, photocopying, recording or otherwise, without the prior written permission of the publisher and/or author.

This edition published in the United Kingdom in 2014 by Obscuriosity Press under the PHOENIX imprint.
obscuriositypress@gmail.com

978-0-9928696-9-4

ABOUT THE AUTHOR

Stuart Holroyd in his own words

Inaptly called an 'angry young man' in the late 1950s, having precociously written a book on modern poets, an 'autobiography of ideas' and an existentialist play, without a trace of anger in any of them. Improbably morphed into family man, educational entrepreneur (school of languages) and text-book author in the 1960s. Improvidently resumed writing full-time in the 1970s, whoring in the literary market place to turn out books on the paranormal, alien intelligence, alternative or 'new age' lifestyles, therapies, sex and what-have-you, as well as a personal memoir (precursor of the present book) and a book on the life and philosophy of Krishnamurti. Inevitably went through a mid-life crisis in the 1980s, resulting in collapse of marriage and business, a new relationship and new life in new places, happy itinerant years and eventual coming to roost in the south of France. Impertinently thought that an old man's recollections of life and love in times past might be for some readers, well, still pertinent. Incorrigibly, having become re-infected with the writing bug, now working on a proper novel.

His Dear Time's Waste
A 1950s Literary and Love Life Memoir

For Gyll

When to the sessions of sweet silent thought
I summon up remembrance of things past,
I sigh the lack of many a thing I sought,
And with old woes new wail my dear time's waste;
Then can I drown an eye (unused to flow)
For precious friends lost in death's dateless night
And weep again love's long since cancell'd woe,
And moan th'expense of many a vanished sight;

William Shakespeare
Sonnet No. 30

PROLOGUE

It was a time of fleeting fame, of stupendous follies and of fretful and fateful love affairs. It was his youth, the time of his life when infinite possibilities narrowed down to very finite realities. He had kept a journal, written and received numerous letters, self-importantly squirrelled it all away. At the time, the way that events were shaping up into a narrative was not obvious, but later it stood out. He wrote it down, ransacking his memory, his journals and letters, for the details, elaborating a bit here and there, particularly in the dialogue, which however was always characteristic of the speaker. It was an unreliable memoir, but a true story, set in an age now slipping into history, nostalgically regarded by some as an age of innocence, though that was not how it appeared at the time.

INTRODUCTION

by A. N. Other

I undertake this task with some reservations, my reluctance having succumbed to the persuasion that there is no one left this side of paradise better qualified to perform it. My qualification is that I have been a friend of SH, though not always a close one, since we were at school together, and also that I have some literary credentials as an academic with a few rather specialised and recondite publications to my name. For the present purpose I have chosen to assume the old cricketing pseudonym for the anonymous and insignificant 'twelfth man'.

Appropriately, I think: I never did entertain the delusion that I might aspire to the first eleven. Nor, I imagine, did SH, at least until he got swept up in the Angry Young Man mania.

In his short Prologue to the present memoir he speaks of his 'fleeting fame'. 'Fleeting' is an apt term for a period of some five years, back then in the 1950s, but 'fame' is an altogether more slippery and anomalous thing. SH wasn't particularly outstanding when we were at school. He wrote some creditable essays and achieved distinctions in exams and could probably have got into Cambridge, as I did, but then he went off and joined a theatre, and the next I heard, some five years later, he had published a book and was being talked of as one of the 'Angry Young Men'. I read the book, it was called *Emergence from*

Chaos, a series of essays on modern poets yoked together by some theory of the variety of religious experiences, and so far as I could make out there wasn't a smidgen of anger in it and as literary criticism it certainly wouldn't have cut the mustard in Cambridge. But soon afterwards he was popping up on television, and in the newspapers and weeklies, and I couldn't help but wonder whether all that fame, notoriety, celebrity or whatever you might call it, would have come his way if it hadn't been for the literary mini-boom of 'angry young mania'. It really was a phenomenon to wonder at.

I was far removed from the London literary scene, a junior lecturer in English at a provincial university, but I followed the developments and read the books with avid interest. They were a motley bunch, the 'Angries', with little more in common than contempt for 'the Establishment' , a term then used for a supposed cabal of diehard traditionalist dullards in the political, social, ecclesiastical, literary and philosophical worlds whose prejudices, mean and petty occupations and aspirations, and sclerotic complacencies and snobberies they hated and reviled. It may be said that youth was ever so, but what was different from other generational divides was that with the help and connivance of the Press, which had its own anti-Establishment agenda, the young writers of the mid-1950s made unprecedentedly rapid progress in destabilising the Establishment apple-cart.

It began in the theatre, with the success of John Osborne's play *Look Back in Anger*, whose anti-hero lead character, Jimmy Porter, railed for the play's duration against the vapid mediocrity of British society and institutions, turning his scorn and anger mainly upon his wife Alison, whose upper-middle-class background he excoriates, regardless of the fact that her marrying him was an act of rebellion against it. Jimmy Porter was not a likeable character, but his was a new voice in the theatre, combining with its raw savagery a saving grace of eloquence and wit. As the novelist Alan Sillitoe put it, Osborne 'didn't contribute to the British theatre, he set a landmine under it and blew most of it up'.

Well, that was how it seemed at the time, particularly to Osborne's young contemporaries, although the supposed victims of the bomb-blast, such as Terence Rattigan and Noel Coward, have posthumously proved surprisingly indestructible, with successfully long-running revivals in the London theatre. But in the latter half of the 1950s the type of the disaffected, radical, bellicose, non-conformist and angry young man was generally believed to be so typical of the post-war generation that any writer who appeared on the literary scene might well be disposed to play up the role, as I think SH to an extent did. I noticed it the first time I met him subsequent to our schooldays, in a dingy Notting Hill café in '59, when he was riding the crest of the wave with his play at the Royal Court Theatre and a new book coming out in the summer: his manner was more assertive, opinionated and uncompromising than I had expected of my rather unworldly and poetry-loving old friend, and towards me, though he was welcoming and friendly enough, I felt he was ill-concealing a tendency to be aloof and patronising. I recall that I came away feeling that the meeting had been a mistake and regretting that I had written to him to propose it, I was surprised, some time later, to receive an invitation to the launch party for his second book, *Flight and Pursuit*.

Retrospectively, the Angry Young Man thing does look like a media hype, a flash in the cultural pan, but when you think of it the 1950s was quite a remarkable time in the London literary world. The later Nobel laureates Harold Pinter (2005), Doris Lessing (2007) and Wole Soyinka (1986) were all at work in London and had productions at the Royal Court Theatre, and V. S. Naipaul (2001), who had been a contender with SH for the John Llewellyn Rhys Memorial Prize in 1958, was publishing his first (and in my opinion best) novels. And none of these luminaries-to-be was at the time counted among the 'Angries', (although Doris Lessing contributed an essay to the touted Angry manifesto, *Declaration*, which I gather she had been asked to do as the token female or maybe, considering her robust views, as an honorary male).

Whatever else the 'Angries' may have been angry about, they tended to spend their most scathing ire upon one another. Although the older generation critics Cyril Connolly and Philip Toynbee heaped extravagant praise upon Colin Wilson's *The Outsider*, the author's near-contemporary Kingsley Amis dismissed the book's prototype as adolescent, self-obsessed and needing to cure his condition by 'ordering up another bottle, attending a jam session, or getting introduced to a young lady'. No literary camaraderie or common cause there, though it could be taken with the proverbial pinch, allowing for Amis's cultivated role-playing as the no-nonsense curmudgeon. There were no mitigating circumstances, though, when factions of the 'Angries' came into direct confrontation, as they did at the Royal Court in the scene SH recounts in his first chapter. Far from being a Movement with a shared agenda, they were on such occasions more like a quarrelsome family.

To permit myself a personal confession here: I was more a fan of Amis than of Wilson and felt rather as he did about *The Outsider*. I had read *Lucky Jim* when it came out in 1954, two years before Osborne and Wilson were heard of, and had immediately identified with the anti-hero Jim Dixon, who like me was a junior lecturer at a provincial university and in order to secure job tenure after the first year was forced to kow-tow to inept and pretentious superiors and turn out essays that threw 'pseudo-light on non-problems'. That phrase seemed to me critically apposite to *The Outsider*, though I wouldn't deny that I was impressed by the range of Wilson's reading, particularly in modern European literature, and by his reputation as an autodidact who had slept out on Hampstead Heath and cycled daily to the British Museum Reading Room to write his book. That represented him as an exemplary Outsider indeed, though a dauntingly earnest one, and I was no more disposed to emulate or aspire to the type than I imagined Jim Dixon would have been.

What the 'Angries' had in common was a working or lower-middle-class background and in most cases, whether by choice or circumstance, lack of a university education. They were bright, intelligent and capable, obviously, but the fact of having got where they were by virtue of their own talents and initiatives made them prone to an attitude of intolerance and superiority towards those of their generation who had pursued a more conventional course of advancement.

Although I am aware that this may be a personal opinion based on my feeling when I met SH in the café and reinforced by my later meeting his friend Colin Wilson, I believe there is enough of a general truth in it to let it stand. In turn one can be indulgent at my age, and recall with a smile the disagreeable qualities of cock-a-hoop youth, which at the time seemed positively repellent. But I do think that arrogance in an individual can get grotesquely exaggerated by his belonging to a group which fancies itself to be a 'movement'. Writers, with rare exceptions, reflect change rather than effect it, and it is one of the more pernicious romantic fallacies for them to imagine that they are the 'unacknowledged legislators' or the fundamental 'movers and shakers' of the world. When the journalist Kenneth Allsop, in his book *The Angry Decade*, bunched together Colin Wilson, SH and Bill Hopkins under the chapter title *The Law Givers*, there was an implicit sneer in the appellation. Literary schools, coteries or movements tend to be regarded with suspicion by English critics, distrusted as a continental thing, and Wilson and SH were courting opprobrium when they called themselves 'English Existentialists'.

They did so knowingly and challengingly rather than naively, however. What they saw as the parochialism, complacency and superficiality of 'little England', compared with the challenging intellectual daring, profundity and relevance of the post-war continental philosophers and novelists was the nub of such anger as they felt. In *Flight and Pursuit* SH derided what he called 'the disenchanted generation', the youngish survivors of WW2 who were disillusioned by what Britain had become, by the squalor, the poverty, the prevailing gloom and greyness, the rationing, the institutional dominance of a washed-up, apathetic and moribund yet older generation, but were content to express their disenchantment in mere facetiousness, flippancy and satire. He picked on Kingsley Amis as the prototype of the writer whose work was an implicit 'denial that life has any moral basis or metaphysical significance.' Amis and his kind, he said, (John Wain, another contributor to *Declaration,* was also skewered as a literary miscreant) couldn't hold a candle to the likes of Jean-Paul Sartre or Albert Camus.

I did wonder, when I read this, what had become of the SH I had known, who had loved the farcical tales of P. G. Wodehouse and radio comedy programmes like *ITMA* and *Much Binding in the Marsh* and had once even written a script for the comedian Terry Thomas. The change to such earnest high-mindedness suggested that Existentialism was as pernicious a continental contagion as the Spanish flu. I suspected that he must have caught it from his friend Colin Wilson.

My first meeting with the author of *The Outsider* was at the aforementioned launch party for *Flight and Pursuit*, held in the run-down Notting Hill house that SH describes at the beginning of the second chapter of the present book. It was a summer's evening and when I arrived the high sash windows on the first floor were open and the hubbub of voices could be heard in the street. Up the stairs the door with the notice 'Beware of the Doggerel' was also open and the room beyond was packed with clusters of standing literati who collectively produced an animated cacophony that I found quite intimidating. I might have turned and given the occasion a miss if SH had not caught sight of me hovering in the doorway and hauled me over to join a small group around CW, who greeted me with jovial familiarity, thrust a brimming glass of red wine from the table behind him into my hand, and said, 'Ah yes, Stuart's school chum. He's told me about how you used to compete with one another to find the most titillating quotes in English poetry.'

I remember that, oddly, but nothing else from the subsequent conversation, except the impression that CW was off duty as the egghead of formidable repute, and far from being the Outsider appeared to be very much inside and at ease with the present company. It was not, as I had expected, an AYM gathering, none of the *Declaration* contributors were there, except SH, CW and Bill Hopkins, and most of the people were of an older generation, writers, publishers, journalists and critics, among whom I did recognise a few, a well-known poet of the '30s, an academic 'talking head' recalled from TV appearances, and the novelist John Braine. It was, I suppose, quite a distinguished turnout for the launch of SH's book, copies of which were in a box under a table and were given out selectively to people as they left, potential reviewers presumably. I was not favoured, and had to wait to borrow a library copy some months later, and later still picked up a cheap remaindered one. The publication was not a success, either critically or commercially, despite the enthusiasm of the venerable publisher Victor Gollancz (who was also at the party) for what he touted on the cover as the young author's 'hard-fought rediscovery of God and religion and the sense of social and human responsibility that ensues.' Gollancz was a shrewd and successful publisher who had both Amis's *Lucky Jim* and Wilson's *Outsider* to his credit, but if he thought that his description might help bring his firm another big seller he must have been deluded either by his own religious bias or by a misreading of the *zeitgeist* and the prevalence of 'angry young mania'.

I can imagine a reader asking at this point why I am writing this Introduction, since I seemingly do not have a high regard for SH's work. I would answer that my remit was to put the present work in context, to sketch out the 1950s background to the tale, and furthermore I write because the present book is different from the published works of the AYM days, and better. I call it a tale, and indeed such it is, a love story, a *Bildungsroman*, a coming-of-age story, a candid, sometimes funny, often moving tale of a love-life triangle, a rather English story really, uncontaminated by even a whiff of a continental Big Idea. It is also a memoir, albeit as SH admits, an unreliable one, for there is some time-shuffling of events in the interest of narrative coherence and development, and there is quite a lot of dialogue which to have recalled verbatim would have required a supernormal memory. It is not within my competence to say whether or not there may be some lying – not an uncommon thing in memoirs - but there is certainly a good deal of invention, or what we may supportively call being creative with the truth.

SH seems to be very fond of F words, (though not of the F word used with such lexical versatility in the present-day vernacular). After his 'fleeting fame', he mentioned in his Prologue his 'fretful and fateful love affairs', which as I have indicated above is what the book is fundamentally about. I have to put in a caveat here, for the 21st century reader. In the 1950s that other F word, feminism, had not yet been appropriated to define a cause or movement, and the social circumstances and male attitudes that led to its being so appropriated were still pretty well entrenched. Girls were, for the 1950s young male, virtually an alien species, objects of adoration, lustful aspiration, wonder and mystery on the one hand, or on the other hand creatures to be scorned, ignored or feared, the two attitudes being largely determined by the individual female's physical attributes, a pretty face and a substantial bust being qualifiers for elevation to a pedestal while the plain and the skinny would be relegated to a disregarded limbo. The international hit musical of the '50s, *My Fair Lady*, said it all, with the metamorphosis of Eliza Doolittle from cockney slut to pedestalled society darling, her father Alfred's lament on his wedding day that 'with a little bit of luck… you can have it all and not get hooked', and Henry Higgins's catalogue of the dire consequences of 'letting a woman in your life'. I would not claim that at the time I was innocent of such attitudes. Nor was SH, and I put in this caveat by way of preparing the reader for some passages that may provoke a rebarbative shock, but might preferably be regarded as typical of the period and even as illustrative of where feminism was coming from when it burgeoned in the 1960s.

Innocent, I just said, and in his Prologue SH said that the '50s was 'an age of innocence.' The word can mean unknowing, naïve, or alternatively, irreproachable, not guilty, and in the latter sense I doubt that it could be attributed to any age, notwithstanding the claims of Rousseau and the book of Genesis. But innocence in the sense of having limits or lacunae of knowledge, being blissfully or burdensomely naïve, specifically in the sexual/moral area, can be attributed to an age, and appropriately I think to the 1950s. The 'facts of life' were conveyed to young people then either by parents with embarrassed or awkward evasions, by teachers with clinical biological frankness, or by other youths who themselves knew little and put what they did know in crude terms that were only good for a giggle. Generally speaking, the imperatives of adolescent hormonal turbulence were the principle drivers of knowledge, but what they didn't teach young lads was that girls underwent the same turbulence of feelings, and moreover (inconceivable, this) that they were endowed with an organ of pleasure quite as excitable, sensitive and demanding as the male penis. The unruly nature of the male member, its tendency to unwonted arousal or emission and its unlovely assertiveness, compared with girls' soft contours and discreet pudenda, further reinforced the view of the female as adorably different, to be worshipped as in the love songs of the day, but also as passive, compliant, a receiver rather than a giver in the sexual act, destined by nature for childbearing and homemaking, and by corollary not creative in the spheres of the arts or sciences (with a few allowable exceptions that 'proved the rule') or capable of abstract thought. It was a view that pervaded the culture, and that in itself validates the designation 'an age of innocence'.

It was also a view that boded trouble, and indeed it brought double trouble for SH, as he relates in this book. The root of his trouble was that the stereotypical passive woman was not the kind that he was attracted to, even though friends tried to persuade him that such was the type best suited to a dedicated writer's needs. Furthermore, he had written a concluding chapter of *Flight and Pursuit* titled *Responsibilities* in which he had effectively philosophised himself into a corner regarding the moral implications of sexually bonded relations. In the book the discussion was cool and confident, but the argument evaporated into hot air in the real life situation that soon ensued, and the cool philosopher was reduced to an emotionally muddled and tormented young man torn between two women, a not uncommon situation either in life or literature, where it has often been played out, both as comedy and tragedy.

There is neither tragedy nor comedy in *His Dear Time's Waste*, but there is humour and there are highly charged emotional scenes. But I overstep my brief, which was to set the book in its background, which I hope I may have done helpfully for any readers for whom the 1950s is a past like 'another country'.

I conclude with a couple of points of necessary clarification. First, with regard to the book: in the early 1970s SH wrote a novel based on his life in the '50s. His publishers asked him to recast it as a frank first-person memoir, which he did and it was duly published with the title *Contraries* (Bodley Head, London, 1976). In 2008 the manuscript of the original novel turned up among a mass of other papers when his son was clearing the attic of a London house that he was selling. They were papers which SH had left in his keeping at the time of his marriage and business failures in the early 1980s. Prompted by their re-discovery, SH embarked on the present book, incorporating previously rejected sections of the novel with the text of *Contraries*, and adding some retrospective views.

Second, with regard to myself: I said at the beginning that I had been a friend of SH from our schooldays 'but not always a close one'. Well, by virtue of a preposterously improbable serendipity, it has turned out that in recent years we have been closer than ever before, living in villages in the south of France less than a couple of hours' drive apart. Both retired of course, in fact both octogenarians, but still writing, as the present book attests. We exchange visits three or four times a year, reminisce, talk about literature, old and new, the writers enduringly beloved and current ones who have impressed, and lament the passing of mutual friends and other contemporaries. On a recent such visit, having read the present book in manuscript, I suggested the title *His Dear Time's Waste*, from Shakespeare's 30th Sonnet, as an alternative to SH's working title, *The Time of His Life*, which I thought misleading, suggestive of a rather jolly time. Maybe 'waste' is conversely misleading, but 'dear times' they were in many ways, as youth always is in retrospect, whatever tribulations may have seemed to blight it at the time.

1

One of the things that irritated me about Joan after I had fallen out of love with her was that she seemed to attract misfortune. Things just didn't go right for her. She was always having money stolen or losing her stupid little Pekingese, or getting the curse on the very day when she had to go for a crucial audition. At first I just thought she was unlucky and vulnerable and I wanted to protect her, and even when I came to think of her as irredeemably one of life's unfortunates I couldn't have conceived that I was to be her greatest misfortune ever.

Her mother had died some months before and she had been looking after her father, a doctor in Leigh-on-Sea. She wanted to be an actress, to go to London and take the theatre by storm. Finally her father took on a housekeeper and let her go. She rented a room in the Notting Hill area, near us, and happened to meet my friend, Bill Hopkins, who brought her round to the house one afternoon. She was twenty-two and had been in London for three weeks. I was twenty-four and had behind me a broken marriage, some half-dozen affairs, two published books and a play performed at the Royal Court Theatre, which together had earned me a reputation as a prodigy miraculously sprung from the lump of the working class. This was in the late 1950s when it advantaged a writer, with publishers and the press alike, to be plebeian, impoverished, arrogant, self-educated, angry and earnest. I ticked all those boxes, though I was rather deficient in the anger department, notwithstanding my being co-opted by the media into the ranks of the so-called 'angry young men'. I was not so much angry as rather smug and self-satisfied, a condition that prematurely successful autodidacts, never having had to sharpen and pit their wits among peers and mentors, are particularly prone to. In my case, however, it was about to be thoroughly chastened.

Despite my affairs and a four-year marriage, which had been founded on adolescent sex and cemented by poverty, I felt that in all my relationships there had been an important element missing. I suppose Joan too was ready for a true love affair, as expressed in poetry and popular song, at her age and after her sheltered life. When we had broken up I told myself that there had been about our affair from the start something theatrical, that we were hamming it a bit, acting like great lovers, kidding ourselves and each other. But perhaps both of us wanted from life at that time an experience that went deep, that gave us a sense of really living rather than skimming the surface of life, and perhaps the wish was strong enough to create the illusion.

I found her beautiful, though she was not conventionally so, not in the manner of the current cinematic sirens, Marilyn Monroe and Brigitte Bardot. But her long dark hair, which she wore sometimes drawn back in a chignon and sometimes loosely tumbling, and her large brown and expressive eyes, captivated me, as did a figure of pleasing amplitude. She was ambitious and had a serious turn of mind, but there was nothing wary or knowing about her, in fact an air of innocence was perhaps the core of her appeal.

I was so stricken that I was rash enough to tell Bill that I was in love, which elicited a characteristic reproof:

'An absurd and undignified condition. It results in impairment of judgment, loss of drive, criminal squandering of time and energy. To say you're in love is to confess to being a mediocrity.'

There was never anything tentative about Bill, and he was never at a loss for words or an opinion. He was Welsh, from a theatrical background, and in conversation was dramatic, entertaining, eloquent and combative. He chain-smoked thin, hand-rolled cigarettes, was usually unshaven and tousle-haired, and had a kind of ravaged look that went well with his wild genius image but was probably produced by malnutrition, sleeplessness and excessive smoking. He had written poetry in his teens, published in small literary magazines that sprang up and subsided like mayflies in Soho in the 1950s, had had a successful career as a journalist on a national paper in his early twenties, from which he had resigned to become a novelist and propagandist. He had recently published his novel, *The Divine and the Decay*, a tale of political and sexual callousness and infamy that the critics had unanimously savaged, raising a wave of derision and opprobrium that would have sunk a less resilient or more sensitive soul, but which Bill rode defiantly, regarding it as an inverse tribute to the singularity of his genius. Despite fundamental differences in character and outlook, we were close friends at the time, and secretly I both envied him for his articulateness and extroversion and scorned him for his unflagging hilarity and overdeveloped sense of the dramatic.

Bill, Tom Greenwell and I had rooms in a shabby house in Notting Hill, and there was a spare room which Colin Wilson and John Braine shared the rent of in order to have a *pied-à-terre* in town. The social centre of the house was Tom Greenwell's room. Tom was unique among us in that he had no pretentions to genius. He had a genius, however, for friendship, and he would dispense to all comers, at all times of day and night, tea, wine when he could afford it, and conversation, which he regarded as an art. Although he was not physically attractive – his nose was rather long, his ears large and his cheeks cadaverous, a combination that got him tagged as 'Mephistophelian' – he counted among his friends some of the most glamorous women in London society. He said that he had been born out of his age and should have lived in the London of Queen Anne's day, and he probably would have held his own with the likes of Pope, Addison and Swift. He worked for the *Evening Standard* newspaper's gossip column, 'In London Last Night', and served as our hot line to Fleet Street, and he wrote for his own amusement sharp little satires in rhymed couplets. The door of his room bore the notice, 'Beware of the Doggerel'. He knew *Omar Khayyám* and a lot of eighteenth century verse by heart, and he affected dandyish waistcoats and a long cigarette-holder.

It was a kind of game with us in the house to mock and expose each other's pretensions. Bill had a way of dropping his chin on his chest and looking at you fixedly and in silence from under his heavy brows, which said, 'Come off it, you can't kid me'. He gave me this look when I told him how I felt about Joan and followed it with his remark about a confessed lover being a mediocrity. We were in Tom's room at the time, and he went on:

'Greta said I should never have introduced you to Joan.'

Greta was his girl-friend, or rather companion for there seemed to be no sexual aspect to their relationship. She lived in one of the small rooms on the top floor, where she worked all day tinting steel engravings for an antique dealer. She scarcely ever ate anything, but lived largely on some slimming compound that she bought from the chemist's. She was wraith-like and unhealthy-looking and smoked incessantly. I knew that she had never approved of me, that she found my keen enjoyment of both food and sex rather gross, and it was typical of her to urge Bill to keep poor innocent Joan out of my clutches.

'Go on, Bill,' Tom said, 'can't you see Stuart's in love? He's gone all soft and romantic and idealistic over this one. Can't you see that stupid, dewy look?

God preserve me from love, all that tumult in the soul, all those soarings and plungings. No thanks, not for me. Love is the wisdom of the fool and the folly of the wise.'

Bill slapped the arm of his chair and laughed. 'Well put, Tom,' he said.

'Not original, dear boy,' he said. 'Acknowledgements are due to my friend Sam Johnson. But it puts it very neatly. And hell, why try to be original? It's all been said before.'

This was said in his contentious tone and accompanied by a flourish of his cigarette holder. Lying on his divan bed, propped up by pillows, he went on: 'We live in a fortunate time. We're the inheritors of centuries of high civilisation, and as we're going to blow ourselves up before long we might as well just enjoy our inheritance.'

Bill's brow furrowed. Joan and I were forgotten. Tom had given the signal that a conversation was about to be embarked on.

'The trouble with you, Tom,' Bill said, 'is that you aren't creative.'

'Don't I create reputations in my column?' Tom countered. 'Not only that, but I destroy them too. I am Savitri and Kali, creator and destroyer.'

'Don't be frivolous, Tom,' Bill said with measured calmness. 'The trouble with uncreative people like you is that you really value life so little that you're capable of sitting back complacently enjoying your precious civilisation and waiting for the big bang to come. You won't *do* anything.'

'What can anyone *do*?' Tom said. 'It's all pre-ordained. Remember *Omar Khayyám*...'

But before he could launch into the quotation, Bill cut in with a mocking laugh: 'Omar bloody *Khayyám*! Don't quote that mindless wog junkie to me in support of your craven fatalism.'

'Wog yourself,' Tom flashed back. 'Bloody Welshman!'

I crept out of the room at that point. They could go on for hours, and I wasn't in the mood to be an audience to a freewheeling conversation that was really a contest of wits. I was in love, and they, mere men of words, could waste their breath on each other.

One of Bill's schemes at this time was to take over a small theatre in Westbourne Grove which had been empty for some time. He had approached the owners 'on behalf of a syndicate of well-known writers' to negotiate a lease, and by way of persuading them that the project was viable he had referred them to the national publicity that had accompanied the performance of my play *The Tenth Chance*, at the Royal Court Theatre some months before. The Royal Court was at the time the most celebrated theatre in London, mainly on account of the innovative management of the directors George Devine and Tony Richardson and the ground-breaking success of their first production, John Osborne's *Look Back in Anger* in 1956. One of their innovations was to try out plays by new writers on Sunday evening

'Productions without Decor'. I don't think Bill mentioned to the Westbourne Grove theatre owners that my play had been one of these one-off productions, but rather had made much of the publicity it had spawned.

The occasion had made me briefly something of celebrity and had contributed to the media merriment of the year. Not that there was anything merry about the play itself. It was conceived as an Existentialist drama, initially titled *Here is Freedom* and illustrative of Jean-Paul Sartre's definition of freedom as 'total responsibility in total solitude', though with a religious conclusion that Sartre himself would no doubt have regarded as a cop-out. It was based on a book I had chanced upon in a second-hand bookshop in Highgate, a translation of the posthumously published diary of a Norwegian resistance leader named Peter Moen who had been captured and imprisoned by the Nazis. A rationalist and an atheist, he shared a cell with a devout Catholic and a foul-mouthed boorish sailor, both of whom were better able than he to adapt to the terrors and humiliations of prison life. A reviewer deplored the 'formulaic triangulation' of characters representative of Body, Soul and Spirit, which was to me a novel interpretation. I thought the play was about pain, betrayal and the break-up and reintegration of a personality. Under torture Peter Moen betrayed other members of the Resistance. His experience brought home to him that rationalism and intellect were inadequate to support the spiritual and moral life of a man when he found himself in an extreme situation. Moen experienced himself as a complete void, a soul with a crying need for God. In the third act of the play he underwent a spiritual atonement, a humbling and healing process, represented in an expressionistic dream sequence which the director had chosen to accompany with a background of moody music from a Bruckner symphony. Towards the end of the act a woman in the stalls – we later learned that it was Elaine Dundy, wife of the critic Kenneth Tynan – got up and left the theatre noisily. Then in the climactic scene, a voice called out loudly, 'Rubbish'. That turned out to be the poet Christopher Logue, who also stood up and made a noisy exit. When the curtain came down there was an outburst and the audience split into factions, boos and catcalls vying with applause and cheers.

The newspapers made much of the ensuing scene in the pub next to the theatre. 'The Angry Young Men get angry with one another', one of them gleefully announced. 'Sloane Square Stomp', trumpeted *Time Magazine*, whose article slyly mocked everybody involved. 'Stuart Holroyd Starts a Storm in the Theatre', said *The Stage*. The scene that caused the media furore happened before I went into the pub. By all accounts Bill, Colin Wilson and Michael Hastings were involved in a scene with Chris Logue and Kenneth Tynan. Colin was reported to have said, 'We'll get you, we'll stamp you out, Tynan,' and 'Tell your friend to keep his filthy mouth shut in future.' To which Tynan replied, 'Stay out of my life, Wilson,' and addressing onlookers: 'There's your supposed leader, your younger generation.' Then there was a scuffle in the course of which Logue landed on the floor. One report had it that he had been dragged down by the hair by Colin, and another that Mike Hastings had pulled his chair from under him. When I went into the pub I was steered away from the corner where all the action was by Sandy Wilson and his partner Jon Rose, who said, 'Keep out of this, Stuart', and led me to the bar where an aloof John Osborne, dissociating himself from the factions, said, 'Terrific! It looks as if the English theatre is waking up at last.'

Bill said later, back at the house, 'It's the best thing that could have happened. You'll get national coverage tomorrow.' And he was right. The story made the front page of the *Daily Express* and the *News Chronicle* and all the other papers carried some mention of the incident. Bill was jubilant. 'This was what we needed all along,' he said, 'a news story that clearly polarises the two camps among the Angries. From now on it's out-and-out war.'

In the afternoon I received a call inviting me to confront Chris Logue on the television news programme *Tonight*. Bill was full of advice as to how I should 'demolish' him. However, I didn't feel any personal animosity towards Logue, nor, I think, did he towards me. Our broadcast confrontation only lasted about five minutes. After the introduction, Logue started by arguing that the theatre ought not to be a place of genteel entertainment and decorous behaviour, but a platform for debate and argument, and if a man found a play's argument objectionable he had a right to say so. The interviewer asked him what he had found objectionable in the play. 'Its sadism and its bogus religiosity,' Logue answered. 'The idea that one can find God by undergoing torture seems to me deplorable, and I object to the idea, implied throughout the play, that we must suffer, and that attempts to check, alter, change or reform our suffering are impudence.'

I replied that nothing of the sort was implied in the play, that it didn't celebrate torture or suffering and it certainly didn't exonerate the torturers. It made a statement that torture is a fact of political life and that a man with the will and the seriousness to do so could grow through the experience instead of being destroyed by it, as in fact the real life Peter Moen himself had done. As for the charge of 'bogus religiosity', it seemed to me that what was deplorable about the contemporary English theatre was that the word 'God' couldn't be used on the stage except as an expletive.

It was Tom, with his journalist's ear for what is today called the 'sound bite', who had suggested that quip, with which the interviewer chose to conclude the confrontation, thereby giving me the last word and leaving Logue feeling piqued and thwarted.

'This publicity is enough to fill the theatre for a month at least,' Bill said afterwards. 'If Devine doesn't put the play into the repertory now he'll be showing where his true allegiances lie.'

Well, Devine didn't, explaining that the theatre's schedule of productions was full for the next few months at least, but he would be happy to retain the production rights on the play and take an option on my next, and I agreed to a contract on those terms for a payment of twenty pounds.

It was on account of what Bill regarded as such shabby treatment of writers, that he argued that we needed our own theatre. 'We need a writers' theatre', he said. 'The directors, actors, technicians, are the minions. The writer is the creative element in the theatre, and as such must have full control. And I mean literally control of every detail, from over-all policy down to the price of seats and the question whether to serve coffee in the interval, and even whether to have intervals at all.'

Thus Bill, as quoted in Tom's newspaper column, prematurely announced the Westbourne Grove theatre project. One of the national dailies picked up the story the following day, and when we went round to see the theatre for the first time, Tom, Bill, Greta, Joan and I, we were accompanied by several journalists and someone from television. The other 'well known writer' of the 'syndicate', Colin Wilson, who had recently had an unwisely publicised spat with George Devine over his rejection of his play, *The Metal Flower Blossom*, was in Cornwall and unable to be with us.

The place reeked of mould and damp and a wan grey light filtered thinly through grimy windows high in the walls. Some of the rows of seats had been overturned and the carpeting in the aisles was worn and full of holes. The place had the smell and look of a dead building awaiting the demolishers.

But Bill was not daunted. He paced the stage and announced, 'This place is going to be the nerve-centre of a theatrical revolution. It will be what the Royal Court was under Granville Barker.'

One of the journalists surprisingly took up his reference to the glory days of half a century ago. 'Granville Barker had Shaw', he called out from the auditorium.

'We have half a dozen Shaws,' Bill countered pugnaciously. 'And don't get me wrong. I think Shaw was the greatest dramatist of this century – so far. But nobody took up where he left off. Shaw's theatre was the theatre of ideas, of intellect. And what have we had since? The drawing room and the kitchen sink. It's time for a revolution in the theatre, and this is where it will begin.'

Tom, mounting the stage, said, 'All Shaw's plays were operas', but no one took up his point.

The journalist asked, 'So where's the money coming from?'

'We have powerful allies,' Bill said darkly.

His enthusiasm was infectious. I stood on the stage and envisaged the auditorium crowded with people applauding a play of mine. I had worked in a provincial repertory company for a year, and was nostalgic for all the fuss and hurry, the noise and the sense of occasion that it involved and that I imagined would make the life of a playwright more rewarding than that of a writer who works in solitude to produce books for anonymous readers.

Joan was standing beside me. 'Isn't it exciting?' she said, gazing out into the auditorium. 'I can just see it, can't you?'

I could see the dark fire-opals of her eyes, the radiance of her face, the tense excitement that possessed her whole body. 'Yes, I can see you holding the stage like a Bernhardt or a Duse, playing the audience like an instrument,' I said.

Joan said, 'I wonder what the dressing rooms are like. Of course you high and mighty writers don't care a damn what squalor the humble actor has to live in.'

'Let's go and look,' I said.

The dressing rooms were indeed squalid. The wash-basins and mirrors had a patina of grease and dust and the armchairs and couches looked as if they had been savaged by vandals.

'You see,' Joan said with an air of triumph, 'utter squalor.'

I had eyes only for her. I drew her to me and kissed her. It was the first time. She was tense and nervous, held me too tight and tried to put too much into it. I realised that she was not only a virgin but virtually inexperienced.

Tom's voice came from below: 'Stop snogging up there, you two. We're leaving.'

'How did you guess, Tom?' I said as I followed Joan downstairs.

He could have admonished my sly declaration, but he just said, 'You forget, I'm a thousand years old.'

Joan didn't mind what people knew or guessed, however. All the way back from the theatre to the house she held my hand and smiled and snuggled up to me, and whenever Mister Gilbert, the Peke, stopped for a sniff or a squirt I brushed her lips with a light kiss and looked into her eyes. I knew that Greta, walking behind, was watching us, and I could feel her resentment, hatred, jealousy or whatever it was, as an active force. But I didn't care. I was in love, and I felt sorry for poor etiolated Greta with her tinted prints, her carbonised lungs and her bland diet.

Covering an entire wall of my room was a montage of press cuttings, letters and photographs. I had been worrying about whether I should take down the sexy Brigitte Bardot photos before Joan came there for the first time, but had decided not to. Perhaps the place ought to be cleaned up a bit though, I thought. One lives with one's smells and doesn't notice them, but to a visitor the room would probably reek of dust, unwashed socks, rotting vegetable matter and cooking. Also there was dust under the chairs and the table and on the floorboards where the ragged carpets came to an end. The long sash windows that looked out onto Chepstow Road were caked with grime, and the bottoms of the curtains were tattered. The place would probably seem dingy and squalid, like the theatre dressing rooms, to a doctor's daughter just up from the country, but on the other hand she might go for the *vie de Bohème* atmosphere. So I had left everything as it was, even the waste bin with its potato peelings, egg shells and tea leaves. After the theatre visit we had all repaired to Tom's room, ostensibly to discuss 'policy', but not even the exciting prospect of having a theatre of our own could confine the conversation to a specific topic, and when Bill and Tom got into an argument about the political implications of Romanticism Joan and I left and went to my room.

'Oh, what a marvellous idea,' she said when she saw the wall montage.

'It's functional,' I said indifferently. 'Anything I see in the papers that I think might come in useful I just cut out and stick up there.'

I knew that she had registered the Brigitte Bardot photos but she didn't ask what function they might serve.

'It must be a mirror of your personality,' she said.

'Of some of my interests,' I shrugged. 'Come and take a seat. I'll make some tea.'

We had been swilling tea for a couple of hours in Tom's room, but she raised no objection. There was a slight awkwardness now that we were alone and there was nothing to inhibit the expression of the passion we had already made manifest to each other and to the others.

But the awkwardness was dispersed when Mister Gilbert nosed over my waste bucket and found a lamb chop bone.

'*Mister* Gilbert,' Joan shouted.

'It's alright, let him have it,' I said. It would at least keep the snuffling creature quiet for a time. He crawled under the table with his plunder and began to gnaw.

I switched on the small table lamp beside my bed and put off the overhead light. The gas fire hissed and gave off a red glow. We sat on the floor in front of it, leaning back against the couch, and drank tea. Joan talked about her family and her home and I watched the expressions of gaiety and sadness that flitted across her face, and the lights in her hair.

'Daddy never approved of my wanting to be an actress. Mummy did. Wouldn't you have thought that when she died he'd have encouraged me, out of respect for her memory if nothing else?'

'He was in love with you; couldn't bear to let you go,' I Freudianly surmised.

'Bosh!' she said. Her fondness for such crude spirited expletives was a characteristic that I was later to find disagreeable, but on this occasion I was too enamoured to regard it otherwise than as a bit of quaint schoolgirl jargon that had happened to survive. 'He's sadistic. He'd just love to tie me down in that gloomy, miserable house. I only stayed with him as long as I did for Mummy's sake, in case it would upset her if I left him just with the housekeeper. I mean, we can't know for sure whether spiritualism is true, can we?'

The question took me completely by surprise. I might have had little compunction about dissembling where matters of the heart were concerned, but matters of the head were a different matter. I said, as noncommittally as possible, 'No, I suppose not.'

'Anyway, after I'd stayed with him a few months I thought she'd not want me to be for ever doing domestic chores and not getting on with my career, so I had to leave, hadn't I?'

'Certainly you had to,' I said. 'Your old man sounds a right selfish bastard.'

She pounced on the word, as if my diagnosis was a stroke of intuitive genius. 'Yes, that's it exactly. He's selfish. He has been all his life. I can't tell you what a miserable life poor Mummy had with him. Even in the last year, when we knew she was dying, things went on just as they always had done. He was selfish to the end.'

'Incredible,' I said, shaking my head.

'Am I boring you with all this?' she said. 'I am rather going on a bit about all my woes.'

'I'm interested,' I said. 'I'm interested in everything about you.'

'You say all the right things,' she said. 'You're such a good man.'

'I shouldn't be so sure about that.'

'You're a good man because you're a man of imagination. It's lack of imagination that makes people selfish and evil.'

I could assent to her last sentence, but to go along with the proposition that men of imagination were necessarily good was an offence both to logic and to experience. But this was no time to cavil.

I said, 'If I say the right things, it's because I love you.'

She glowed. 'I mustn't talk about them any more,' she said. 'All that's past and gone. From now on life's going to be very different.'

'Yes,' I said, taking up her abrupt change of mood, 'I shall write you a play and you'll become a great actress.'

She raised her head to be kissed. She was more relaxed than the time in the theatre, but still tried too hard. She had seen too many Hollywood clinches. I broke it and looked at her softly so that she wouldn't construe it as a reproach when I said, 'More gently, more relaxed, just let it go and go with it.' She did, and it was better. I said, 'Lie with me on the bed.'

She looked nervous and awkward, and said, 'I don't want to be a disappointment. You might well think that at my age and having been to drama school… '

I cut her short. 'I know, you don't have to tell me, and you don't have to worry. I only want to lie close to you, hold you in my arms and kiss you occasionally.'

I really did intend just that. I believed that this was a love different from all before, and wanted to demonstrate it. But I had not put down in myself the atavism that looks to the woman to be the guardian of the profounder values of life and secretly disrespects her when she too readily gives what a man ardently solicits. Poor inexperienced, trusting Joan knew nothing of such male perversity. She was in love and felt herself loved, and must have felt that nothing bad or wrong could come of giving herself completely to her gentle and considerate lover. She was unresisting under my hands and I was powerless to halt the old familiar process of sexual escalation, to consciously engage all my experience in giving her pleasure and satisfaction. But my satisfaction was chiefly in accomplishing hers, and it was bewildering and galling to find that the pleasures of love were not consonant with the degree of genuine feeling one had for the loved one, and that sex with Joan was not much different from how it had been with other women.

But, 'Oh, they're so wrong,' she said afterwards, 'all those people who say it's overrated. It's the most marvellous experience I've ever had. But I always knew it would be with the right man.'

'The man who loves you.'

'Yes. Will you always?'

'Always.' The declaration had always stuck in my throat before, but now it came with ease and confidence.

Tears welled into her eyes as I gazed into them.

'What's the matter, silly?'
'I'm so happy, and so frightened.'
'Of what?'
'Of it ending. It's bound to one day, isn't it?'
'Not necessarily. People go on loving one another throughout a lifetime,' I said, and part of me hoped that such a marvel might be possible while another part recoiled with horror at the idea of lifelong fidelity.

Joan snuggled her head into my chest and whispered, 'Do it again.'

I said, 'I need a little time to recover. We'll have another cup of tea first.'

'I'll make it,' she said, and got out of bed and pottered about with the tea things quite nude. She was aware that I was watching her every movement and was a little awkward.

'You have a lovely body,' I said.

'My thighs are too short,' she said with a suggestion of a pout.

'Yes, and your neck as well, and your feet too big, your nose too long, your bum too plump and your breasts way too large. God knows why I love you.'

She jumped on the bed and laughingly thumped me with a pillow.

'You're supposed to be making tea,' I admonished.

Between lovers, I thought, there must be scrupulous honesty. The decay of love set in when one of the partners hid or dissimulated their thoughts or feelings. I was resolved not to do that. I needn't confess to her my disappointment with the first time, but I could let her know that it could be better. To help her to make it better would itself be an act of love.

She was a willing pupil. 'Stay with me this time,' I urged when she was back in bed. 'We'll take it gently and make it long. Don't close your eyes. Stay with me all the time. Feel my rhythm as I feel yours, and let them come together.' She did so and it worked perfectly. All that spoilt it was the fact that I had been completely unprepared for this night's turn of events and had to practise *coitus interruptus.*

But that didn't matter. It was an omission that could be rectified the next time. I went to sleep that night with Joan nestled in my arms as trusting as a child, happy in the contemplation of a sequence of next times stretching to eternity. Nothing, I felt, could injure or abrogate such love.

We seemed in those first weeks marvellously compatible. We explored each other's loneliness, and with the avidity of lovers for total possession we talked about our lives in the past. I had never thought of mine as particularly interesting. For me, life had only really begun when I moved down to London at the age of eighteen. But Joan probed beyond that. She wanted to know everything, and she was so easily amused and so readily moved to sympathy that I found myself telling her things that I had almost forgotten because they had seemed irrelevant.

She wanted to know about my parents, as she had told me about hers. I told her they were currently living in Canada, having emigrated there not long after I had left home in 1952. Dad had served as an army truck driver in the war, and Mother had moved from our home town of Bradford to Cleveleys, a part of the seaside town Blackpool, where she had had a job as billeting officer for evacuees. Instead of taking in kids herself, who would have been playmates for me, she chose to accommodate two women civil servants, also evacuated from the South to work in government offices at Norcross, so I was brought up between the ages of six and eleven in a small house with three women. Two other women were also prominent in my life at that time, my widowed grandmother Mabel King, an active and vociferous socialist and early feminist, although the term was not then in use, and her sister my Great Aunt Annie, who had retired to Blackpool with a nest egg accrued from a bakery business in Bradford. Her husband, Uncle Ralph, a veteran of the First World War, was, I heard it mysteriously said, under her thumb, but for me he was a unique male influence who taught me to play cricket and even allowed me to handle his Home Guard rifle, a privilege I was forbidden after giving a widow neighbour the fright of her life by training it upon her from an upstairs window. When Dad returned from the war it was perhaps too late for him to take up a father's role, or more likely he was disinclined to contest the influence of Mother, who had gained assurance from her wartime independence and responsibilities, and who I later learned still harboured resentments towards him on account of some pre-war peccadilloes. He conceded and accommodated to her independence, registering only mocking or humorous protests, as on an occasion that endeared me to him when he greeted her late return from choir-practice at the chapel and neglect of preparing supper with: 'That's just you all over, praise the Lord and bugger the old man!' It was his initiative, however, that took them to Canada, where they both found work and prospered more than they would have in indigent post-war Britain.

At the age of eleven, through my mother's persistence and on the advice of the headmaster of my primary school, I became one of the early beneficiaries of Labour's Education Act and was enrolled as a day-boy at Arnold House public school in South Blackpool, where I became a powerless rebel against a system which sought to turn out officers and gentlemen and graduates of the more august universities.

I particularly loathed having to travel to school on the tram dressed in rough khaki uniform every Friday for an afternoon of playing soldiers in the Combined Cadet Force, and I hated the public school system of prefects and monitors and the bullying that went with it. But the years passed and eventually I became a prefect myself, elocution classes expunged my Yorkshire accent and replaced it with what was then known as the King's English, and I came to appreciate the compensations of playing cricket for the school and having dedicated teachers who awakened and nourished my love of language and literature.

I told Joan all this gradually in our conversations, and I also and probably more interestingly told her about my modest start in the theatre, how at the age of fourteen I had attached myself to a summer show that had come to Cleveleys every year. It offered an unsophisticated, even crude kind of entertainment to the seaside holiday crowds, but to me it represented a glamorous world of colour, freedom and opportunity. For me the theatre was an exciting alternative world to home and school, and I liked theatre people because, being themselves rootless and egotistical, they had no tedious counsels about what I should do with my life. Also, there were young dancers and chorus girls in the show, not much older than me, and a young singing and dancing prodigy named Roy Castle, whom I befriended. I got myself a part-time job as a spotlight operator, and later graduated to stagehand, a job which put me in exciting proximity to the girls and afforded me on occasion glimpses into their dressing room. From Roy I learned that I had better look out for some of the older members of the company because they were 'queer', and had sometimes given him a rough time when they were on tour. At the time I was not aware that male passions are not necessarily focused exclusively on girls, and without Roy's warning I would have been quite unprepared when the show's comedian cornered me in the 'props' room one afternoon and tried to pull my pants down, although even so I panicked and probably over-reacted. When the boss of the company asked the next day whether anyone knew about the mess in the props room and the empty fire extinguisher I was relieved that my assailant acted as puzzled and innocent as I did.

In the second season I made my first appearance on stage – as the back half of a pantomime horse. It was an undignified debut, but a first step onto the boards before a live audience, and the indignity was mitigated by the anonymity of the occasion. The following year I put in a more creditable appearance as one of three piano-accordionists in an ensemble 'Dutch number'. By dint of prolonged practise on the instrument I became passably proficient at playing three tunes, and after further practise before a mirror acquired a stage smile, which I managed to keep fixed even in some terrible moments when my playing lagged behind or raced ahead of the other instrumentalists. Musicianship was decidedly not one of my talents. I thought that comedy writing might be, though, and tried my hand at it, and later some of my material was used in the show; which was how I came to write for Terry Thomas.

The famous comedian was appearing in the summer show at the Blackpool Opera House and came down to our theatre one Sunday evening to take part in a special charity show. The 'Dutch number' was part of the evening's entertainment, so, wearing my Dutch costume and assuming by virtue of it a status of equality with the star, I offered to write a script for him. It was no doubt out of amused indulgence of my youthful opportunism that he agreed to let me try, but I took the matter very seriously and two days later I sent him my script, with a brief note saying that if he chose to use it my fee was two guineas. He replied courteously, inviting me to have tea with him at the Opera House. I went one evening after school, and over tea and cake he took my work to pieces, dispensing praise and criticism in a professional manner that quite charmed me. I went away not at all disappointed by his decision that the script contained too little material that he would be able to use to be worth two guineas. The incident was worth much more to me for the reputation it gained me among my friends and at the theatre, where I never let on that he had rejected my script.

My years of part-time involvement with 'the Show' were fun and I could amuse Joan with tales about them, but my graduation to the 'legitimate' theatre of 'weekly rep' didn't afford quite so much amusement. When I was turned down for national service on medical grounds at eighteen I wrote a letter to the manager of the Jack Rose Repertory Company in Blackpool recommending myself as a young actor and writer of promise and got the producer of the summer show to sign it. Weeks later I received a reply offering me a job as Assistant Stage Manager at £3 a week. I was overjoyed. I had a real job, had chosen a career. I had rejected the way prepared and laid out for me by parents and teachers, who on the strength of my A-level exam results had urged me to apply to read English at Oxford or Cambridge, as a friend of mine with similar results had successfully done, and had embarked on a way of life in which the future was not boringly predictable, more of school, but excitingly challenging and full of opportunities.

The trouble was, I was the world's worst actor. I was too shy and introspective to be able to play-act, project myself into a role. By the time I told Joan about it, I could look back on my year in the theatre with humour, but at the time it had been one long experience of humiliation, of the ruin of self-image and the frustration of ambition. I turned up at the theatre on the first Monday dressed in my best suit, thanks to my mother's ministrations, and was immediately set to work to make an awning out of wood and dirty canvas for a 'Riviera set' which was required for that evening's play. After twelve hours of continuous work on that first day, which included sitting offstage following the prompt copy throughout the performance, I went home exhausted and with some of my illusions about life and about the theatre severely shaken. Life was so much more hectic, mundane and businesslike than it had been in the summer show, so much less fun, and the people were different too, altogether more sober, reserved and hard-working. Nobody was singing Pinocchio's 'Hey diddle-dee-dee, an actor's life for me.' Oh no, acting was a job, and a tough one, and my status in the company as a.s.m. (no capital letters now) was to be at everyone's service, for getting together and setting up the stage sets and props, for following the prompt script in the mornings at rehearsals of the following week's play, and even for fetching beer from the pub around the corner between shows on Saturday nights. I was allocated some walk-on parts, as a policeman or a servant, and managed even in such minor roles to demonstrate that I would never be even a competent actor. I was incompetent too even as a.s.m., omitting to put essential props on stage and even on one occasion neglecting to give the signal to the stage hands to bring the curtain down on a very dramatic act ending, literally leaving a poor actor fuming and fretting upon the open stage. I fell so far into disfavour with the company that I thought the only way I could redeem myself was by writing a play. So I wrote one about Thomas Chatterton, the brilliant boy poet of Bristol who was driven by the world's neglect and incomprehension to commit suicide at the age of eighteen.

I gave copies to the producer and the manager of the company, and waited in suspense for weeks to be acclaimed the boy genius of Blackpool. But it didn't happen. The producer said the play was 'promising but a bit too wordy' and the manager said hypocritically that he didn't think they would be able to give it the production it deserved. So I packed up the theatre and went to London.

London in the autumn of 1952 was a city still slowly recovering from the war. It was scarred and dingy and there were extensive rubble-strewn bomb sites. Tramps slept on the Embankment and under the Charing Cross arches, garish whores touted for clients in the streets of Soho, greyness was everywhere, on the few television screens that existed, in clothes and faces and sometimes all-pervasive when the smog descended. It was a poverty-stricken and run-down city, but for me it was romantic and exciting and just what I had expected from my reading of Dickens.

I found an attic room in Pimlico for thirty shillings a week. It was rather like the room Chatterton had died in according to Henry Wallis's painting: small, with the ceiling sloping on two sides, and with a little window overlooking the rooftops. It was furnished with the bare necessities: a bed, an upright chair and a tattered old armchair, a washstand, a small table and a chest of drawers. There was also a gas fire and a gas ring, the latter to be used, a notice on the wall stated, only for boiling and not for frying because of the fire risk. The landlady, however, was a kindly disposed woman, and she let me use her own gas-cooker in the basement on the odd occasion when I indulged myself in a fry-up.

Food was still rationed, and you had to produce a little brown book for the butcher or grocer to clip coupons out of whenever you bought anything. This didn't inconvenience me as I had to make strict economies anyway. My only income was the dole, which was just over £3 a week. Twice a week I walked to the Westminster employment exchange in Horseferry Road and 'signed on' as an out of work actor. One advantage of my year with the repertory company was that it qualified me to belong to the actor's union and to hold an Equity card, which was another thing that Joan and I had in common.

Either because for some reason I ceased to qualify for the dole, or because £3 a week was too exiguous an allowance to live on when half of it went on the rent, I eventually had to seek a job. I got one clearing tables on the breakfast shift at the Lyons' Corner House near Piccadilly Circus, starting at six o'clock in the morning. 'Joe Lyons' was at that time apparently a favoured employer for out of work actors, particularly those of a homosexual orientation. They were funny, outlandish and camp to a degree, and two of them tried persistently to cajole me into sampling their sexual predilections, assuring me that I would not thereafter be interested in girls. I didn't believe them, and was able to decline their proposition civilly and without recourse to a fire extinguisher, a decision they accepted with exaggerated expressions of gracious chagrin and regret for my loss.

Joan was entranced and amused by the tales of my theatre and early London experiences, but naturally even more interested to know about my marriage. I had known Anne Freeman, a Cleveleys girl, since we were both sixteen, and with her had discovered, prematurely for the time, the delights and torments of sex. I had had pangs of juvenile lust for some of the girls in the summer show, but none of them would concede to my entreaties even a view of a completely naked breast, not to mention a touch or holding of the coveted object. Anne had no such inhibitions, and within a short time of our first meeting and gauche fumblings I was going to a back-street chemist's shop in Blackpool, school cap stuffed in pocket, at first nervously but later quite confidently, to buy condoms. Anne was the adoptive daughter of a rather elderly couple who were often out of an evening playing bridge, which afforded us opportunities to play quite other games that they apparently never suspected, and it wasn't long before, as was quaintly said then, we 'went all the way'.

When I left for London it was on the understanding that eventually Anne would follow me. In my Pimlico garret I was often tormented by my memories and frustrated sexual desire. In the early 1950s post-war scarcity and rationing extended to the market in visual sexual stimuli, and young men weaned from puberty on *Lilliput* and *Men Only* with their coy pin-ups, and perhaps if they were lucky an occasional ogle over *La Vie Parisienne*, didn't have much to go on when it came to fantasising about sex. Anne had the starring role in my erotic imaginings, and supporting roles were played by girls seen on tube-trains or buses or in art galleries. I once ventured to speak to a girl in the National Gallery and even persuaded her to go to the theatre with me to see Donald Wolfit in *Volpone* at Hammersmith, but I was too inexperienced in effecting a smooth transition from cultural to carnal communion, and when I tried to kiss and touch her I received a sharp rebuff. I went out some evenings to Soho to look at the incredible women who would sell sexual services for a pound or less, but found them too gaudy and brazen in proclaiming the fact, and knew that for me they would offer not fulfilment of fantasies but only disappointment, shame and self-disgust.

My letters to Anne became more romantic and passionate, and eventually in spite of her parents' opposition she joined me in Pimlico, renting the room below mine for appearances' sake although we slept and ate in my room. She got a job as a typist, and as we could then afford an extra pound a week for rent we moved to a larger room in Belsize Crescent, telling the landlady that we were married. Then we married for real, at Hampstead Register Office on a clear, crisp day in February 1954, and both pairs of parents came down from Blackpool for the occasion, my mother bringing with her a wedding cake that she had baked some two months before in anticipation.

That was about all I told Joan at first about my life. She was later to learn more about the four years when Anne and I remained married, about our meeting and friendship with Colin Wilson and his girlfriend Joy, about the various jobs we did and moves we made, about my literary work and first publications, and about how the marriage gradually broke down as we grew out of our adolescent romance and both succumbed to a need to make love with others that we were inevitably attracted to. Joan thought that the dissolution and break-up was a sad story, and was even more saddened when I insensitively said that life was a process of continual growth and that for two people whose paths happened to cross and who found they had affinities at a particular time to shackle themselves together for fifty years seemed not only foolish but life-denying. I was talking about myself and Anne and the fact that we had been lovers since we were sixteen or so, but Joan thought it was sad anyway, probably reflecting on my assurance of 'always' when we first made love.

During the first weeks of the affair with Joan I thought and talked a lot about love. There was what we considered a spiritual element in our relationship. When we met, Joan had been reading the *Life of Saint Teresa*, which I proceeded to read too, and we both found in the expression of the religious transports of the Spanish nun a passion which paralleled and mirrored our own feelings. When I philosophised about love with Joan, saying that a true understanding of love does not conceive of it as something that is 'mine', but as something of which one can be the expression, she would have certainly assented with Saint Teresa in mind. Love, I said, is a process of giving out which is endless and inexhaustible because what is being given out is not coming from you but through you. 'Oh yes', said Joan, thinking perhaps of acting and inspiration and the divine spark. It follows, I said, that we should not regard love as a commitment willingly entered into but as a revelation of the primal committedness of our being to the world through a particular person who focuses it. Her assent to this was rather less enthusiastic, though she no doubt allowed for the fact that I had something of a reputation as a philosopher and was inclined to talk in this way.

'Yes', she might have said but didn't, 'but what about sex?'

She did say, one night after we had made love, 'I couldn't bear the thought of you doing that with someone else.'

'I don't want to,' I said, and it was quite true. 'I think it works so well for us because we have brought sex and love together. Sex in itself is the root cause of the "my love" way of thinking, which gives rise to possessiveness and jealousy.'

That was a palpable *non sequitur*. But if Joan saw it as such she didn't say so. I think that perhaps a touch of *folie de grandeur* had jammed up her feminine intuitions. We were, after all, the great writer and the great actress, and so our love had to be something unique, impassioned and spiritual, not possessive, selfish, muddled and human like that of lesser beings.

So there was no question of marriage, though we did have something of a honeymoon. It was in Cornwall, at the expense of the National Film Board of Canada. They were going to Cornwall to interview Colin Wilson and wanted Bill and me to go too. I said I would only go if Joan could come with me, and of course Joan couldn't go without taking Mister Gilbert. So early one autumn morning we all set off from Notting Hill crammed into a van and a car: six film men with all their equipment, Bill, myself, Joan and the dog. The director was a burly Canadian who talked at length and graphically about breaking in horses, and who wanted to stop for a 'noggin' every couple of hours. The journey took fifteen hours, but the beer was free and it was fun to be able to take one's mistress to Cornwall on expenses.

A digression is called for here, so capricious and ephemeral is literary reputation. In 1958 Colin was what would today be called a celebrity. Within three months of the publication of his book, *The Outsider*, two years earlier, he had become, to his own and his friends' amazement, something of a national figure. 'At twenty-four, with his first book, Mr Wilson steps straight into the front rank of major writers,' one of the papers had trumpeted. He was inundated with offers from publishers, newspapers, magazines, television programmes, hostesses. His book quickly sold over 50,000 copies and his name became known to millions. The publicity was not all favourable, however, for he represented different things to different people. To his admirers he was the working class autodidact and hero who had fought his way to the top. They made much of the fact that he had left school at sixteen, worked as a laundryman, a hospital porter, a washer-up, had lived rough in Paris and London, sleeping out on Hampstead Heath by night and cycling in to work in the British Museum reading room during the day. To academics his success was symptomatic of the erosion of standards of sound scholarship and the contamination of British culture with the pretentious and sinister poison of European Existentialism. Literary people were on the whole more generously disposed, and conceded his vitality, originality of theme and astonishing breadth of reading, but some deplored the inelegance of his style, and Arthur Koestler dismissed the book as 'the work of a young man who has just discovered that genius is prone to *Weltschmerz.*' Colin characteristically took the acclaim as his due and the criticisms as the drivel of fools. It was the notoriety that he was unprepared for. His opinions on numerous topics were eagerly canvassed by journalists and television interviewers, and he, like many a young man before and since who has suddenly found himself listened to, and as befitted an 'angry young man', enjoyed being outrageous and shocking. He was always good 'copy' and inevitably the media men probed further into his background and private life. They dredged up the fact that he had a child by and had married a woman ten years his elder, had left them in Leicester some three years before and was now living with a woman to whom he wasn't married. To the image of the cocky and opinionated young genius was added that of the unprincipled and callous lecher. It was distressing not only for him but also for Joy's parents. One evening the father went round to their flat in Chepstow Villas and demanded that she return home with him and never see Colin again. There was even talk of a horsewhipping. At the time of the intrusion Colin and Joy had dinner guests, among them the egregious Gerald Hamilton, the 'Mr Norris' of Christopher Isherwood's Berlin stories, who must have tipped off the press, for it was all over the newspapers the next day. The story was embellished with a real horsewhip and served up as a symbolic drama, a confrontation between the old order and the new, the righteous anger of a father and gentleman of principle and the effrontery and cynicism of the upstart. Cartoonists had a field day. It was too much. Colin and Joy fled to Ireland for a while, and when the storm had abated in the teacup they gave up the London flat and moved into a rented cottage in Cornwall. When he was talked about in London, it wasn't uncommon to hear such terms as 'come-uppance' and 'nine days' wonder' associated with his name, but Colin kept writing and produced another two books both of which got a luke-warm critical reception but nevertheless went into several impressions. After eighteen months in the cottage he decided to settle in Cornwall and bought a larger house.

It was a charmless house, a post-war brick and pebble-dash structure, uncompromisingly functional inside and out, situated on a hillside overlooking the sea and with two acres of long grass around it. There was nothing about it to suggest that Colin had adopted the role of the cultivated man of letters. The furniture was cheap and ordinary and the interior lighting and decoration haphazard. Only the crowded shelves of books and records in every room represented a discretionary disbursement of cash. Everything else about the place declared that although Colin had become a man of property nobody was going to be able to accuse him of being a man of taste.

Such was the house we and the Canadians came to after checking in at the Fountain Inn in Mevagissey, and where they were to do the interview with Colin on the second day. They were not going to traipse all the way down to Cornwall, though, without getting a bit of local colour for the folks back home, so the producer designated that the first day should be devoted to me and Bill, striding along beaches and cliffs in earnest conversation.

He chose Pentewan Bay for the main film sequence. This is a sandy bay about a mile wide which in summer is packed with caravans and tents. A stream running down from the china clay pits around St Austell turned the sea white for about a quarter of a mile out. It was a bleak November day and a bitter wind was cutting in from the sea and up the valley. Bill, Joan and I sat in the car with the heater on while the technicians set up their equipment. Mister Gilbert scampered around stupidly in pursuit of seagulls, then yapped to be let into the car and jumped all over us with sandy paws and underbelly. Within seconds the warm air in the car was fetid with the pungent smell of wet dog. I was glad when the producer signalled that they were ready for us.

But they weren't. They kept us standing around for ten minutes while someone attended to the power supply. I said I thought it was all a waste of time and we ought to be at home getting on with the job of writing.

'This will be an historic documentary,' said Bill, rolling a thin cigarette with shaking fingers. 'Surely that's worth suffering a little discomfort for.

'I don't see why history has to be made in this God-forsaken place,' I said. 'It could just as well be done in the bar at the Fountain.'

'Too cosy,' said Bill. 'The great writer today has to be an ascetic.'

The producer instructed us to walk towards the camera in conversation and to stop about ten feet away, where the recording equipment could pick up our voices. To make it look natural, Bill could stop to light a cigarette at that point.

That reminded me of an occasion in my brief inglorious career as an actor, when I, a non-smoker, had had to light a cigarette on stage. The cigarette had stuck to my lip make-up and when I tried to remove it my fingers had slipped along to the lighted end and I had exclaimed involuntarily at the pain. Another dramatic moment ruined. It was the story of my life as an actor.

We followed the producer's directions, strolled up to within ten feet of the camera and paused for Bill to light his cigarette. The wind blew out three matches but he managed it with the fourth.

'When you think of it, Stuart,' he said conversationally, 'the literature of the last decade in this country has totally lacked imagination and drive. There hasn't been one monumental character created, not a single new idea developed. Between the wars we had Yeats, Eliot, Joyce, Lawrence. What have we had since? A generation of literary pygmies.'

'Yes,' I agreed, 'the generation that came through the last war seemed to have been creatively crippled by the experience, to have lost their nerve. Whereas in France...'

'Cut there!' said the producer, stepping forward in front of the camera. Sorry, but we're having trouble with the sound. The wind doesn't help. You'll have to come a bit closer. And Stuart, try to look a bit more natural, less wooden. Perhaps it would help if you lit a cigarette too.'

'I don't smoke.'

'Well, just try to forget the camera. We'll take it again from the beginning.'

We walked away from the camera and then, on a signal from the producer, back towards it. Bill lit his cigarette and began, 'When you think about it, Stuart, the literature of the last decade...'

'Cut!' They were still having trouble with the sound. The producer apologised and went to confer with the sound technician in the back of the van. He called out that there would be a ten minute break.

Mister Gilbert had given up seagull chasing and settled down to smell quietly on the back seat, Joan took my hands and rubbed them vigorously when I got into the car beside her.

'Incompetent idiots!' Bill exploded. 'How do they expect us to have a coherent conversation if they're going to interrupt every few seconds?'

'I don't know that I can be coherent anyway,' I said. 'It's unnatural, standing out in the middle of Pentewan Bay in a gale shouting at each other about modern literature. The Canadians will think we're nutters.'

'Or fanatics,' Bill said. 'That's alright, that's the image we want to cultivate. But we must plan what we're going to say, and under these conditions it's got to be pithy and to the point. What were you going to say about France when they cut us short?'

'Just that Existentialism emerged out of the Resistance, out of the experience of men in extreme situations.'

'Right, and for them questions of freedom, betrayal, solitude, anguish and death weren't merely academic, they were daily realities. That's the stuff. But we don't want to give Sartre and Camus too much publicity. This is a programme about English writers.'

'Who by comparison have been narrow and parochial, preoccupied by subjects of class… '

'And personal relationships, as in the Bloomsbury gang.'

'Yes, and have cultivated the qualities of sensitivity and charm at the expense of energy and imagination.'

'Good. Great stuff. And we'll go on to talk about the need to create heroes. The writer today must dare to be great and to tackle great themes.'

'Right. And to do that he needs to have a sense of crisis. Greatness is a response to a challenge, an extreme situation.'

'How about throwing in a reference to Elvis Presley or the James Dean cult,' Bill said, 'just to show that they're symptoms of a crisis in our civilisation? The kids are frightened and lost, and they react by looking up to hero figures and leaders.'

'I nodded. 'A good point.'

We spent another hour and a half, intermittently stopping and starting up again, and at the end of it the producer said, 'We ought to be able to edit four or five minutes of usable material out of that.'

'Do you wonder that film stars are neurotic idiots?' Bill said.

'Come on, I'll buy you a noggin,' said the Canadian.

We had arranged to meet Colin after the filming for a drink at the Fountain. He was already there when we arrived, in the middle of a group that a tourist might have taken for local fishermen. Most of them had weathered or bearded faces and wore duffle coats and thick roll-neck jerseys of coarse wool. Some were refugees from broken marriages or uncongenial jobs, others unsuccessful writers or artists who for the most part had minimal talent but whom obstinate dedication or fear of change, or sheer laziness, kept reconciled to a life of poverty and hardship. As they set little value upon property or money, they had few inhibitions about sharing what others had gained by hard work or good luck. Colin was popular with them because he always kept their glasses full and was often good for a touch. He would never let anyone buy him a drink in return. His generosity was legendary, but it was also, I thought, ambiguous. There was less in it of convivial benevolence or indifference to money than of old-fashioned lordly magnanimity and unwillingness to put himself under the slightest obligation to anyone.

His manner was not in the least lordly, however. He would lambast other writers as fools or mediocrities and assert as a matter of palpable fact that he was the greatest writer in England, but he was not condescending towards present company. He enjoyed and indeed told the odd dirty joke, and would listen to other people's opinions and experiences. In the group at the Fountain that morning he was conspicuous only in that he was cleaner shaven and looked younger than most. He was wearing a thick blue fisherman's jersey and baggy brown corduroy trousers. He retained something of the look of the school swot, high brow, thin mouth, small eyes behind thick glasses, short back and sides haircut; and when he moved or shook hands he did so jerkily, as one not quite at ease with his body. He was quite tall and broadly-built, but no one would ever take him for a sportsman of any kind.

Nor was Bill at all interested in sport, though he had become quite keen on darts recently. He had a theory that a man of strong enough will could exercise power over inanimate objects and he played darts with intense concentration and determination. As soon as we got to the Fountain he challenged the Canadian producer to a game. The producer cheerfully accepted, and bought a round of drinks first. Joan and I sat at a table, where Colin presently joined us.

'How did it go, Stuart?'

'It was bloody cold, and they said they only got four or five minutes of usable material out of it.'

'That's quite a bit in film time. Enough to make an impression. You know, Stuart, I'm convinced it's vital that we get ourselves known on the other side of the Atlantic. I've already made a breakthrough there; *The Outsider* is selling well and I'm going out to do a lecture tour in a couple of months.'

'That's great,' I said, 'but I don't think Houghton Mifflin have even sold out the first impression of *Emergence from Chaos*,' referring to my first book and its American publisher, 'and to judge from the reviews there won't be any demand for a second.'

Colin nodded thoughtfully. 'Of course, you and Bill have suffered from the backwash from my publicity. Those bastards the critics got embarrassed because on second thoughts they reckoned they'd praised me too extravagantly, so when your books came out they savaged them.'

'Well, you had advertised us as the only other two geniuses in England,' I pointed out.

'Why not? It's true. The buggers were just too mean-spirited to admit it. Still, they'll come round. We just have to keep producing work and ignore them. What are you working on now?'

'Another play.' I reached across the table and took Joan's hand. Colin, I thought, had pointedly ignored her. I was faintly annoyed.

'Good,' Colin said. 'But you should get down to another serious philosophical book. We've got to put English Existentialism on the map. Sartre is too pessimistic, too low-key. Husserl's important. His concept of 'intentionality' is central to the new Existentialism. Look, why don't you come and put in a solid stint of work down here? Get another book done. You could stay in the chalet and have meals with us.'

That proposal, too, pointedly ignored Joan. 'I'll think about it,' I said.

'For some reason, he hates me,' Joan said when we were preparing to go to bed in our hotel room that evening. It was a small room, cheaply furnished, heated by a one-bar electric fire and lit by a central hanging light bulb with no shade. The paintwork was dark green and the walls were covered with a mottled brown wallpaper against which hung three tawdry paintings of harbour scenes. The room did nothing to alleviate a feeling of depression that had been building up in me all day. We had spent the afternoon watching the filming of the interview with Colin at his house and the evening in the Fountain bar. The day had sapped my energies. I had found prolonged conviviality and playing the role of the celebrity quite exhausting, and what I wanted from Joan was tranquillity, warmth and love.

'He doesn't hate you,' I said a little tetchily. 'I admit he's been rather cool, but he tends to be with everybody until he gets to know them well.'

'Cool, you call it? It was as if he was trying his best to make me feel superfluous.'

'I know,' I said, 'but take no notice. You're not superfluous. You know that. I need you. Come to bed now. It's been a wearing day. I want to relax, with you in my arms.'

Bless her for being so easily conciliated, I thought when she came to bed.

Colin had said that evening, when we had found ourselves side by side in the Gents at the pub, 'I don't know why it is, Stuart, but she gives me the willies.'

I had thought to say, 'You are speaking of the woman I love', but such a riposte, which suggested a follow-up challenge to swords or pistols at dawn, would have been too melodramatic. I had answered tamely, 'She's an intelligent and understanding girl and I'm very fond of her.' It had been a kind of betrayal and had contributed to my feeling of depression.

Joan fell asleep quickly, lay in my arms, breathing deeply and evenly. But sleep eluded me. Thoughts and memories raced through my brain with a momentum of their own. I found myself thinking about a young man in the pub, a short fellow with a little goatee beard, hollow cheeks and mournful eyes, whose wife had just had a baby, and who was gloomy about the world it would live in, where if we were not all incinerated in a nuclear holocaust or poisoned by Strontium-90 the planet would become overpopulated and there would be tooth and claw battles over diminishing resources. Counterpointing his dire lamentations, the juke box had belted out a miscellany of Elvis Presley numbers which kept being repeated throughout the evening, one of which was being re-run in my sleepless brain. 'Love me tender, love me true, all my dreams fulfil, for my darling I love you, and I always will.' The words were banal and the sentiment glib, but they were apparently what every woman wanted to hear. 'Will you always?' Joan had asked on that first night. Perhaps Tin Pan Alley and the American musical were to blame for our generation's naivety about love. It was easy to sing, 'And I always will', but how could one know? It was what they called a white lie. White lies, like white mice, relentlessly gnawing at the roots of love, with small betrayals, ephemeral irritations and disappointments as their accomplices. So it had been with Anne. I thought about the time she had confessed that for six months she had been having an affair with one of the directors of the publishing firm she worked for. She had enjoyed rubbing it in, describing the luxury flat he took her to, the carpeted bathroom, the lights that could be dimmed, the silk dressing gown and satin negligee he'd bought her, and his gentle expertise in the art of love. She'd meant to hurt me and she had, but it wasn't jealousy, it was more humiliation, the thought that it had been so long and so successful a betrayal. The memory could still bring back a spasm of anger. It was crazy, this headlong rush of unconnected thought. Like an engine idling with full throttle out but no gear engaged: tremendous thrust but no drive or direction. That was one of Colin's images, his way of deploring human laziness, typical of his fondness for the argument by analogy, trying to throw light on mental processes by comparing them with mechanical ones. Anne hadn't given him the willies, in fact he'd quite liked her. Maybe he too had been a lover, but it was unlikely, I couldn't see how they could have had the opportunity. The publisher lover must have been in his forties, he'd been in submarines during the war and had published a book on his experiences. The night she told me about him we had had such a row and she had rushed out of the flat at two o'clock in the morning and I had chased her down Haverstock Hill and a police car had stopped us and we were berated for disturbing the peace. Probably not an unusual occurrence for them, witnessing marital rows. In the end two bitter, angry, empty people spill it all out, tear each other apart and trample all over the shreds of their love.

Love me tender, love me true, all my dreams fulfil. And here, dreaming in my arms, lay Joan, sweet girl, soft and trusting, doctor's daughter from Essex, a good woman fallen into a den of literary lions.

2

Our Chepstow Road house was part of the property empire of Peter Rachman, whose name was later adopted to describe a sinister kind of ruthlessly exploitative landlordism. The practice of 'Rachmanism' was said to consist in buying or otherwise forcing sitting tenants out of their homes in order to maximise rents from overcrowded immigrant families, or from prostitutes, and the typical Rachman property was characterised as old and run-down. The name had not acquired its sinister connotations when we occupied the house, and our rents, of thirty shillings a week per room, were generous rather than exploitative. No doubt the girls in the basement rooms made a more substantial contribution to the Rachman fortune, but they seemed to ply their trade quite independently and without coercion, and to earn enough not only to meet their rents but also to run MG sports cars.

Rents were collected, in cash, every week by Rachman's son-in-law, a cheery cockney called Les, who was sometimes accompanied by his blonde, plump, overdressed wife. He followed the careers of his literary tenants in the papers with great interest and was an avid reader of Tom's *Evening Standard* column.

Whatever the house yielded in rents, nothing was ploughed back and the place was certainly a typical Rachman property in its state of dilapidation. On the exterior, the stucco was flaking away, and the inside was dingy and shabby. The hall, stairs and landings were all brown and dirty white, and the stairs were laid with green linoleum. There was a bathroom on the first half-landing with a sliding door of frosted glass. The bath was served by an ancient rusty gas geyser, which for a shilling in the meter would produce enough hot water for a bath, though it made alarming explosive and roaring noises in doing so.

My room was on the first floor, overlooking Chepstow Road, and on the same floor at the back was the guest or out-of-towners' room. Bill had the corresponding room on the second floor as a work room, and the one above mine belonged, as the warning on the door announced, to the demon doggerel poet, Tom Greenwell. A narrow staircase lined with bookshelves led up to Bill's attic bedroom and Greta's studio. The only source of water in the house, apart from the bathroom, was a tap on the second floor half-landing with a shallow triangular sink fitted into the corner below it. As Tom said, the place had 'all modern inconveniences.'

As befitted the social centre of the house, Tom's room had the most lived-in appearance. The furniture was the nondescript junk of bedsitters, but around it Tom had contrived an atmosphere of studied decadence. Tacked to the wall above his divan bed was an Arabian carpet with an embroidered harem scene. On the other walls were two large prints, one of Burne-Jones's '*King Cophetua and the Beggar Maid*', and the other, called '*The*

Penitent', depicting a naked girl kneeling before an altar with a group of severe robed nuns looking on. Slotted in all around the mirror were invitations, postcards, photos of friends, many of them strikingly attractive women. On a hook beside the fireplace hung a mask of the Devil, with little horns, florid cheeks, bushy eyebrows and drooping moustache. 'My doppelganger', Tom called it, though for all his affected decadence and diabolism no one had ever known him to be other than courteous, generous and sympathetic. On his desk there was a small portable Olympia typewriter and a square cut-glass decanter which an elaborately engraved silver label announced was for 'Crusted Port'. The room was always warm, for from the moment of the first autumnal chill Tom kept an oil-fire burning day and night, which produced not only warmth but also a pervasive smell of paraffin fumes. He sometimes lit joss-sticks to counteract the smell, and when he had one burning and had his red bedside lamp on the atmosphere of decadence was complete.

The house generally, and Tom's room particularly, drew visitors like a magnet. It was not only the association with people and events currently in the news, though this was no doubt part of its appeal, but also a sense of its being a haven of disorder, a place where there were no set times for anything, where life's normal primary concerns, with eating, sleeping, earning a living, took second place, and primacy was given to conversation, creative work, friendship and the organisation and execution of grand designs. Life began about midday and would go on until three, four or even five in the morning. People called in at all times of day or night and could be fairly confident of a welcome in one or other of the rooms. There were fellow writers and journalists, people in television or publishing, and a host of seekers, malcontents and misfits who found the conversation and the atmosphere of the place stimulating. The spontaneity, too, was engaging. If someone suggested going out for a meal, to a party or to see a particular film or show, or roaming round the junk shops in Portobello Road, or taking advantage of the availability of a car to drive out to see Shaw's house at Ayot St Lawrence, others would fall in with the plan and an enthusiastic little group would be formed for the venture. Droppers-in and hangers-on never quite knew what they might get involved in. 'But when do any of you work?' some of them asked. My answer was that I liked to write between about eleven o'clock at night and four in the morning, though in fact I often spent several of the night hours talking in Tom's room, for Tom returned from his evening gossip-foraging and 'putting the paper to bed' shortly after midnight. Bill worked more spasmodically, at odd times of the day or night for an hour or two, or in two or three-day spurts, when he would go down to his mother's house at Streatham in South London and was incommunicado. He made out that writing for him was a tremendous travail, a matter of grappling with his 'angel', and indeed when he returned from his

Streatham trips he often looked worn-out, though he never showed anyone what he had written and I often wondered whether his 'angel' might not be of flesh and blood.

Early one evening not long after we had returned from Cornwall I was with Tom and Bill in Tom's room and took the opportunity to tell them about a plan I had.

Bill's reaction was prompt and predictable. 'What? Bring Joan to live here? It's crazy, sheer madness. You're a writer. You need solitude. Besides, you should know by now that all relationships based on sex are short-lived.'

'This one isn't based on sex,' I said. 'Sex is just a part of it.'

Bill smiled as if to call my bluff. 'Anyway, no writer should be tied to one woman,' he said. 'You need variety, you need material, you need the satisfaction of conquest. Most great men are prodigious womanisers.'

'Prodigious bastards,' Tom put in. He was standing in front of his mirror struggling with a starched shirt-front and bow-tie as he had to cover a charity ball at the Dorchester that night.

Bill ignored him. 'Just think, Stuart,' he went on, 'in a few months or perhaps weeks you'll meet someone you want to take to bed. And where will you take her when Joan is here?'

I shook my head and smiled. Bill, poor shaggy titan, would never know the satisfactions of true love. 'You don't understand, Bill,' I said. 'All that's over.'

Bill laughed outright. 'Man's capacity for self-deception astounds me,' he said.

From one professed Existentialist to another, an accusation of self-deception was a serious one. The term was a rendering of Sartre's *mauvaise foi*, literally 'bad faith'. A cardinal sin in the Existentialist ethic was man's tendency to lie to himself for the sake of comfort or convenience or to suppress recognition of the full implications of a situation in order to enjoy an immediate advantage. Bill's accusation was comparable with charging a Cardinal with heresy.

I took it with suitable gravity. 'It's not self-deception,' I said. I really believe that "the unexamined life is not worth living", and I tell you I've examined this idea and my motives very carefully.'

'But you're in no fit state to judge your motives or the situation,' Bill objected. 'On your own admission, you're in love, which means that your senses and judgement are temporarily deranged.'

'Bill's right,' Tom said. 'The examined life is fine as an ideal – a bit dull, perhaps, but worthy – but the question is, who examines the examiner? Who but his friends?'

I said, 'I didn't bring this up as a matter for discussion. I just wanted to tell you what I propose to do.'

Bill shrugged. 'So we can't dissuade you. I should have thought your own experience might, though. After all, you've been married once.'

'This isn't the same.'

'Perhaps, but it will be almost as difficult to get out of supposing you ever want to, and if you don't it will be virtually a marriage, won't it?' He smiled, pleased with the irrefutability of his logic.

'Marriage,' Tom said, 'was best defined by Ambrose Bierce as 'a community consisting of a master, a mistress and two slaves, making in all, two.'

'Bill laughed. 'Touché, Tom, touché,' he said.

Well, the Devil always has the best lines, but though the sequel was as disastrous as Bill and Tom predicted I didn't see it as a vindication of cynicism or of the view that the artist is necessarily a 'prodigious womaniser' off duty and an aloof spiritual colossus on. We were all three playing up our roles, Tom as the Cynic, Bill the Great Writer, me the Lover, and though the question was whether Joan should come and live with me what we were really talking about was love, and none of us knew much about it. I thought I did, that I was more passionate, more daring, more life-affirming than Bill or Tom. I had no conception of the pain that lay behind Tom's cynicism. He had formerly been married and had a house and a well-paid job at the Central Office of Information, and had had his world shattered by the breakdown of his marriage. During the Chepstow Road days he was just putting the pieces of his life back together again. I didn't know about any of this until much later. I regarded Tom as an amusing, generous but rather superficial cynic. I knew nothing about pain, nothing really about love.

Yet at the time I was proposing to write a book titled *The Dialectics of Despair*. I had it all worked out in chapter headings and notes, the 'human condition' tabulated and analysed, and the way beyond despair, the way to a 'higher integration' clearly mapped. In the book would be paraded for the edification of the parochial English all the great themes of Existentialism: the death of God, the problem of subjectivism, the elusiveness of reality, the otherness of nature, the illusoriness of freedom, the sense of the absurdity of life and the world, the distinction between 'authentic' and 'inauthentic' existence, dualism, angst, and in the last chapters a way out would be shown, a way that Nietzsche, Kierkegaard, Sartre and the rest had not had the will or the insight to find for themselves. I wasn't entirely clear what the way out was, but I was confident that it would emerge in the writing and would have something to do with the reinstatement of God and religion, of love as a vital, unifying force, and of a philosophy that rejected Cartesian doubt and solipsism as its starting point and regarded man and nature as many-faceted interdependent entities involved in an evolutionary process of growth. It was to be a great, sweeping definitive book, but it never got written, for suddenly life, love and pain became more real.

I had a lighter, but connected, literary project on at about this time, a long story titled *The Man Who Couldn't Despair*. I put the hero through a whole gamut of literary suffering: betrayal, torrid love affairs, brooding guilt, solitariness, alienation, persecution, but endowed him with a faculty that enabled him to rise above it all, to experience moments of joy, of vision, of life affirmation that quite cancelled out the rest. I conceived it as a philosophical comedy, in the manner of Voltaire's *Candide*. It was the poorest, the saddest, the most desperate thing I ever wrote. At the time, conscious of no weakness, no vulnerability, no fears, no desperation in myself, I imagined that I wrote out of my strength. I had no conception of the hurts, the losses, the shuddering shocks that can negate life utterly. I could go through hell, but I wouldn't particularly notice it, or would embrace the experience as grist to the literary mill.

The ending of my marriage to Anne hadn't devastated me as Tom's divorce had him. In fact it had been quite amicable, the marriage mutually acknowledged as a stage in life that had run its course and must inevitably come to an end. We had remained adolescent lovers, had not developed our precocious love life into something more profound and emotionally bonding, and after the first couple of years we had both been led by curiosity or simple lust into affairs with others. We were complaisant and accommodating about one another's affairs. We considered we were being civilised and rational. We regarded sex as one of the pleasures of life and came to accept that variety was its spice. We had Eros tamed and domesticated, no longer mighty and godlike with the power to drive a person to madness or death for jealously or love, but on a par with the *lars* and *penates,* the little household gods.

'We're more like brother and sister,' I would explain when some girlfriend expressed surprise that I should be on such good terms with my wife and her lover. And it was true. After all we had been through together since we were kids in Cleveleys, we had a relationship that we felt couldn't be abruptly terminated.

When Anne got involved with my friend, the playwright Michael Hastings, I took myself off to Germany for three months so that we could 'see how things worked out'. They eventually worked out to everyone's satisfaction, though not without a good deal of emotional upset and soul-searching, with Anne and Michael living together, my moving into Chepstow Road, and our remaining close friends for years thereafter. I was a sort of brother, or even father-figure, to both Anne and Michael for a time, and would reconcile them when they quarrelled, as they often did, and be a confidant to each of them separately. And I confided in Anne, at least I did until the affair with Joan started. She heard about it anyway, and when she learned that Joan had moved in with me she was apprehensive and I had to assure her that I had no intention of marrying Joan.

Joan understood that too. Our love was spiritual. It didn't need ratifying by Church or State.

We had very serious conversations. I gave her Tolstoy and Dostoevsky and Hesse to read and we talked about their books and about religion and God.

We were both a bit God-obsessed. I had written a chapter on 'The Riddle of Nobodaddy' in my second book, *Flight and Pursuit*, and of course Joan had read St Teresa, and she said she could understand the appeal of a life of devotion to God.

'Even if it meant taking a vow of chastity?' I asked.

We had this conversation over a table in Jimmy the Greek's dim basement restaurant in Soho after eating a plate of Jimmy's excellent and cheap stuffed vine leaves.

'I must admit I'd find that very difficult,' Joan admitted. She smiled and reached across the table and took my hand.

'It's not necessary,' I said. 'Sex too can be a form of worship.'

'Oh yes, I feel that,' Joan said. 'Though when the church people say "God is love" that isn't what they have in mind, is it?'

'No, they mean benevolence or forgiveness. But the religion of the churches has always been concerned with reconciling man to his unhappy lot, with offering respite from "the weariness, the fever and the fret" of life. I don't think that seeking refuge in God, whether philosophically or by going to a monastery or a nunnery, is the real religious life. It's not rest or respite we need from religion, it's a sense of participating in God's creative activity, not escaping reality but entering more deeply into it.'

'Yes,' Joan said. She was an avid listener when I talked like this. Now she was frowning slightly. 'But does this mean that God is just a force of nature?' she said. 'I mean, you can't love an impersonal force, can you?'

The restaurant was full and a waiter gave me the bill, obviously hoping that we'd go. I ordered two more cups of tea. 'No, I'm not proposing a naïve vitalism,' I said, leaning closer to Joan across the table so as not to be overheard.

'I believe that God is both immanent and transcendent, both existence and essence. He can be loved in His immanence, through man and nature, which is the way for most people, or in His transcendence, which is the way of the mystic. You know the lines of Blake's Angel:

Little creature, form'd of Joy and Mirth,
Go love without the help of any Thing on Earth.

Well, that's the way of the mystic, and it's difficult. That's your Saint Teresa.'

'And the other way?'

'The other way is to love the creator through His creation, and to participate in the process of creation. For me all love is physical.'

Bill would have hooted with laughter if he had been witness to this scene. He was convinced that such talk was just the deployment of a weapon from my seduction armoury. He had read my books and accepted them as contributions to 'our' literary project, but I never thought that he had much affinity with or regard for their religious and philosophical ideas.

He and Tom soon got reconciled to having Joan about the house. She accommodated herself to the routines willingly and unobtrusively. Usually the day began with tea and the day's papers in Tom's room between eleven o'clock and midday. Tom would be in carpet slippers, with a short red silk dressing gown over his pyjamas, and Bill would appear, unshaven and uncombed, in shirt and trousers that he might have slept in, and they would smoke cigarettes and discuss the papers, appraising them with the eyes of professionals, comparing the different treatment of subjects, the choice of lead stories, the make-up of front pages, tracing where a story 'broke' and how it was taken up by other papers, and pointing out who had managed to get into and who had been left out of the gossip columns. It was a bit technical for me to contribute much, but Joan and I often joined them, read the news and listened to their commentaries.

A great disappointment to all of us was that Bill's theatre scheme didn't get off the ground. He had had the financial backing all lined up, he said, but hadn't been able to reach an agreement with the owners of the theatre about the terms of the lease. The falling-through of the scheme put him in Fleet Street's bad books for a time, for the press had given it a good deal of publicity, and he found it difficult to get anything in the papers, though Tom did all he could through his column. It was Bill's firm belief that 'we must keep our names before the public', and he gnashed his teeth and got quite eloquently malicious when such people as Billy Graham, Lady Lewisham, Liberace, Elvis Presley or Russian space dogs seemed to be getting all the publicity. However, he had a project brewing that they would all have to sit up and take notice of, he said, though as yet it was too early to tell even his closest friends about it. Meanwhile we would throw in our lot with the English Stage Company at the Royal Court so far as our theatrical work was concerned, and as a platform for our ideas we would use the columns of *Time and Tide*, the editor of which was hospitable to 'angry young men' particularly if they would contribute reviews or articles to the magazine for three guineas a thousand words.

One weekend soon after Joan had come to live at the house I took her and Bill with me to a conference on 'The Search for Meaning' at which I had been invited to speak. It was held at the R.A.F. college at Cranfield in Lincolnshire because some high-ranking R.A.F. officer had taken up religion in his retirement and was a prominent member of the Centre for Spiritual and Religious Studies, which put on the programme.

'You must be joking,' Bill said when I suggested he come with us. 'You mean people will actually spend a weekend in the sticks in midwinter hoping to discover the meaning of life?'

'All expenses paid for me and any guests I want to take,' I said.

'Well, I suppose it'll be an experience,' Bill said.

'Of monumental irrelevance,' Tom said, 'but you should go, Bill, because you're always knocking people for not asking fundamental questions. Here's a bunch that do, and I hope they bore you rigid.'

They did. Bill, Joan and I sat through a series of lectures and discussions on the first day in which scientists, psychologists and theologians concurred that love was the answer to the problem of the meaning of life.

'A bunch of bloody mediocrities,' Bill said as we ate in a brightly-lit refectory that evening.

'No doubt,' I said, 'but the funny thing is that they're right. The only trouble is that with them it's the *idea* of love that is the answer to the *idea* of meaninglessness.'

Bill grimaced. 'Seems to me you're turning Christian, or worse, taking up the tepid humanism of whoever it was wrote "we must love one another or die".'

'Auden,' I said.

'Typical,' Bill said. 'Look what happened to the 'thirties. A generation of maudlin commie mediocrities. All they proved is that you can love one another *and* die.'

I had to give my talk on the morning of the second day. The Air-Marshal introduced me as an 'angry young man' and the audience of about a hundred and fifty settled down, perhaps imagining they were about to be harangued by a latter day Savonarola.

I had roughly prepared my talk and reduced it to a page of prompt notes. I began: 'Any comprehensive philosophy must be, among other things, the critic of satisfactions. Unless it can criticise the satisfactoriness of other ideas, a philosophy of meaning is bound to get bogged down in relativism and admit the equal validity of as many meanings as there are people who entertain them. So let me say this at the start: the merely mental satisfaction is not enough. Man's hunger for meaning cannot be satisfied by knowledge or by scriptural truth. It is a hunger for more life. Love, we have heard it said, is the answer, the meaning. All very well. But the answer to what? Merely to the question: what is the meaning of life? That's not enough. No concept of meaning has any validity that is not hard won from a vision of meaninglessness.'

I went on to expound a 'vision of meaninglessness'.

'He gave them a dose of the old Existentialist horrorshow,' Bill reported to Tom when we got back to Chepstow Road in the evening, 'and they loved every minute of it.'

'Of course they did,' Tom said. 'The God-hungry are always gluttons for punishment. Just look at that.' He pointed at the picture of 'The Penitent', the kneeling naked girl surrounded by grim nuns. 'God preserve me from the godly.'

'That's a prayer, Tom, be careful,' I laughed.

'A rhetorical one, Stuart, I assure you. I know very well that I have to do the preserving. All I ask is that nobody interferes with my happy sins in the holy name of what might not exist.'

'I agree with you about the godly, Tom,' Bill said, 'but what *do* you believe in?'

Tom plucked his cigarette holder from his mouth and frowned. 'It's not a line we sell. You must remember that I'm of the Devil's party. We don't recommend the wares of the Other Place. And we don't think much of the idea of life everlasting if it means spending an eternity of tedium among the righteous and the godly.'

'But Tom,' Bill said, 'people with your views find *this* life tedious. A man has to have an obsession, and none of the things you profess to believe in are worthy of being obsessive about.'

'You damn well leave my beliefs alone,' Tom said. 'I don't mind a man having obsessions, so long as he doesn't thrust them down my throat. Worthy, indeed! You know, with your value-judgements you belong among the godly party. And, for your information, I don't find this life tedious. I enjoy every minute of it.'

'But enjoyment isn't what it's about, Tom,' Bill persisted. 'The question is, what do you hope to achieve?'

'Hope to? I've achieved it.'

'What?'

'The complete life.'

Bill laughed. 'Then isn't it about time you died?'

'Not at all. I said complete, not completed.'

'Sophistry, Tom. In a man without purpose the will dies, and a man without will is a vegetable.'

In discussions of this kind, Bill would sit back in his chair and smile when he had made a point. Tom, by contrast, was all movement and gesture, and would frequently get up and walk about the room. He jumped up from his chair now and went to his desk where he searched among a litter of papers.

'Just let me read you a couple of stanzas from a recent composition,' he said.

Bill sank in his chair. 'The man doesn't write for publication but for persecution', he said.

Tom paced the room and recited his lines with vigour, making little stabbing gestures in the air with his cigarette holder.

> 'Is Man no more than what he is – a Man
> Slow dragging out his unimportant span?
> No punishment, no hope, and no reward;
> No good, no bad, no Devil and no Lord?
> Then let us part-existence justify
> With just one bright and self-convincing Lie,
> For smallness does not fit this mortal scheme,
> Where Truth itself is swallowed by the Dream.'

'What you're in fact advocating is bad faith,' Bill said.

'I call it the necessary illusion,' Tom said. 'To me, faiths are neither good nor bad, neither true nor untrue. They're just necessary.'

'For others, but not for you,' I put in.

'I tell you, I believe in beauty and brandy. One needs fewer illusions as one grows older. And you must always remember that I'm a thousand years old.'

'And you don't look a day over fifty,' Bill said.

Such was the mood and tone of those late-night discussions in Tom's room. We laughed a lot, mocked each other, scored points, but the issues were fundamentally serious ones. Joan listened attentively, and though she rarely contributed she often took up points with me afterwards when we were alone. 'I've learned so much in these weeks,' she said once.

Joan had had a 'steady' boyfriend down in Essex before we met, and for weeks after moving in with me she worried about whether and what she should tell him. I thought she agitated herself unduly about it and told her simply to write and tell him she'd fallen in love with someone else. Eventually she did write and tell him, but only, she said, after she'd decided that she wouldn't be able to go back to him even if we split up.

'I'm sorry I've been such a bore about it,' she said after she had sent the letter, 'but he did ask me to marry him.'

'You don't want marriage,' I said. 'You're going to be a great actress.'

Joan was convinced of that too. If only she could get a break, a chance to show her worth. She was out two or three times a week, seeing her agent or attending auditions, but the hoped-for break proved elusive.

'Oh, I wish I could show you how good I can be,' she said. 'I'd like to do Saint Joan.'

'It would certainly be appropriate, and I'm sure you will one day,' I assured her, but when she kept getting turned down I began to wonder.

I began to get a bit impatient too. I had envisaged our life together as that of two hard-working artists pursuing independent careers. Joan would be out at the theatre in the evenings, and perhaps at rehearsals in the mornings, and I would have the place to myself and be able to work in peace. We would be together for meals, for a bit of socialising, and to make love, and life for each of us would be full and eventful and we'd have a lot to talk about, spending so much of our time in different worlds. That was how I had imagined it would be.

'You're so lucky,' she said, 'being able to use your talents without being dependent on anyone else. All you need is a quiet room and a typewriter.' I was sympathetic and reassuring.

'You must find it boring, having us around all the time,' she said on another occasion. The 'us' meant her and Mister Gilbert, the Peke. If any proof were needed of the depth of my love for Joan it lay, I thought, in the fact that I had taken in her dog as well. And it was the dog that I first fell out of love with. At first he had wanted to sleep at the foot of our bed and I had kept kicking him off until he got the message that if he wanted a good night's sleep he'd have to have it somewhere else. Joan hadn't protested about that, but Mister Gilbert had other irritating habits. He rushed about aimlessly and excitedly and got under my feet, he yapped when he heard anyone on the stairs, and once or twice a week he somehow got out and wandered off down Chepstow Road and we had to get together a search party to find him. After a month or so of this I broke off diplomatic relations with Mister Gilbert. I refused to buy or dish up his food, cowed him when he yapped by barking back, and was so reluctant to help search for him that it was clear I didn't care if he got lost.

But it wasn't only the dog. After a couple of months I began to get irritated with Joan. She talked too much about the theatre and boring theatrical people, and when she sat reading for long hours I felt it was with the attitude of being a good girl and letting me work. Furthermore, the work wasn't going well. How do you write about 'The Despair of Europe' (Chapter One of *The Dialectics of Despair*) when you're being continually driven to desperation by a bloody Pekingese? One needed detachment, objectivity, conditions conducive to the contemplative life, to do justice to such a theme. I didn't at the time think that I was falling out of love with Joan. It was just that we were living too cramped a life, seeing too much of one another. When an opportunity arose to get away for a while I jumped at it.

Among the occasional visitors to the house was a writer named Paul Rowland. I say writer, which was what he had always aspired to be, but he had not been published though he was in his forties, and was earning his living as a resident teacher in a private school. He had a cottage in Sussex which he was only able to use in the school holidays and had offered the use of it to any of us who might feel like getting away from London for a while to enjoy 'the eternal sanities of nature' (he talked like that), and he was delighted when I said I would like to take him up on the offer.

Joan understood. She said jokingly that she knew that if she was going to hold me she would have to do so loosely and on a long rein, and so, tenuously tethered and loosely held, I went to the country to work.

The journey from Charing Cross was like a liberation. Paul had given me instructions how to get to the cottage, getting off the Hastings train at Battle and then taking an hourly bus towards Heathfield. It was a fine autumn day, and south of Tunbridge Wells the forests of the Weald were a symphony of shades of green and brown, with here and there a patch of flaming red, and when I contemplated the vistas of country from the train window I felt a sustained joy. One forgot how stifling London was, how rarely one experienced there a spasm of sheer delight in things seen.

From where I got off the bus, following Paul's directions, I could see the cottage down in a valley, two fields away from the road. There were woods on two sides of it, and on the green hill rising beyond it a copse of dark trees stood out sharply against the skyline. Paul had told me where the key was hidden and given me written instructions about the domestic arrangements. Water had to be fetched in buckets from a stream about thirty yards away. It was quite pure because it came from a spring further upstream. Light was provided by paraffin lamps, which had to be handled carefully so that the mantles wouldn't break. There was a wide, open fireplace with a stack of logs beside it, and there was plenty more fuel to be found in the surrounding woods. The village store was about half a mile away by a short cut over the fields. In a cupboard in the kitchen I would find tea, coffee, sugar, evaporated milk and cans of stewed steak, baked beans and sausages.

It was already getting dark when I arrived. The cottage had been empty for weeks but it still smelled of wood smoke and paraffin. I soon got a fire going and the oil lamps lit and made myself a meal. I spent the evening reading in front of a log fire, and before turning in took an exploratory walk along paths through the woods. The ground was crunchy with frost underfoot and the sky was clear and brilliant with stars, which seemed so much closer than they ever did in London. When I went to bed I left a window partly open, and was lulled to sleep by the sound of the steady rush of water.

The conditions were ideal for the contemplative, creative life. I had two literary projects current at the time, the book provisionally titled *The Dialectics of Despair* and a play with a part for Joan. Although the *Observer* critic, Kenneth Tynan, had savaged *The Tenth Chance*, sneering that I 'had hardly started Shavian'. His counterpart on the *Sunday Times*, Harold Hobson, had given the play a favourable review, as had one or two other critics, so I was not entirely disabused of my potential as a playwright. And of course I had a contract giving George Devine's English Stage Company an option on my next play. The role that I was trying to develop for Joan was that of a woman in an unspecified Eastern European country whose husband was acclaimed a hero after the success of a revolutionary uprising of which he was a leader, but with a counter-revolutionary overthrow was arrested as a traitor and executed, only to be reinstated as a national hero years later. Despite a lot of reading, and research into the 1956 Hungarian Revolution, the play wasn't going well. It wasn't working up its own momentum, and I couldn't get the characters to live and breathe. Joan had enthused about the play and the part, and if I put aside the project I feared it would be a let-down for her. Perhaps I also feared that an admission of failure in the project would indicate that the whole elaborate framework we had created around ourselves was insubstantial as smoke, and that all the talk of genius, fame and true love was nothing more than an exercise in mutual deception.

So I sat in the cottage and fancied that I was working immensely hard because I found the subject uncongenial and brain-wracking. There were in fact quite a lot of things more congenial than writing to be done. There were stores to be got in from the village shop, there was firewood to be collected and sawn and chopped up, water to be brought from the stream, meals to prepare and eat. I enjoyed the chores, particularly the wood-chopping with a long-handled axe. To aim and swing the axe accurately was an acquired skill, requiring a good eye and a steady hand, and to split a log clean down the middle with one blow was very satisfying. When a good log fire was blazing in the hearth in the evening there was nothing more agreeable than to enjoy a long undisturbed read in front of it. It was a very pleasant life, marred only by the necessity to show something for it.

I had been there about a week when, one Saturday morning, Paul turned up unexpectedly. I felt mildly irritated at the intrusion at first, but could hardly make him unwelcome in his own cottage, so I made us a meal of corned beef, mushrooms, onions and Branston pickle fried up together and served on a bed of rice, which was one of my very limited repertoire of dishes. He enthused over it and we spent the rest of the evening chatting agreeably in front of the fire.

Paul had read some of my work and expressed non-specific approval of it, but his interests were not literary or philosophical. He had his own philosophy of life, however, and his conversation was full of observations on the delusions and absurdities of modern man and all his works and laments over his loss of innocence and departure from the wisdom and common sense of unsophisticated people. He and his three brothers had been brought up by a father who had had them schooled to be stalwart English gentlemen and a religious mother who wanted them to pursue spiritual vocations, and Paul and at least one of his brothers appeared to have been serially influenced by these irreconcilable ambitions. When their father had died they had squandered their considerable patrimony in a manner befitting gentlemanly English reprobates, then proceeded to live rather austere and otherworldly lives in remote cottages. Paul, however, had been more consistent and truer to his mother's memory, for his younger brother, Brian, had married two years before and had a son and was now living at his in-laws' house in Battle. One of the reasons Paul had come down was to pay him a visit, which was arranged for the following day, and he suggested that I should go with him.

We met Brian and his wife in a pub in Battle at lunch time and afterwards went back to the bungalow where they were living. Both brothers were in their forties, and though Brian was the younger he looked older, thin, ill-looking and unkempt, wearing baggy brown corduroys and a grey sweater that was too big for his frame and moth-eaten. I later learnt that he had only recently been discharged from a tuberculosis clinic. He was animated and funny, however, and he and Paul clearly enjoyed one another's company. Both were gifted and accomplished raconteurs and were happy entertaining the crowd that gathered around them in the pub. I laughed with the others at their tales and jokes, but I noted that Brian's wife, Susan, was rather detached from the fun and had a look that said that the scene was all too familiar. That she and Brian were married was curious, as he must have been at least fifteen years older. Susan was about my age, with features distinguished by high cheek bones, full lips and a strong chin. She employed neither make up nor hair style to enhance her good looks. I thought that the child, not yet two years old, must have been the reason for the marriage.

I was accustomed to seeing silent, domesticated background women and was in the habit of ignoring them. Susan kept in the background, said little, attended to the child, made tea, coffee, and later a meal, and seemed every bit the busy, dutiful wife. But there was something about her that proclaimed a difference, an independence. It was in the way she looked on and listened as the men talked, with an air of detached amusement. It was in the way she went about her work, the way she sat and sometimes smoked a small cigar. It was above all in the way she sometimes looked at me throughout the day. My antennae picked up the message that this was a marriage on the rocks.

While she was preparing the meal in the early evening she suddenly turned to me and said, 'Would you mind coming to help me in the garden? I need to pick some spinach for supper.'

'Love to,' I said, 'fresh spinach will make a nice change from all my canned grub.'

It was getting dark. The 'garden' was more like a wilderness of long grass, brambles and looming fruit trees. Susan had a torch. 'I'll lead the way,' she said, and took my hand. Her hand was hot, dry and rather rough. It was a long, slender hand without much flesh on the bones. I found the feel of it strangely exciting.

We ducked under some low branches and emerged into an open area where the ridged earth indicated there might once have been a vegetable garden.

'The spinach is around here somewhere,' she said.

We both looked around at the indistinguishable undergrowth and laughed. I took both her hands and looked into her eyes.

'I've been looking at you all day,' I said.

'Yes, I noticed. Your eyes have been positively burning me up.'

Her eyes now had a disturbed look. She tried to draw her hands away but I held them tighter and she didn't resist. Nor did she resist when I drew her closer and kissed her, though she reciprocated the kiss with only the merest tremor of consent. I tried to make it more intimate and open-mouthed, but she broke away and said breathlessly, 'We must get the spinach. They'll begin to wonder what's happened to us.'

We found the spinach. A lot of it had run to seed. As we picked the leaves she went on talking as if nothing had happened. Her father had bought the bungalow when they returned from India in 1947. It wasn't a very pretty house, but he had bought it for the four acres of land. He wanted to keep chickens – 'You can't keep a retired army officer and a chicken apart', she laughed – but then he had been offered an administrative job with the army in Germany, and when he had gone nobody had attended to the land, which had gradually reverted to jungle. The police had once found that a remote corner of it was being used as a dump for stolen petrol.

I listened sulkily and picked spinach and wondered what the hell she was doing. She had led me on all day with her looks, had contrived this expedition into the jungle, and now she was keeping me at bay with her bright chatter. When she decided that we had picked enough spinach I tried again.

'We're not going back until I kiss you again,' I said.

'Alright,' she said, 'but only if you promise to hold all the spinach and not to drop it.'

I accepted the terms and the implication that this time I would have to keep my hands to myself. But this time she kissed me. While I clutched an armful of spinach she insinuated slender arms around my head and neck with nervous, bony fingers, and planted on my lips an inexpressibly tender and firm kiss which shuddered through me like an electric shock. But she made it brief and then stepped back a pace.

'There you are,' she said, 'you unscrupulous seducer of other men's wives.' But she was smiling and there was no reproach in the words.

That night back at the cottage, I couldn't get to sleep for thinking of her. I went over the events of the day, remembering the looks she had given me, her tender kiss, the feel of her curiously rough hands. And I remembered telling Joan some time before that I didn't want anyone else because with her for the first time in my experience love and sex had come together. And it had been true at the time.

Poetry and pop songs, novelists and neuroscientists, have acknowledged and variously lamented, celebrated or coolly analysed the ephemerality of love. For some, to find and enjoy an enduring love is the ultimate fulfilment of life, for others, particularly the young, it is to want an ignoble settlement with life, to purchase ease at the cost of intensity, adventure, freedom. The literary lover as hero, the Don Juan, Casanova, Lord Byron, is the man who moves from conquest to conquest, who never puts down roots, who has the resilience to suffer the agonies of love as well as embrace its joys. He values freedom above all, and is never so free as with the new potential lover, who affords him the opportunity to choose himself anew, to shed the accumulated dross of life hitherto, to wear a new mask, assume another personality; a truer one, to be sure, than the tarnished and compromised one that he will now shed.

It had initially been like that with Joan. I was the great writer, she the great actress, so ours had to be a great love affair. It was a strain to keep it up. There was domesticity, the dog, always problems with money, Joan's failure to get work, the unglamorous day-to-day struggle with words and ideas.

Susan had chided me, but rather coquettishly I suspected, as the unscrupulous seducer, and I imagined she thought of me as the literary Lothario from the big bad city who came into her life one Sunday afternoon and bulldozed through the proprieties and her inhibitions. Well, it wasn't a new identity. I had lived the life of the sexual freebooter between separating from Anne and getting involved with Joan, and although I had wanted and professed a deep and enduring love it was not exactly dismaying to find that with Joan it was too demanding and constraining a thing to sustain.

However, I didn't see Susan Rowland again at this time.

Just a few days after our meeting a letter came from Joan saying that she had got a small part and a job as stage manager in a touring company, starting in Leeds the following Monday. So I returned to

London and spent a couple of days and nights with her before she left.

Of course I didn't say anything that could spoil her excitement about getting the job or undermine her confidence. It may well be considered a craven, ill-judged and cruel stratagem to substitute kindness for love, but that was what I did. Joan was only able to pay occasional visits to London during the weeks that followed, when the show came within striking distance, so I reckoned I could keep up the pretence that things between us were as they had been at least for as long as she kept the job. I thought that with separation and the passing of time her own ardour might abate and the final break become easier. I reasoned that after losing her mother and becoming alienated from her father, it would be too cruel a blow for her to be abruptly dropped by her first lover. Also there was a chance that she might meet someone else while on tour. Thus I debated the situation with myself, worrying over fine points of morality while continuing to commit the major sin of still sleeping with a woman I no longer loved and hoping for some turn of events that would accomplish my deliverance without leaving me with the inconvenience of a guilty conscience.

I reoccupied my room and resumed my independent London life with a degree of relief that I think did not go unobserved by Bill and Tom, though they refrained from comment, colluding in the pretence that the only thing that had changed was that Joan had found work. They didn't even say anything when I was sometimes out for the evening and didn't return to the house to sleep. Though there came an occasion when they could no longer keep up the act.

'So what are you angry about?' people sometimes asked on a first acquaintance, and I would answer: 'First and foremost, about being saddled with that damn silly journalistic tag.' The 'angry young man' label raised expectations that I was neither temperamentally nor ideologically disposed to play up to, and it prompted sneering or supercilious comments that themselves gave rise to an angry response. The only dubious advantage the label conferred was being solicited by publishers and magazine editors to submit projects or articles, instead of having to submit work to them, and also being invited to parties and dinners where one might meet distinguished older writers or contemporaries, and maybe on occasion encounter the possibility of an interesting liaison. One such occasion was a party given by a privileged young man, then studying at Cambridge but with the use of a grand and spacious family home in Kensington. It was a relaxed and merry party, generously lubricated with champagne and red wine, and with the music of Buddy Holly and Elvis Presley blasting out an irresistible urge to dance. Dancing was not one of my accomplishments. I had attended Saturday evening ballroom dancing classes when at school and learnt how to waltz, quickstep and foxtrot with a degree of clumsy competence, but rock and roll were not then on the agenda, though from watching others I saw that one could get away with jigging about to a basic beat, so I invited an attractive girl whom the host had introduced me to as 'Lynne, my bluestocking friend' to join me on the floor. She was no better at rocking and rolling than I was, and we shook and shuffled and gestured vigorously enough for a few minutes before retiring breathlessly at her suggestion to sit the next one out with a drink. I asked her why our mutual friend had called her a bluestocking, and she laughed and said, 'Isn't that what all you Brits call a woman with intellectual pretensions?' The accent was American, the tone mocking, the expression amused and provocative. I dissociated myself from the anachronistic prejudices of academe and asked her what she was studying. She was reading English literature at Cambridge, at postgraduate level, currently writing a thesis on the 17th century metaphysical poets. Our host had introduced me with the usual crass label, which I also dissociated myself from, telling her that my first book had been about varieties of religious experience expressed by modern poets. We spent the next hour or two talking animatedly. Bill, I noticed, was observing from across the room the intimacy and intensity of our conversation and interactions, and when the time came to leave and she accepted my invitation to come back to my place, an acceptance that held for me a vertiginous promise, he came over and joined us. He raised an eyebrow when I told him that Lynne was coming over for a nightcap, and suggested that we shared a taxi. Bill was never a man of tact; he regarded it as a virtue of the pusillanimous. Also it was a kind of game with him to spike my guns.

When we got back to the house he suggested a drink in Tom's room. It was as well that he did. Tom managed to get across to me the message that Joan had arrived and had gone to bed because she was tired after the journey. Bill watched my discomfiture with amusement. His look said, 'Let's see you wriggle out of this.' But Tom, on this occasion, rendered me a sterling service, by engaging Lynne in a discussion of the poems of John Wilmot, the Earl of Rochester under King Charles II, with whose scurrilous and erotic works she showed a surprising familiarity, indeed an appreciation that would have been considered unbecoming in any English bluestocking. This made me all the more intrigued by the possibility of getting to know her better, although on this occasion it was clearly not going to be possible, and when Tom eventually announced that it was time he turned in, I duly had to wriggle. Although nothing had been specifically proposed regarding the sleeping arrangements, there had been the aforementioned promise in the air, and Lynne was clearly bewildered when I escorted her to the spare room and settled her down for the night with an elaborate show of chivalrous solicitude. When I came out of the room Bill leaned over the banisters above and said, 'Crafty bastard! But you won't get away with it. You'll be dragged down to hell, there to burn for a million years alongside Don Giovanni.'

I said, 'And a damn fine Leporello you make, Hopkins.'

Bill went away chuckling.

I felt exhausted, and I experienced what is commonly described as a sinking feeling but was more like a sense of my entire guts collapsing into the pit of my stomach and messily coalescing there when I saw Joan brightly sitting up in bed reading.

'You're late, darling,' she said. She put down her book on the bedside table and held out her arms, and I called on resources I didn't know I possessed for my second act of spurious chivalry within the space of five minutes.

We both realised later that that must have been the time when she got pregnant.

Joan's show folded after a few weeks and she returned to London. I contacted Paul to see if I could use the cottage again, but he regretted that it was currently being used by Brian, which I thought was odd but didn't of course question. So I phoned Colin to see if I could stay for a few weeks in the chalet that he had recently had built in his garden. 'As long as you like, I'll be glad of the company,' he said enthusiastically.' I told Joan that I really had to work full stretch on the book and the play now. She was clearly less enthusiastic than when I had gone down to Sussex, but she didn't demur.

I took the train from Paddington to St Austell and then the bus to Mevagissey. I had arranged to meet Colin in the Fountain. His car was being repaired and he had cycled over from Gorran to meet me. We had a couple of drinks and talked about our work before setting out to walk the couple of miles back over the cliff path, which Colin said was shorter than going along the road. It was getting dark, and after about half a mile a light drizzle began to fall. There was a head wind and the sound of the sea below us.

'I'm glad you didn't bring Joan with you this time,' Colin shouted. 'Is that all over?'

'Pretty well,' I shouted back into the wind, 'though she's living in my room at the moment.'

'So Bill told me. I thought that was a fatal move. Still, you can stay down here as long as you like. I'm off to the States next month, so you'll be able to have the whole place to yourself. What are you working on now?'

'The Despair book is coming along, and I've got about half a play written.'

'That's good. We've got to keep churning the stuff out. Make them take notice.'

We walked on in silence for a bit until the path widened and we could walk abreast.

'I'm sorry if I was a bit curmudgeonly about Joan when you were down last,' Colin said. 'I suppose it comes down to our having different ideas about women. I need a woman to make me human, not to remind me that we both have minds or, worse still, souls. You know Heine's lines:

> Your body's love I still desire,
> For it is young and fair,
> Your soul can go and hang itself,
> I've soul enough to spare.

'No,' I said, 'but I did feel at first that with Joan something more than a physical relationship would have been possible.'

'The romantic fallacy.'

'Maybe,' I said, 'but I still believe a really profound relationship with a woman can add a dimension to a man's life.'

'I dunno, Stuart,' Colin said, 'any man who needs anything added to his life is pretty well a dead loss.' Colin had a singular tone of voice for such statements, casual but at the same time lamenting. He often prefaced his more outrageous assertions with 'I dunno'. He went on: 'A man should be able to spend a lifetime just thinking. Women get in the way of a man's thinking, particularly so-called intelligent women with their bright chatter. I should have thought that after splitting with Anne you'd have steered clear of the type for evermore.'

'Joan's not the same type,' I said.

'No, but she gets in your hair just a much, doesn't she?' he laughed. I didn't deny it.

The walk got more arduous. It was uphill, and there were fences and gates to climb and muddy patches to negotiate. We struggled on in silence for a while. With my rucksack slung on my back I felt like

Pilgrim fleeing from the City of Destruction. I thought of London and Joan and the analogy didn't seem inapt.

Colin insisted on carrying my rucksack for a while, and I pushed his bicycle, which was scarcely less laborious. At last we reached the top of the hill and stopped to rest. A few yards in front of us the cliff fell sheer away. We could hear the crash and drag of the breakers on the rocks and shingle below, and from the direction of the great rock-island that loomed a mile out to sea there came the deep and dolorous clang of a warning bell.

'That's Gorran over there,' Colin said, pointing to a cluster of lights about a mile away. 'It's all downhill from here.'

It was downhill but not without hazards in the fading light. When we got near the village we had to scramble through hedges and over ditches and tramp round the muddy peripheries of ploughed fields. We were both sodden and exhausted when we reached the house.

'Why didn't you get a taxi from Meva?' Joy said brightly.

'Because it wasn't fucking raining when we set out,' Colin said. 'And I had my bike with me, didn't I?'

'You could have left it at Lionel's.'

'Well, I didn't. And now I'm wet and hungry, so dig out some food while I have a shower and change.' He stomped off and left me to settle in and shower at the chalet.

'I think you'll find everything you need there,' Joy said. 'I made up the bed and put the electric fire on this morning, so it should be warm. If you need anything else just give a shout. Of course you'll have all your meals here with us.'

'Thanks for everything,' I said, and gave her a kiss.

Joy was serene, the soul of equanimity. Colin raged at her one minute and petted her the next, and she bore it all with an air of surprise and humour. She may have seemed the little background woman, but she always looked as if she had a secret, a little inaccessible rock-island of a self from which she looked out upon the world. She was no domestic paragon, however. Her kitchen was equipped with every item of domestic paraphernalia on the market, but she was blithely unconcerned about keeping it tidy, and the long kitchen table was always piled up with open cans of pet food, messes of left-overs, as yet unwashed crockery, as well as books and papers. Joy would spend hours in there, and emerge from time to time with plates of sausages, eggs and baked beans. The cuisine was basic and unsophisticated, which was how Colin liked it, and meal times were flexible and dependent on his mood. He might get hungry in the middle of the afternoon, or in the evening suddenly during the second act of *Tristan and Isolde*, and would bawl out, 'Joy, I'm hungry, feed me', whereupon everyone present would be duly fed. Joy was unperturbed by what would later be regarded as such intolerable male chauvinistic boorishness, and always maintained her air of amused serenity and unconcern. It occurred to me once that while Colin and I talked earnestly about religion and mysticism in the sitting room we were quite unaware that we had a real live mystic sitting there coolly in the kitchen.

Colin was a queer mixture of the ascetic and the *bon viveur*. He spent lavishly on fine wines, malt whiskies, books and records, but cared little for what he wore or ate or what his surroundings were like. As his guest, one had to be prepared to quaff wine like a Dionysian reveller and at the same time listen to a lecture on philosophy or literature or to a complete performance of some obscure operatic masterpiece that he had recently discovered. It was a basic belief of Colin's that a man must strive to transcend the merely human condition and be able to focus his mind like a laser for long periods of time, and it seemed to be a function of his hospitality to provide the conditions for practice in such concentration.

Sometimes as we sat around the fire in the evening, talking and listening to music, he would launch into a speech as if he was practising for his forthcoming U.S. lecture tour.

I recall one such occasion particularly vividly because it was, though I was unaware of the fact at the time, on the last night of my stay and preceded an event that was to change my life for ever. We had been talking about Existentialism and how we might develop a distinctive English school of the philosophy. Colin was sitting slumped in his armchair, head bowed and chin on chest, brow furrowed with concentration, pursuing his train of thought. He didn't look at me. I could see only the glint of the firelight in his glasses.

He said, 'We've got to get beyond Existentialism, Stuart. The Existentialists have got stuck with this image of man inhabiting an alien, meaningless world in which he feels accidental, mediocre and mortal. According to Sartre, man *creates* meaning. I'd disagree. I'd say that man *perceives* meaning. Meaning is all around us. If we feel accidental and mediocre it's our perception that's at fault. We're functioning at too low a pressure. Sartre is obsessed with the subject of how the gaze of another person can narrow or distort our sense of identity. It's true that I might experience a distortion of my self-image if I'm caught looking through a keyhole, for instance, but to base a whole philosophy on the fact, as Sartre does, is ridiculous. Why not base a philosophy on the opposite experience, on those moments that Maslow calls "peak experiences", when we perceive the wide network of relations between things?'

Maslow was a new name to me. I said, 'Who?'

'Abe Maslow. He's important. You must read him.'

He stood up, crossed to a bookshelf, and handed me a copy of a hefty tome titled *The Farther Reaches of Human Nature*.

He went on to expound what he called 'the relational theory of consciousness', saying that reality is a network of interrelations and human consciousness operating at its correct pitch is the full perception of these interrelations He quoted the poet Yeats sitting at the café table and suddenly feeling that 'I was blessed and could bless'. Such experiences, he said, show that meaning is not something we impose on the world, but is always there, as a reality outside us, but most people are too mentally lazy and easily discouraged to screw their consciousness up to that pitch.

Although much that Colin said when he talked like this had my assent philosophically, I found his rather hectoring tone and his dismissive denigration of human frailties disquieting and unsympathetic, carrying as it did the implication that one was not prone to such frailties oneself.

The phone had been ringing for some time. Soon after it stopped Joy came into the room and said the call was for me. I was at first mystified, then apprehensive when Joy handed me the receiver and whispered 'Joan'.

I didn't get around to reading Maslow's theories about peak experiences and the hierarchy of human needs for quite some time, because Joan's news left me no alternative but to promise to return to London the next day.

His Dear Time's Waste - Stuart Holroyd

3

Proust was impenetrable, irrelevant. Soon after the train left St Austell I had taken out the book, as was my custom on long train journeys which afforded an opportunity for a good read. I remembered how absorbed I had been on the journey down, how the deeply satisfying, sensuously rounded Proustian sentences had drawn me so intensely into his world that they had heightened my perceptions of the world around me. But there were no such subtle literary epiphanies to be had on this return journey. The real world had presented me with quite other things to think about.

Had Joan got pregnant deliberately? The question had arisen when I had talked over the situation with Colin, who as well as being cynical about Joan's purpose had in his way tried to be helpful by suggesting that I get in touch with a former girlfriend, Carole-Ann, who had had an abortion. At first I had thought the idea that Joan had wilfully got pregnant was preposterous, but it was a possibility that nagged. She had known, surely, that our relationship was not as it had been, that love had cooled and that my going to Sussex and then to Cornwall was indicative of the fact. But to get pregnant with the hope or expectation that it would bring us together would have been a pretty desperate gamble. However, she had asked me on the phone what she should do, which suggested that the abortion option was on the cards and by implication discredited the deliberate stratagem idea. But even if not exactly deliberate, it was her fault in the sense that she must have miscalculated her safe period, and I felt resentful that she was now burdening me with the decision of what to do.

Well, one thing I would do soon after I got back to London was get in touch with Carole-Ann. It was arguable that it was because of her that I had become involved with Joan in the first place, so she would surely be willing to help with the question of how to get an abortion, having had one herself.

Carole-Ann was also in the theatre, in fact at the time quite more definitively so than Joan, although she didn't boast thespian talent or ambitions. She was appearing in the long-running Michael Flanders and Donald Swann West End show, *At the Drop of a Hat*. By way of contributing a bit of a diversion from Flanders and Swann's repertoire of droll and witty musical numbers, and to arrest at least half of the audience from any tendency to torpor that might be setting in, she had a couple of walk-on appearances as a stereotypical scantily clad 'blonde bombshell', a provoker of suppressed 'Wow!' murmurings and furtive lustful urges. My quite unconstrained urges were awaiting her some nights when Mike Flanders drove her home after the show to her flat in Putney, and she would accommodate and reciprocate them with wondrous generosity. For a 1950s girl, her sexuality was uncommonly uninhibited, and it had got her into a bit of bother with a former boyfriend, whose child she had had aborted a short while before we got together. Mike Flanders had arranged and paid for the abortion, and I was sure that he and Carole-Ann would be willing to help with advice and introductions for Joan. It seemed it had all been quite straightforward and unproblematical for Carole-Ann, who had ambitions that she didn't want thwarted by a pregnancy. She aspired to be an opera singer and was having lessons, and she was as uninhibited with me in her singing as in her love-making, practising her soprano scales, or the Queen of the Night's aria from *The Magic Flute*. She was the queen of my nights for those weeks in Putney, and it might well have gone on and the affair with Joan never have started, but for a rather surprising twist in the situation.

One afternoon Carole-Ann turned up unexpectedly at Chepstow Road. I was working but delighted to see her, particularly as the sight and fragrance of her stirred anticipations that literary aspirations would gladly temporarily cede to. But she had a rather curious and serious look, and had come to consult me, she said, on a rather urgent matter. Oh Christ, not pregnant again, I thought. But no. The problem was that she had had a proposal of marriage from an opera singer whom she had met at her singing lessons. I imagined a soaring tenor virtuoso with matching phallus and felt a pang of jealousy. But it turned out that she hadn't been to bed with him and hadn't accepted his proposal because she wanted to talk to me about it first. I was slow to grasp her drift, the point that she was in fact giving me first refusal. But when I grasped it I promptly declined, explaining that I had only recently been divorced and now wanted to devote my full time and energy to my work. In that case, she said, we had better not see each other again. 'One last time, then,' I suggested, and as ever, generous in the impulse and uninhibited in the act, she brought joy to my day, as she said I did to hers, though tinged with the sadness of finality and parting. Afterwards I walked her to Notting Hill tube station, where we said fond farewells. It had been a curious affair, laced with sex, fun and fondness, but with never a mention of love.

I realised during that train journey that Joan must have got pregnant the night when I had brought the American student Lynne back to the house. It couldn't have been any other time, for that had been the only time we had slept together during the weeks she was on tour. It would somehow have been more tolerable if the pregnancy had resulted from something more like a genuine act of love. It was ironical and cruel that it had resulted from a dreary and dutiful act of copulation in which there had been no love or tenderness but only covert resentment and crude precipitation.

The train slowed as we approached Paddington. It was dark and there were lights on in the rows of grimy tall terraces that backed onto the railway, giving glimpses of people going about their lives in shabby rooms. Shabby, grimy, grubby, were apt terms for the streets around Paddington in the 1950s, and for the lives of most of their inhabitants. I didn't exclude myself from the reflection, and as I hitched on my rucksack and set off to walk the short distance home through the now quiet streets I felt an unwonted affinity with the shadowy derelicts of the London night.

Joan said, 'I want to go through with it, Stuart.'

'But you said on the phone that you wanted to discuss it, and would do whatever I decided. Was that just to get me up here?'

'No, you'd have had to come anyway, wouldn't you? I've been thinking it over, that's all. And I've been talking to my father.'

It was the morning after my arrival. I had crept into the house and spent the night in the spare room, daunted at the thought of a night-long scene after my journey.

'Your father!' I said scornfully. 'I could remind you of some pretty bitter things you said about your father.'

'He is a doctor,' she said, adding, 'and he's the only person I have to turn to now, isn't he?'

'So why bother to get me to come up from Cornwall?'

'Because you are the father.'

The word made me wince. It made me angry too. It was ridiculous, it was emotional bullying, to drag the idea of fatherhood in.

'You said you wanted to discuss it,' I said. 'Now it seems there's nothing to discuss. You've made up your mind.'

'I'd like to have your child,' she said. 'What have you been thinking? That I should have an abortion?'

'Frankly, yes,' I said. 'I know it's illegal, and that there are problems, but I know people who could help. I'd work to get the money, even if I have to get a job for a while.'

I considered that a fair acquittal of my responsibility in the matter, and no small sacrifice as any short-term job would no doubt be uncongenial.

Joan was sitting up in bed wearing a blue quilted bed-jacket. Her hands encircled a steaming mug of tea as if for warmth. I wondered whether it was my disenchantment or her pregnancy that made her face look flabbier than before.

She shook her head and said ruefully, 'It was over between us before this happened, wasn't it? I thought it was when you went down to Sussex, but I didn't want to believe it.'

This cheered me a little. That she had been a party to the error of stringing along the affair after its natural demise removed some of the responsibility from my shoulders. The fact that she had gone on loving escaped me.

'I worked out when it happened,' she said.

'So did I.'

'It was that weekend when I came back unexpectedly, wasn't it? And that girl who slept in the spare room and was drinking tea in Tom's room when we went up there the next morning was one of your mistresses, wasn't she?'

'I never slept with her,' I said.

She emitted a sharp laugh. 'Poor man. Did I spoil it for you?'

I said testily, 'Shall we keep to the point?'

'Meaning, let's be practical and logical and not drag in those messy things called emotions. Well, I'm sorry Stuart, but I can't be as cool about it as you are. You see, I am emotional, and I am, though God knows why, still in love with you, you great oaf.'

I felt trapped. I recalled Anne Whitefield and John Tanner in Shaw's *Man and Superman* and saw Joan as the eternal predatory female, more than a match for the male with her formidable life force and emotions. She looked so assured and satisfied now, sitting there in her bed-jacket.

I said, 'I can't believe that, not after the way I've treated you.'

'You can say and write reams of highfalutin stuff about love,' she said, 'but you don't know the first thing about it, do you?'

I was nettled. 'My writing doesn't come into it,' I said tamely.

'You fool,' she said, 'everything comes into it. You can't neatly divide life into compartments. It's all one great bloody mess.'

'This situation certainly is,' I said.

She got out of bed suddenly and searched for her handbag among the litter on the sofa. I watched her, tried to see if there was any evidence of a bulge, but her nightdress was too loosely fitting. She took a packet of cigarettes from her bag and lit one with shaking fingers.

'I need help,' she said.

'Well, I've offered to help.'

'You've offered to pay for an abortion.'

'It's no big deal,' I said. 'It's a simple operation. You're out the next day.'

She said, 'But it's murder, isn't it? It's taking a life. It's already alive. It's a person. They kill it when they drag it out. I couldn't bear to have someone do that to my child. Well, could you?'

The way she put it turned my stomach. At the same time a hard knot of resentment formed in me at the way she insisted on talking about my child.

'I take it your father wants you to go through with it,' I said.

'He's a doctor. His job is to save and preserve life.'

It sounded pious, but it was irrefutable.

'And what does he expect me to do?'

'He expects us to get married, of course.'

'Of course!' I put sarcasm into it.

She was silent for a time, seeming preoccupied with burning holes in a screwed-up bit of cellophane in the ashtray on the floor with the end of her cigarette. Suddenly she looked up and her eyes were full of tears.

'Is it such a terrible prospect?' she said.

I was going to say, 'It's a bloody impossible prospect,' but there flitted across her face for a moment an expression that took me back, reminded me of the innocent, trusting and adoring Joan of three months before. I felt suddenly tender towards her.

'It wouldn't work, Joan,' I said. 'I mean, marriage is supposed to be for life, isn't it? I know myself too well. I wouldn't be capable of that sort of commitment.'

A tear escaped and she quickly brushed it off her cheek.

The confusion of my feelings quite choked me up. I wished more than anything that I could speak out clearly and with assurance and take the situation in hand. I felt that the poverty and shabbiness of my feelings reduced me to a dumb nothing. Perplexed, defeated, self-pitying and suspicious, I was Sartrean man, my self-image distorted, destroyed by the gaze of the other. Joan's eyes were full of hurt and reproach.

We must base our philosophy on our peak experiences, Colin had said. That was good and true, and philosophically all very well, but life raised problems more thorny than being caught looking through a keyhole.

Bill was delighted to see me back. I had come at the right time, he said. The new project that he had hinted at some time before but had kept everyone in the dark about was ready to be announced to the world. He had launched a new political party. The Standard had carried a paragraph about it the day before, the Sketch had picked up the story and given it five column inches, and he had just had both the Mail and the Chronicle on the phone.

'The Spartacans are going to be big news tomorrow,' he said.

Tom explained: 'Spartacus was a character who raised a rebel army of slaves against the Roman Empire and got himself and most of his followers crucified. Bill would insist on the name. I think he must have a political death wish.'

'Don't give us that Freudian crap, Tom,' Bill said. 'I grant you Spartacus was a bad strategist, but he led a revolt against the greatest military and political power the world had known and he damn near brought it off. That's why he's our man.'

'Isn't he a bit obscure?' I said.

'Fabius was obscure to the great unlettered British public, but that didn't stop the Fabian Society making its mark,' Bill said.

Tom chuckled and said, 'It didn't help either.'

Bill rode it. 'Basically, you're right, Tom. There's nothing in a name.'

'A fanatic by any other name would smell as foul,' Tom declaimed.

'There you're wrong, Tom.' Bill took him up seriously. 'Fanaticism is what is needed today. Public life in England shows all the signs of a democracy in decline: shameless materialism and cynicism, class antagonisms, lack of vision. We need to make a clean sweep and a fresh start under new men, selfless men, men of vision, in short, fanatics.'

'Tom held an imaginary microphone in front of Bill's face and said in the manner of an interviewer, 'And what, Mr Hopkins, will be your first act as Great Dictator, I mean as Prime Minister?'

Bill said, 'My first act, Tom, will be to line up all cynical reactionary bastards like you and have you mown down.'

'I see I shall have to start my own party,' Tom said. 'How's that for a slogan: Cynical Reactionary Bastards of the World Unite!'

'Lousy,' Bill said, and grimaced.

He had given my name to the papers as one of the founder members of the Spartacan Society. I protested that he shouldn't have done so without consulting me.

'You might not have agreed,' he said. 'Writers are inclined to be so pussyfooting where politics are concerned. I've put Col's name in too, as he'll find out when he sees tomorrow's papers. People like you and Col have to be press-ganged.'

'Yes,' Tom said with a laugh, 'and what a formidable bloody Press Gang it is: William Hickey, Cassandra, Paul Tanfield, and of course *In London Last Night*. You don't stand a chance against that gang, Stuart. You'd better submit with good grace and join the ranks.'

The project turned out to be more interesting than I had at first thought. Bill had been negotiating with a publisher to bring out at regular intervals volumes of Spartacan Essays. He reckoned that with the names that Bill gave him as potential contributors he could probably sell over five thousand copies of each volume. It would mean a regular income from royalties and – more important – a platform for our ideas. Could I afford to opt out?

'It depends on what you mean by our ideas, Bill', I said.

'I mean exactly what I say: your ideas, mine, Colin's. We've got to get together and hammer out policies. In England today there's no public debate of the real issues. The important questions aren't even being asked, much less discussed. The job of the Spartacans will be to bring them into the open. We shall be the intellectual power house of this society.'

This was the beginning of a discussion that went on for weeks. Some time before, no doubt, I would have participated in Bill's scheme with more enthusiasm, but at this particular time I felt that, with my own house in such palpable disorder, it would be preposterous to presume to set the world to rights.

'It seems to me that you've lost your nerve,' Bill reproached.

I thought he could be right, but I argued: 'I haven't. I just don't think I've got anything useful or original to say on political subjects. And I've no desire to exercise political power. I think this century has had too much of demagogues and ideologies.'

'That's the politics of the nursery,' Bill said. 'Keep your nose clean and don't have anything to do with strangers. It's not good enough, Stuart. We've got to be committed.'

'To what? People like you, Colin and I are *déracinés*. We have no class interests to defend or promote.'

'Precisely, and that's our strength. Class-based politicians are always fighting today's battles in terms of yesterday's victories. Our commitment is to the future. And I tell you, we'll get a following. People are fed up with politicians who try to capitalise on the old and crumbling antagonisms between the privileged and underprivileged, the boss class and the working class. They want vision, ideas, leadership.'

It is not surprising that, with the publicising of such views, the Spartacans were regarded in some quarters as proto-fascists. Journalists and writers with leanings to the left regarded the movement as a sinister symptom, and there was talk of the younger generation's disenchantment with democracy. But as Bill predicted, we gained a following. Private and public meetings were held, discussions and lectures organised, and before long the Spartacan Society was able to boast a nucleus of some forty or fifty members. Bill energetically organised, publicised, proselytised. Colin loyally supported him, though I think he was as sceptical as I was of the value of action on a political front. I remained a fellow-traveller, chiefly out of loyalty to Bill, though I felt all along that my incompetence to handle the problems of my own life disqualified me for any kind of leadership.

Of course, Bill and Tom knew about Joan's condition. It made no difference, and little was said about it. It was our problem, not an uncommon problem, and I was grateful to them for being sympathetic, not taking moral attitudes, above all for not saying 'We told you so.' There was one occasion, though, when Bill came down to my room and after we had talked about other things for a while he suddenly asked Joan:

'What's going to happen about the baby, Joan?'

'What can happen?' she said. 'It'll be born.'

'So what about your career as an actress?'

It was a question that hadn't arisen in our discussions, and I pricked up my ears for her answer.

'I'll probably have to take a rest for a year or so,' she said.

'Then what? How can you be out at a theatre every night, or away on tour, if you've got a kid to look after?'

'We'll cross that bridge when we come to it,' Joan said firmly. She was, I thought, every bit the brave little woman with brave little clichés, and I felt guilty that everything about her irritated me so unreasonably.

'Drop the subject, Bill,' I said. Joan and I had had another harrowing scene that afternoon. 'We've had enough of it for today.'

'Speak for yourself,' Joan said. 'It's a relief for me to talk to somebody who can be reasonable about it.'

'Bill can afford to be reasonable,' I said. 'He's not involved.'

'Alright, I won't say any more,' Bill said. 'But you're wrong about my not being involved. When I see two of my friends being the ruin of each other I can't help being involved.'

'You have an overdeveloped sense of the dramatic, Bill,' I said. 'Nobody is being ruined.'

'I hope not,' Bill said. 'But it does seem to me that recently you've suffered a loss of confidence.'

'Well I can't say I have total confidence in the Spartacan project, if that's what you mean,' I said. I knew that it wasn't what he meant, but I wanted to deflect the discussion from the personal, and I went on: 'This century has seen a whole series of projects radically to change the world, and the world is in more of a mess than it was fifty years ago. I think the most urgent thing today is not to embark on some futuristic project, but rightly to understand the mess we're in. We need to get back to concrete facts, to understand facts as they appear, events as they happen, without invoking any abstractions to explain them.'

Bill screwed up his nose. 'You sound like one of those damned linguistic philosophers. But let me take you up on those terms. You say we shouldn't explain facts by invoking abstractions. What I take it you mean is that we shouldn't twist or change or misinterpret the facts in order to fit them into our preconceptions.'

'I mean more than that,' I said. 'I mean that having preconceptions makes you misinterpret the facts.' I felt myself warming to the argument. It was a relief after the acrimonious emotional sessions with Joan to get onto something abstract and safe.

Bill nodded, thought a moment, then said, 'Would you say that this world is an ideal place, Stuart?'

I recognised the tactic. He was doing his Socratic act, contriving a series of seeming guileless questions that would lead up to a sharp knock-out blow. I played along with it, saying, 'Of course it's not ideal.'

'You can imagine it better?'

I parried it. 'I can imagine some features of it better.'

Bill chuckled. 'Your reservation doesn't invalidate my point. If you can imagine some features of it better, and those features are not yet to be met with in the world as it is, they are, quite literally, preconceptions, or abstractions if you like. Granted?'

'Okay.'

'And what is going to make those features realities? What is it that brings about change in the world?'

'That's the crux of the matter, isn't it? I would say thousands of incalculable things.'

'By incalculable you mean that you can't calculate them.'

'I mean that no one can.'

'Wrong,' Bill said emphatically, thumping the arm of the chair. 'You're right that this is the crux of the matter. I'll tell you how changes come about in the world. Because they are engineered by men of vision, men of ideals. Ideals, preconceptions, abstractions, are different words for the same thing. The man of vision is continually setting himself goals to aim at, and by the same token the highest form of society is the one that is continually evolving, that is informed with ideals and led by men of vision. England today is a stagnant society. It's our job – the job of the Spartacans – to make it a dynamic society, to define its goals and give it ideals. I don't see how you can deny it. In fact you can't, because you've said as much yourself, in your Declaration essay.

He referred to a collection of essays, touted by the publisher as 'the manifesto of the Angry Young Men', that contained quite disparate tracts by myself, Colin and Bill, John Osborne, Kenneth Tynan, Lindsay Anderson, John Wain, and as a token woman among our number, Doris Lessing.

I had originally submitted as my contribution an essay on Existentialism, but the publisher had asked for something 'a bit more controversial', and it was true that I had come up with an expression of views similar to those just expressed by Bill. But now they had a hollow ring.

I tried to explain why.

'You know, Bill, I'm not sure that all this straining onwards and upwards, all this setting up challenges for yourself and strenuously pursuing them, isn't finally life-denying. We delude ourselves with the supposed realities promised by ends and aims, and can never know what the consequences of our actions are going to be. I've been coming round to the view that Eliot put in *The Rock*:

Take no thought of the harvest,
But only of proper sowing.

'Don't quote that Tory high church royalist to me as an authority on anything,' Bill said. Then he leaned forward with an expression of earnest concern. 'You know, Stuart, it seems to me that what you've said adds up to a quite fundamental change in your ideas.'

'Yes, it does,' I agreed, 'but of course one's ideas evolve and change. Thinking is a process, it's not a condition of mulling over established views.'

Bill shook his head. 'This change isn't an evolution,' he said. 'It comes close to a kind of quietism or to old Tom's brand of Omar Khayyámic fatalism. It worries me. Ah well, must get some work done.' He stood up abruptly and made for the door, pausing to put a comradely arm around my shoulder as he went. 'Do me a favour, Stuart, if you intend to break with the Spartacans leave it for a while. In a few weeks' time we can make it out to be a break over a specific point of policy. The press will lap it up. Remember the furore caused by Wells' break with the Fabians.'

Reluctantly, because Joan had repeatedly asked me to, I agreed to discuss our situation with her father. I had met him before, during our first weeks, and on that occasion he had stood me a lunch and confided to me that he considered Joan much improved since she had come up to London. He had even gone so far as to hint that he was aware of the real nature of our relationship and was quite prepared to connive at it.

But on our second meeting there was no offer of a meal, no nod and wink, no man to man camaraderie. He came to the house and to our room with as little ceremony as he would have shown had he come in a professional capacity. Joan greeted him briefly and then left the room, throwing me a look as she went that had a suggestion of smugness, and said, 'You've had this coming to you.' Her father seemed rather less confident, even a bit flustered, as if he couldn't separate his righteous paternal indignation from the petty irritation he felt over his recent rail journey from Leigh-on-Sea. It was quite a hot day and he was wearing a heavy dark suit. Beads of sweat stood out on his brow and the bald top of his head. He was a short, heavily-built man and his teeth had conspicuous gold fillings. His manner was brisk and nervous. He ignored my offer of tea and would not sit down.

'There's no point in beating about the bush,' he said, 'I understand from Joan that you have refused to do the decent thing by her.'

The phrase confirmed my fear that we were not going to discuss the situation at all, but rather to engage in a useless duel of clichés. It would be difficult to avoid in a situation that was itself a cliché, but I held back an instinctive scornful response to 'the decent thing' and sought words that would be conciliatory enough to bring him to discuss the matter reasonably.

'Well, what have you to say for yourself?' he demanded irritably.

'For myself, nothing,' I said. 'You may find it hard to believe, but it's not myself I'm concerned about. It's Joan.'

'But not concerned enough to marry her.'

'Is concern a good enough basis for marriage?'

'Presumably you felt more than concern when you made her pregnant.'

'I sincerely believed that I loved her.'

That drew his derision. The trouble with my type was that we spent so much time examining ourselves that we didn't know from one minute to the next what we sincerely felt or believed. He supposed that when I found out she was pregnant I'd conveniently discovered that I no longer cared for her. I told him it had happened before that, as Joan would confirm. We had virtually separated when I went to Cornwall. I had come back because I had wanted to help her.

'By getting her to have an abortion? Which is not only dangerous, but illegal too.'

I said I respected her reasons for not wanting to have one. But marriage was out of the question. What would it be for? Just to give the child a name? Surely to marry without love was just to stunt two lives in cringing observance of a social convention, and one that was changing anyway.

Yes, I had all the answers, he said, but one day if I was lucky I'd stop baying for the moon and learn that life only really begins when a man can put himself and his precious freedom and independence in the background and devote his life to someone else.

'Or something else,' I put in.

The doctor sighed and smiled. 'Yes, I know you writer types fancy that the service of your art is the be-all and end-all. But I've done a bit of reading, and it seems to me that all that's worthwhile in literature is an overspill from life. You can choose to shun life and spin your clever webs of words, but they won't ever add up to anything, believe me.'

It shook me that this little provincial doctor could so precisely formulate my own secret apprehensions. I had suspected a degree of hypocrisy in what he said, remembering things that Joan had told me about him, but now I saw him as a man who had had disappointments and disillusions in life, who had himself perhaps experienced the decay of love, but who had in a fashion, and not discreditably, come through. But I felt that I still had to fight back.

'You speak as if to avoid marriage is to shun life,' I said. 'I don't think that's true, and I don't think you can accuse me of shunning either life or my responsibilities. I have, after all, stayed with Joan.'

'But withdrawn your affections,' he sneered.

'I tell you that had happened before all this came up.'

I had deliberately not said 'before she got pregnant', but he seized on the implication and said,

'In other words, you have the morals of an alley-cat.'

He knew he had the upper hand with that. He strolled over to the window and looked out onto the traffic in Chepstow Road. He had his back to me when he concluded:

'Well, I see I misjudged you. I thought you were a mature young man whose influence on Joan could only be for the good. But I was wrong. You've let her down badly. You've not only caused her a disillusion that she'll take years to get over, but you've also managed to ruin her chances of success in the career she'd set her heart on. Well, we'll make sure that you don't get away with it scot free. You're going to pay for your mistake, my boy, and if you don't do it willingly we'll slap a paternity suit on you.'

'That won't be necessary,' I said.

'We'll see,' he said.

I resolved that it wouldn't be necessary. Confronted by the little doctor, who clearly held all he imagined I stood for in very low esteem, I decided that I would stick by Joan and see her through her pregnancy if only to prove him wrong. We reached a kind of accommodation in the days that followed. Joan, in fact, was so accommodating that I sometimes suspected that she was engaged in a subtle campaign to gain by stealth what she and her father had failed to gain through moral or emotional coercion. There were no tantrums, no demands, and she accepted without demur my insistence that she shouldn't seek or accept any financial help from her father.

Although we were quite poor and such income as I had from occasional articles and book reviews was a pittance, we eked it out and Joan performed little culinary miracles on our single gas ring. I took to working late in the spare room and going to sleep there about three or four o'clock in the morning. It was understood that we should no longer sleep together.

Then one day two simultaneous and unforeseen events changed things quite fundamentally.

Joan had a hospital appointment for an ante-natal examination, and I went with her. It was another of those little things I did, like seeing her father, because I felt guilty that I was going to abandon her and in the circumstances it was the least I could do. I sat for over an hour on a hard uncomfortable chair in a bleak and dimly-lit waiting annexe in an out-patients department. At first I sat where I could command a view of the ante-room where about a dozen women were waiting to be summoned into the doctor's or gynaecologist's presence, but then an elderly nurse who looked as if she had had her face starched as well as her uniform asked me to move, 'because some of the girls get embarrassed'. The implication was that I had chosen that seat in order to indulge in a bit of cheap voyeurism, as perhaps I had, though there was nothing to see out of the ordinary, except occasionally a woman quite decently wrapped in a dressing gown. If I was stealing a view of anything in that ante-room, it was of an exclusively female world that at once fascinated and repelled me. They were all presumably strangers to one another, and yet most of them were talking quite animatedly. Joan, I noticed before I was moved on by the starched nurse, was as communicative as any of them, laughing and talking with her neighbour. What about? I wondered. 'You'd be surprised' she said when I asked her afterwards. 'Obstetrics and men,' I surmised, and she said 'Maybe' in a tone that conceded that I was right; but what was surprising was not what they were talking about, but the manner, the animation, the lack of inhibitions. I supposed it to be a kind of comradeship in misfortune.

Most of the women were dowdy and plain, and among them Joan shone. She was not yet very far into her pregnancy, and could still wear a belted skirt with a short-sleeved summer blouse and high-heeled shoes, but it was clear that even in her later stages she would not look anything like some of those grotesques. Seeing her there among the others in the ante-room, chatting away happily in a female world and looking attractive and clearly differing from the others in that she cared about her appearance, I quite warmed to her.

Sitting across the room from me was a little old lady in a shabby black coat. After a while a young ambulance man came in and approaching her with open arms and a merry smile said, 'Come into my arms, you bundle of charms,' and as he helped her to her feet asked, 'What are you doing in this place then, love? Been a naughty girl, have you?' The woman chortled as she trudged slowly to the door with the ambulance man's help. 'Come on, love, I'll race you to the ambulance,' he said, and she chortled again and said something I couldn't catch in a quavering voice. The scene affected me because I felt by contrast with that young man my own emotional bankruptcy. His sympathies could reach out to an old bag of bones, but mine were all knotted up with guilt and resentment and couldn't even extend to the girl I had not long ago regarded as my first and only love.

When we got back from the hospital there was a note by the phone in Bill's spidery scrawl saying that Joan was to call a Mr Davis at a Gerrard number, urgent. The message sent her into a tizzy of excitement. Mr Davis, she explained, was her agent, and his phoning could only mean one thing: that she had got the part she had auditioned for a couple of weeks before in a play that was to open in Oxford. She phoned, and the Davis man confirmed her hopes. Suddenly she was radiant, transformed, joyous. She embraced me and danced about the room.

'This could be my break, she said. 'If the show is a success in Oxford, it could move into town. Isn't it wonderful news?

'But how long would you be able to stay with it? Do they know you're pregnant?'

'Of course I didn't tell them that. But if I wear the right clothes I can disguise it for weeks. A pregnant woman doesn't have to look like a tank. It's all a matter of posture. The doctor said I have a very good carriage. And, just think, it will mean money. We'll have some money.'

She so much wanted me to share her excitement. And I did, though I didn't much like the financial inducement. I could imagine her father accusing me of letting her work and living off her earnings.

'Pooh! It doesn't matter what Daddy thinks,' she said when I expressed my misgivings. 'It's my break. We must celebrate.'

Bill, Greta and Tom were generous and genuine in their congratulations, and Tom proposed that we should celebrate the occasion by dining out together that evening at the little Italian restaurant we occasionally went to in Notting Hill. We spent a merry couple of hours there, and returned to Chepstow Road to extend the merriment with drinks in Tom's room, and at the end of the evening we had become so mellow and relaxed that the customary routine of my working late in the spare room was subverted, and when Joan said, 'Why don't you stay with me tonight?' the idea seemed but a natural culmination of the celebratory mood and didn't have the ominous implications it might have had another night. 'We don't have to make love,' she added. 'I've come to terms with the fact that you don't find me attractive any more.'

'I thought you looked very attractive at the clinic today,' I said, alcohol no doubt spurring the imprudence, which I then compounded by adding, 'You quite stood out among all those frumps.'

'I'll take that as the nearest you can manage to a compliment,' she said. 'Don't stay if you don't want to.'

'It was meant as a compliment,' I said. 'And yes, I'd like to stay.'

'Oh, goody. So how are we going to arrange it? Do I go on the floor or do you? 'Or' – and this with a mischievous throaty-theatrical delivery – 'do we risk it top to toe?'

'We might even risk it back to back,' I said.

Which we did, for a time. I went to bed first, keeping my day-shirt on, and lay there listening to the familiar little sounds she made as she prepared for bed, removing her make-up, brushing her hair, undressing. I was feeling the effects of the alcohol, but I was wide awake. Then Joan slipped into the bed as if not wishing to disturb me and turned to switch off the bedside light. We lay motionless for a long time, each listening to the other's breathing and knowing that we were both still awake, and knowing too as time passed and neither of us dropped off that something would have to happen.

After the wine, the celebratory mood, the long period of celibacy, we were voracious for one another and made love as never before. In the ensuing mood of relaxation and intimacy Joan said, 'that was just like the early days.' Then, after a reflective pause, 'Don't you think it a shame not to take advantage of the time when we can do it without there being any danger? We have, after all, come to an understanding about the baby and I've accepted that we aren't going to get married, but do you have to keep so aloof and distant?'

'Just like the early days,' I said, ignoring her questions and affecting sleepiness and satiety. 'Let us sleep now.'

'I can't help still being in love with you,' Joan said before she fell asleep.

If I had reflected at all before sleeping with her that night, it was to think that it would be a one-off situation, an isolated act with no strings attached, a mutual relief and pleasure. But the simplicities of the night disappeared with the coming of day. The logic, both mine and hers, no longer resolved itself in a cosy complicity. It ran up against dead ends, tangled itself in the non sequiturs of the heart. The way things had been going before, Joan would never have said she was still in love with me. Her confession, I realised, made nonsense of my idea of what had happened the night before. She had not used me as I had used her. I had made the mistake of thinking that her need for sex was like my need, a need to alleviate a kind of cramp. That she was pregnant with my child and that she had done it with love, were facts that I had blindly, or alcoholically, set no store by.

The next morning I noticed that there was an unaccustomed bravura in her manner, a lightness and vigour in her movements, a confidence in her speech, and above all a lack of shyness. When she got up she stood naked, surveying herself in the mirror.

'Do you think my breasts are getting bigger?' she said.

'Not noticeably.'

'I think they are. They feel heavier.' She weighed one in each hand, still contemplating herself in the mirror. 'Didn't they feel heavier to you?'

I resented this reference to the intimacy of the night and said sharply, 'No.'

'They wouldn't when I was lying flat, would they?' she said, either not catching or ignoring the note in my voice. 'Look, those are the milk glands.' She came over and sat beside me on the bed and pointed out the cluster of little white pimples around the bud of her nipple. 'It's funny they develop so early, isn't it?'

She wanted to involve me in what she called 'the extraordinary and miraculous process of making a human being.' That was another change: she began to talk as if she was actually enjoying being pregnant. I must have been manifestly unresponsive and recalcitrant when she did so, for on an occasion a few days later she said, 'I'm worried for you, Stuart. I'm worried what this is doing to you.'

That was ironical. I laughed. 'Doing to me? But you're the one who is going through it. You needn't spare any of your sympathy for me.'

She was wide-eyed, earnest, soft-spoken. 'I don't think I'm the only one going through it. I think you are too, even if you won't admit it to yourself. In fact I think it might be worse for you because I still love you and that helps. And it's because I love you that I want you to gain something from this, which you won't do by shutting yourself off, grudgingly doing what you imagine is the right thing, and just biding your time until I'm out of your hair.'

Pregnancy was supposed to make a woman cow-like and of-the-earth-earthy, not intuitive and articulate. I was a little awed by this new Joan. I wanted to take her up on the word 'grudgingly', but didn't because in the circumstances it would be a mere cavil.

'Don't you know what to make of me?' she said when I didn't reply. 'Do you suspect that I'm just being a cunning female? For what it's worth, I can promise you that I'm not. It's you I'm thinking of, not myself.' Her large brown eyes found and fixed mine with a look that was composed and compassionate.

Logic was called for, recapitulation, time to think, to get bearings. I found myself falling back on the glib techniques of the debating platform. 'You say you want me to gain something. Alright, I accept that, but...'

'Please, Stuart! Please don't go on like that.' She swung forward and her hair swept the floor. 'If you don't know what I mean, it's no good talking. You can't get at it that way.'

I contemplated a cascade of shining hair in the sun's beam, a figure bent double – in mirth or in exasperation? – a woman who a few months ago would have been a barely-noticed passer-by in the street and was now inextricably linked with my life, my future, but was still a stranger. She flung her head back and said, 'You don't have to try so hard. You only have to accept the fact that you are going to be a father. That's all I ask. It isn't much. You don't have to marry me. You don't even have to support me. Just live it through, really live it, and don't shut yourself off and get embittered.'

Her words sank in, but they didn't change anything. How did one accept the fact that one was going to be a father? A woman, with the child growing in her, might go through a spiritual change parallel with the physical one, but I doubted whether a man, even when he was in love with the woman and wanted the child, ever got such joy or satisfaction out of impending fatherhood as a woman did out of motherhood. 'That's all I ask,' Joan had said. 'It's not much.' But what was for her 'not much' was for me impossible, and the demand only drove me deeper into sullen and resentful introspection.

When I took her to Paddington to get the train to Oxford the following week, Joan was full of excitement and apprehensions about what she was embarking on. I saw her off with encouraging and reassuring words, but as I watched the train draw away it was with a happy sense of liberation from her tenacious and terrible love.

His Dear Time's Waste - Stuart Holroyd

4

Colin regarded Bill rather as Matthew Arnold regarded the working classes, as 'our playful giant.' His attitude to the Spartacan project was one of benign indulgence, and it was with such a regard that he had agreed to give a talk to a gathering of the Spartacan Society and guests. When Colin hit London he did so with the violence of a hurricane. If you were in his path you got swept up in a round of parties, social visits and sessions in pubs and clubs that demanded a high degree of physical, intellectual and alcoholic endurance. The festive note was struck at the start, for he moved in with crates of booze and brimming with bluff bonhomie. On this occasion he arrived a day earlier than expected. It was late afternoon and we were all in Tom's room when he walked in, his tall, rangy figure clad as usual in bulky jersey and baggy trousers. He smiled boyishly, pleased at the minor sensation his appearance had caused. Bill greeted him effusively, with a pumping of the hand and a slap on the shoulder, as befitted a meeting of comradely giants.

'Great to see you, Col,' he said. 'It's about time you spent some time in town instead of skulking down there in the country. There are great things happening.'

'You mean this Spartacan business?' Colin said with a laugh. 'Still playing the political power game, Bill?'

'Someone has to if English society is to get the shot in the arm it needs.'

'I suppose so,' Colin conceded genially. 'So how's it going with the Spartacan essays publisher? Proving a bit of a Fabian is he as regards coming up with an advance?'

'Afraid so.'

'Typical. But let me show you what I found in that bookshop near the Cathedral in Salisbury on the way up.'

He opened a bulky parcel and proceeded to thrust books at each of us, with a brief eager comment on each as he did so.

I was simultaneously invited to appreciate an edition of *The Egyptian Book of the Dead*, an obscure eighteenth century clergyman's journal and an illustrated copy of de Sade's *120 Days of Sodom*.

After about half an hour Colin announced that he had to go and meet someone and asked for help to get some things from the car. I said I would move my things out of the spare room and went downstairs with him.

'Been using the place as a refuge from Joan?' he said when we were alone in the room together. There was a note of amusement in his voice.

'I've been working here at night. I find I get more done in the early hours when there aren't likely to be any interruptions.'

He pointedly ignored my evasion. 'I thought it was a mistake to have her come and live here in the first place. How are things working out? Did you contact Carole-Ann?'

'No point. She wants to go through with it, and then probably have the kid adopted.'

He looked dubious. 'I've heard that before. They never do when it comes to it, though.'

'She wants to get on with her career.'

Colin shook his head. 'Damnable business,' he laconically sympathised. 'Where is she anyway?'

'In Oxford. She's got a small part in a production at the Oxford Playhouse.'

'That's good,' he said ambiguously.

The meeting he had to get to was with a girl named Fanny who had sent him an essay she had written on his work. 'A surprisingly intelligent and perceptive piece for a seventeen year-old convent girl,' he said. 'Why don't you come along? She's going to have a friend with her. We'll get Bill to come too. Afterwards we can go on to Sandy and Jon's. I promised to see them this evening.'

I hadn't seen Sandy and Jon since the evening of the production of *The Tenth Chance* at the Royal Court, when they had ushered me into the bar away from the commotion that had produced the headline 'The Angry Young Men Get Angry With One Another'. It would be good to see them again.

In the car Colin told us about an American he was to meet the next day who was in London buying material from young writers on behalf of a university that was accumulating a library of original manuscripts, drafts, letters, diaries, jottings and items from what he called 'file thirteen', meaning the waste paper basket. Colin had brought with him a bundle of his original manuscripts for which he was getting five hundred dollars, and he had suggested to the American that he should get his university to invest in material from me and Bill too.

Colin had arranged to meet the convent girls at a bar on the Bayswater Road which had a forecourt with tables and sunshades. He introduced me and Bill as 'the only two other geniuses in England today' and left us while he went to order drinks. Fanny was a petite and slender girl with shoulder-length hair that she kept tossing back, revealing an intelligent, animated face with features a little too sharp to be called beautiful. Her friend, known as 'Bunny' though really called Marion, was taller, more generously fleshed both in face and figure, blonde and of the two the prettier but the less vivacious. Both girls wore colourful summer dresses of a length and cut that would certainly have been frowned upon by the pious sisterhood that had until recently been charged with their education.

'Colin says you wrote an excellent essay on his work, Fanny,' Bill said. 'Are you going to be a writer?'

'I'd like to be,' she said, 'only it's not a thing one decides to be, is it? I mean, I want to write, but one can't call oneself a writer until one's published something.'

Bill frowned. 'Let me give you a tip, Fanny. Drop this "one" affectation. Only BBC mandarins and royalty speak like that nowadays. Always speak your mind and don't hide yourself or your opinions behind the impersonal pronoun.'

The other girl giggled, it wasn't clear whether at Fanny's being admonished or at Bill's sententious tone. Bill turned to her. 'And what do you want to do, Bunny?'

'I think I might be a model,' she said.

'Artist's model, fashion, or photographic?'

'Oh, fashion,' she said with an emphasis that suggested there was something disreputable about the alternatives.

'Hmm, I doubt that you'd make it in the fashion line,' Bill said.

'Why?'

'Fashion models invariably have small breasts. In haute couture, as they ridiculously call it, the favoured figure is not the fully feminine but the gamine, the rather boyish. How do you explain that?' He cocked an inquiring look at each of the girls in turn. Fanny took it up.

'I suppose haute couture has more to do with elegance than with sex appeal.'

Bill nodded, considering it. 'Yes, you're probably right.' He turned to the other girl. 'So it's photographic, not fashion, for you Bunny, and a great success you should be at it.'

Colin returned with the drinks. 'What have you been saying to her, Bill?' he said. 'The girl's gone as red a beetroot.'

'He's been telling her that her breasts are too big,' Fanny said, clearly delighting in her friend's discomfiture, but with a look towards Bill that suggested an admonition.

'How ungallant, Bill.' Colin looked appraisingly at Bunny. 'I wouldn't say that. Certainly not. But how did the subject come up in the first couple of minutes after you'd met?'

'I said that she hadn't the figure for fashion modelling,' Bill explained, 'and if Bunny wants to be a model she'd stand more chance as a photographic model.'

'Quite right.' Colin nodded vigorously, took a draught of his beer and turned to the girl. 'And if you ever want to get some practice, Bunny, my Brownie is always at your service.'

'Oh, come on, both of you,' I put in. 'You're embarrassing her. Talk about ungallant, Col.'

'Yes,' Bill said, clicking his tongue in remonstrance. 'The double entendre is the wit of the travelling salesman. The girls have a right to expect better of a literary giant.'

'Well, we're here to talk about Fanny's essay, aren't we?' Colin said, comfortably settling into literary giant mode. 'It was very insightful and well written; better than much of the stuff written by many so-called literary critics. Thoughtful, too, in that you had reservations.'

'Well yes,' Fanny said, 'I have problems with the idea of the serial murderer as a type of Outsider, given that you've generally represented the Outsider as a kind of hero figure.'

'This is a mistake many people have made,' Colin said. 'The Outsider is neither a hero nor an anti-hero, he's a psychological type, and the book is a scientific psychological study as objective as a thesis on microbiology.' He went on to explain how extreme, pathological or aberrant phenomena and behaviours enable the understanding and definition of things that might not otherwise be perceived.

The low-geared rush-hour traffic growled along Bayswater Road. Across the road Hyde Park, lush with spring foliage, offered lover, poet or recluse a make-believe rural retreat. My attention drifted away from Colin's familiar disquisition. The forecourt tables filled with suited men disgorged from offices, either accompanied by secretaries, typists or even wives, or clustered in groups laughing at jokes or solemnly talking business. Colin was addressing all his attention to Fanny, and Bill had started talking to Bunny. I overheard that she lived in Barnet and that Daddy was a solicitor with a firm in the City.

'Catholic?' Bill asked.

'Oh no,' the girl said. 'Daddy's a confirmed fence-sitter in everything, but for some reason he believes in nuns. I couldn't tell him that half of them are lesbians, or at least they were at our convent.'

They laughed. Bill had apparently been forgiven his initial impropriety. I realised that I had not so far contributed anything to the occasion, so I stood up and proposed to buy everyone a drink.

'Must make it a quick one,' Colin said. 'I told Sandy and Jon we'd be there about six.'

'Oh, are you leaving us so soon?' Fanny said.

'Of course not. You're coming with us.'

It seemed that Colin collected namesakes rather as he collected fellow geniuses, for he counted among his wider circle of friends the novelist Angus Wilson and also Sandy Wilson, the composer and librettist of the hit show *The Boy Friend*. It was through Colin that Anne and I had met Sandy and his friend Jon Rose in '56. Jon was an Australian who had come to London some ten years before aspiring to fame and fortune as a singer, and he and Sandy had formed a cabaret duo before the success of *The Boy Friend* changed their lives. He was a tall, slim young man, extrovert and garrulous and in voice and manner flagrantly and joyously gay. Sandy, by contrast, was rather self-effacing, had a long, furrowed and melancholy face that would have qualified him to be cast as Cervantes' 'knight of the sorrowful countenance', but with a friendly smile that was like a sunburst over a railway siding.

Sandy and Jon's place was a small house overlooking Hampstead Heath. Jon answered the door and, unfazed by the size of our party, ushered us in with effusive greetings. The front door opened directly into a large sitting room with a carpet so thick that you felt you were wading through it. There was a large mauve studio couch with matching armchairs, a long, low, glass-topped table, and two bronze Apollo figures serving as standard lamps. Numerous little bulbs set in a blue ceiling gave the effect of a night sky. The Apollo theme was taken up by the plaster pediments of an arch which led into another room where there was a grand piano. The general impression of having stepped out of the day into a plush nightclub was augmented by the music issuing from a concealed hi-fi system, a recording of the other hit musical show of the day, *My Fair Lady*.

Sandy turned the volume down and came through from the other room to greet us. He said to me, 'You've just missed your ex. She stayed with us for a few days last week.'

'Anne did? How come?' The news was perplexing. Anne had always been more at ease with Jon and Sandy than I, but I didn't know they had become so close.

'Had some sort of tiff with Michael,' Jon explained; 'We're Heartbreak Hotel here, don't you know? Anyway, yours truly did his agony aunt bit and they were soon all lovey-dovey again.'

Colin said he had brought something for Sandy and presented him with a wrapped record.

'Oh no!' said Jon with affected horror, 'not another of your dreary Teutonic heavyweights. Since meeting you, Sandy has been going on as if he'd be content with nothing less than being right up there with Wagner or Alban bloody Berg. The new show is terrific, but he's come over all morose and worried as hell about it.'

'It's Carl Orff's *Carmina Burana*,' Colin said. 'Magnificent stuff, and certainly not dreary. Just give it a hearing.'

'Christ, he's trying to educate me now!' Jon said. Hopeless task: doesn't he know that Frivolity is my middle name? Jon Frivolity Rose: yes, it has a ring. Now, how about drinks for everybody? Whiskey all round?'

Nobody demurred, so Jon poured large whiskeys in heavy cut-glass tumblers. Fanny and Bunny, who had drunk *Babycham* before, looked at the glasses, and at each other, with some dismay, but took tentative sips.

'I thought *Valmouth* deserved better,' Colin said, alluding to Sandy's musical adaptation of Ronald Firbank's high camp novella which had had a mealy-mouthed critical reception and a short run at Hammersmith some months before. 'It's typical of the fucking critics to murder the next work after one that's been a runaway success, as I know all too well. You just have to plough on. So how's the new show coming along, Sandy?'

'Don't ask Sandy, he's going through menopausal depression,' Jon said. 'I tell you, it's going to be good, a masterpiece. Sequel to *The Boy Friend*, ten years on, and musically of the thirties too, more Cole Porter than the Charleston. Do you know what Noel Coward said to Sandy when we had dinner with him? He said, "There are three good lyric-writers today, Cole, myself, and you". So come on, Sandy, shake off the black dog and give our guests a treat. Give us, *Whatever Happened to Love?'*

'Not now.'

'Yes, now,' Jon insisted, 'if only as a compliment to present company.' He raised his glass to each of the girls in turn and they responded with a sip and a giggle.

Sandy trundled with mock reluctance over to the piano, took some time to compose himself and then launched vigorously, and as requested, into *Whatever Happened to Love?* the number from his show, *Divorce Me, Darling!*

We all applauded the performance. Colin had strolled over to the piano in the course of it, and afterwards he and Sandy spent some time thumbing through the score. Jon took the opportunity to tell us a bit of his life story.

'All this,' - he waved his glass at the room in general - 'is new. Before *The Boy Friend* we hadn't a bean between us. I believed in him, though, knew he was a fucking musical genius. Worked to keep us going. Now the ice cream factory, that was a revelation. Put me off ice cream for life. A pittance, virtual slave labour, men venting their resentment by pissing into the vats. Then there was the glass factory. More vats, big ones of molten glass. There were these gantries above them, nice warm place to have your lunch sandwiches in winter, but one poor bugger stumbled and plunged down into one of the vats, and before he reached it he turned into a beautiful blue flame, like a tongue of fire leaping out of the vat, and no trace of him was ever found. I kid you not.'

This last was addressed to Bill, who had laughed his incredulity.

'An original way to go,' Bill said.

'Yes, I sometimes think I owe my life to that poor bugger, because if ever I feel suicidal I know that by the time I could get a job again in a glass factory the urge will have passed.'

Colin and Sandy came to join us. We sat around for another half hour, mostly listening to both Jon and Sandy enthuse about their recent discovery of dianetics, the 'science of the mind' central to Scientology. It was, Jon said, a wonderful and effective technique of spiritual regeneration, of clearing the mind and body of the dross of 'engrams', which were some kind of negative and cluttering residue of past experiences, even going back beyond childhood. Both he and Sandy had, with the help of a trained 'auditor', benefited hugely from the technique. Their enthusiasm was such that the subject was not open to discussion or argument and it would be churlish to show anything but indulgent interest, so we drank our whiskey and listened and nodded, expressing interest even to the point of promising to peruse some literature that we (excluding the girls) were given, and it was in what Fanny described as a 'rather squiffy' state that we eventually left Jon and Sandy's.

Scientology, Colin said when we were in the car, was the creation of a science fiction writer called L.

Ron Hubbard, and in his opinion was a pseudo science and a crap religion, but Sandy and Jon were good friends and if they wanted to believe in it and found it helpful he wasn't going to argue.

Bill said he had found the experience surreal, the ridiculous room with its Apollos and stars, Jon's talk about a man turning into a tongue of fire and the nonsense about engrams.

Colin said with a laugh, 'What irked you was that you weren't able to get a word in about Spartacanism. And you were right. I think Jon Frivolity Rose would be a hard nut to crack.'

'Nut is the word,' Bill said.

'I thought they were sweet, and fun,' Bunny said.

'Women often like queers,' Bill observed.

We dropped Bunny off at Hampstead tube station to get a train to Barnet and took Fanny to her parents' home in Maida Vale, where, with uncharacteristic courtesy, Colin opened the car door for her and, talking in a manner that suggested he was arranging something, accompanied her a little way along the street before kissing her on the cheek and waving a smiling goodbye.

Oliver Moxon's spacious Chelsea house seemed an oddly inappropriate place for a meeting of a subversive political society. Everything about it proclaimed a vested interest in the class-structured, privilege-ridden order that the Spartacan philosophy, as Bill expounded it, regarded as a brake on the advancement and effectiveness of the man of genius and vision. But Oliver himself was quite a catch, with his wealth and political experience, which, though it hadn't gone beyond the hustings, was more than any other founder Spartacan could boast of. He had stood as a Liberal candidate in parliamentary elections, and his politics, he declared, were those of Edmund Burke. But Bill had persuaded him that there was room for all shades of opinion in the Spartacan movement.

About fifty people had gathered for the meeting that Colin was to address. There were few seats and a lot of us had to sit on the floor. I knew quite a number of the people there and recognised several of Bill's recent catches – a pretty actress, a publisher, a septuagenarian titled lady, some writers and journalists – and there were others whom I couldn't place although their faces were familiar. Among these was a young woman sitting across the room talking to a man dressed rather conspicuously in a plain respectable business suit. I racked my brain to place her, but unsuccessfully.

Suddenly Bill was standing before the assembly with his arms outstretched above him, as if acknowledging the roar of a crowd after a sporting triumph. The gesture had the desired effect of reducing the loud hubbub of conversation to a low murmur. He proceeded to introduce Colin and thank him for coming up from Cornwall for the occasion, and Colin stepped forward, acknowledged the scattered applause with his boyish smile and a nod, and launched into his talk. He spoke initially about some recent research which had demonstrated that in a colony of rats there were only five per cent of the population that possessed leadership qualities, and that without them the rest became malleable and quite without initiative. The fact that the same applied to human beings, he said, had been proved by the behaviour of American prisoners subjected to Chinese 'thought reform' techniques during the Korean War. The implications were clearly that in human societies the effective political power ought to be in the hands of the five per cent minority who were equipped to exercise it, and this would not happen while political advancement depended on class or party loyalties.

I suddenly remembered where I had met the young woman before. The expression on her face as she listened reminded me. She had worn the same expression listening to the brothers, Paul and Brian. It seemed long ago, with all that had happened in the interim, but it was only a few weeks.

She became aware that I was looking at her, looked up and gave me a smile of recognition. She held it just long enough to tell me that she too remembered the intensity of the looks we had exchanged that day in the pub and back at the house while the brothers entertained one another. If she remembered that, she must remember too the twilight expedition into the wild garden to pick spinach, her taking my hand and above all, our kisses. Now she had looked away and down, seemingly paying attention to Colin's speech, but I could see that the ghost of the smile lingered and thought that she too may be reminiscing.

When I turned my attention back to Colin's talk he had switched into his hortatory mode, urging that what was essential was a further advance in human evolution, which could only be accomplished by increasing the powers of the mind.

'We are not yet creatures of the mind,' he was saying. 'We shun pure thought because after a time it bores and depresses us. We have in us a very useful shut-out mechanism, which enables us for example to listen to music and concentrate on it and shut out the loud ticking of a clock or the cries of children playing. But try to listen to a Bartok string quartet right through, and what happens? Before long you find that this clever and useful psychological mechanism has shut out the music as well, that the initial concentration has gone and you're listening with half your mind. The trouble is that though we have this shut-out mechanism we don't know how to control it. The next step in evolution will be taken by those who learn to control it, who don't get bored or depressed after spending half an hour in the world of the mind, because for them the world of the mind is the natural and proper element, the only element in which they can live.'

Susan, that was her name. I wondered who her companion was, and what she was doing here. I had gathered when we first met that her marriage to Brian was on the rocks, and I thought now that maybe it had finally foundered and the smiling tailor's dummy who now sat beside her had barged in to snap her up. Maybe he had been on the sidelines all along, waiting his chance. Or maybe she had been in the habit of casually flirting, and I was just one of several conquests. It was she, after all, who had initiated the expedition into the garden. Maybe, maybe... I smiled at the thought that my present mental processes were a fine example of the inattentiveness that Colin was deploring. He had got on to the subject of Existentialism. I recognised the words he had spoken to me in Cornwall when I felt he was rehearsing for his coming American lecture tour, and my attention drifted again.

Somehow she looked younger than I recalled. In Battle she had been associated in my mind with her roles as mother and housewife and had had a somewhat harassed look, which would not be surprising if she had marital problems. Tonight she didn't look at all the housewife, but rather a self-aware young woman groomed for an evening out, wearing a skirt and sweater that revealed her figure without unduly emphasising it, her hair lightly styled to frame a face distinguished by her full lips and high cheek bones.

Now Colin was talking about Albert Camus, the French author of the other book with the title *The Outsider*. 'Camus's work can be understood as an exploring and defining of the conditions necessary for a truly human life,' he was saying. 'Camus says that creation must be corrected. What he means is that the results of man's mischief must be redeemed by an effort of man's intelligence and humanity. But the question is, what then? We are in life and the world, whether we like its conditions or not. We have an obligation to life itself. The thing that defines life is the urge to change, and the thing that distinguishes man from all other life is that in him this urge can become conscious and subject to the workings of the will. So the new Existentialism holds that a person only truly reaches what Malraux called "man's estate" by establishing the will to change at the centre of his consciousness and his life. Not to "correct creation", but to become it and to advance it, both in our own lives and in our society, must be our aim and the focus of our efforts. Thank you.'

There was some puzzlement at his rather abrupt conclusion, but then some scattered applause, which gathered momentum and assurance when the elderly titled lady called out, 'Well said young man. I agreed with every word, at least every word I understood.' That made people laugh and clap more. Bill stood up and thanked him for his 'thought-provoking and brilliantly reasoned contribution to Spartacan philosophy', adding that he hoped Colin would expand his ideas in the first volume of Spartacan Essays.

There followed a question-and-answer and discussion session for half an hour or so. When the meeting broke up I crossed the room to where Susan Rowland was standing. 'Hello, how's Sussex?' I said, intending the question as a reminder of our last meeting. She answered, equally inanely, 'Oh it's fine, or was this morning when we left,' but I knew from her expression that she too remembered what had happened in the garden those weeks ago, though there was nothing to indicate whether for her the memory was a regrettable or an agreeable one.

She introduced her friend as Bruce Willard, 'my escort'.

Bill had met the brothers and Susan on a visit to Sussex with Paul, and he suggested after the meeting that she and Bruce should join us back at the house for a drink.

'Well, we have to drive back to Sussex tonight,' Bruce said.

Susan said, in a tone that settled the matter, 'It's early yet. We can go back for a little while, then drive down when the roads are clearer.'

Colin had another appointment to go on to, but Tom joined us and after hearty leave-takings from the rest and a brief and intense conspiratorial exchange between Bill and our host we filed down the oak-panelled staircase, across the resounding parquet hall and out into Chester Square.

Bruce led us to a sleek white Jaguar parked a short distance away, and while he fumbled in his pockets for his keys Bill said, 'What do you do, Bruce? I trust it's something shady because anybody who earns this sort of money by honest means must have to sell out the best part of himself to get it.'

He laughed, but it didn't really take the sting out of the remark. Tom did, however, saying, 'Take no notice, Bruce. Bill speaks with the traditional rancorous voice of the bumming classes.'

'It's not rancour, Tom, it's envy,' Bill said, resorting to frankness to exculpate himself. 'I enjoy the creature comforts. I just don't like having to pay for them, and I don't want anyone else to pay for them, unless like Oliver back there they have a private income and don't have to sweat their guts and soul out to do it.'

'So up with privilege, eh?' Bruce said slyly. I was reluctantly impressed.

Bruce drove through the London traffic with ease and dash. It was one of the much-publicised psycho-sociological axioms of the 1950s that cars were sexual symbols, and that a handsome, bronzed brute of a man at the wheel of a sports car was irresistible to women. Bruce was, undeniably, handsome and, moreover, bronzed – I later learned that he was on leave from a job in Africa – and although Susan had introduced him as her 'escort' I thought that if he aspired to be anything other he certainly held all the cards.

'Well, are you converted, Susan?' Bill asked as we drove through Knightsbridge.

'Whatever to?' Susan said with a laugh.

'Spartacanism, of course.'

'No, Bill,' she said. 'But don't let it worry you. After all, I'm only a woman.'

'One thing I deplore,' Bill said, 'is people who parade their misfortunes as excuses for intellectual flaccidity. You can't help being a woman, Sue, but you can help not having opinions.'

She was unimpressed by the epigrammatic weight of the reproach. 'I do have opinions, Bill, but I don't always want to air them,' she said.

Back at the house, while Tom was dispensing glasses of wine borrowed for the occasion from Colin's stock, Bill took another tack and asked Susan if he could count her among the founder members.

'I don't think there would be any point, Bill,' she said. 'For one thing, I live in the country, but also I don't see that there's anything to be converted to.'

'You'd have to come to more meetings to judge of that,' Bill said.

'I don't think I'd be able to do that. But why should you bother about converting me? When I say I'm only a woman I'm not being sarcastic but, like most women, I'm quite content to leave to you men the job of setting the world to rights.' Despite the disclaimer, there was in her voice an edge of teasing sarcasm.

'Traitress!' Bill theatrically exclaimed. 'If Mrs. Pankhurst could hear you she'd turn in her grave.'

'I think it must have been quite fun to be a suffragette,' Susan said, 'and to have all those pompous Edwardian gentlemen running rings round themselves and getting apoplectic.'

'You can't win, Bill,' Tom said, 'it's a case of an irresistible force meeting an immovable object.'

'On the contrary, the difficulty of arguing with someone like Susan is that she won't stand her ground. She's no immovable object, she moves all over the place. It's like grappling with smoke.'

'I'm sorry, Bill,' Susan said with mock contrition, 'I didn't know it was one of the rules of this sort of game that you had to offer yourself as a sitting target.'

'You don't, you just have to be intellectually consistent.'

'Isn't that a lot to ask of a woman?' Her tone was still level and her manner playful, in contrast with Bill's comically exaggerated but not entirely affected exasperation. 'I mean, every man knows that women can't really discuss because they can't help bringing in emotions and personalities.'

'I know a lot of women who don't,' Bill said, rather losing his grip in a rush of inappropriate magnanimity.

'And I know a lot of men who do,' Susan struck back sharply. 'In fact I think the real difference isn't to do with emotions at all. It's a question of knowing the rules of the game. Sessions like this evening must be great fun. I mean, it's like belonging to a chess or bridge club, isn't it?'

'You compare the Spartacan Society to a bridge club!' Perhaps he became the apoplectic Edwardian gentleman to amuse her or to dodge the implications of the argument by turning it into farce. 'You're a lost soul, a soul wandering in the void,' he declaimed. 'Sartre is wrong; hell isn't other people, it's the triviality of one's own mind.'

'A sound Miltonic principle,' Tom obligingly glossed. 'Dear old Milton, after sounding off about "Man's first disobedience" and all that guff, has to face up to the fact that it wasn't man, but woman, who picked the apple. And as in his book disobedience was more of a virtue than a crime – after all, his chums had cut off the king's head – he was loath to give little Eve the credit for it.'

'What are you going on about, Tom?' Bill said, but Susan put in, 'It's interesting, let him finish.'

'So what does he do?' Tom went on. 'He portrays her as an idle little featherbrain with time on her hands and nothing better to do than casually pick forbidden fruit. And when she realises what she's done he puts into her head the idea that perhaps God wasn't watching anyway.'

He stopped abruptly. Bill said, 'Yes, Tom?' in a tone of indulgent inquiry.

'It's like you said, the cardinal sin is triviality of mind. It's the traditional Puritan indictment of woman. As a traditionalist, it cheers me to find grass-roots Puritanism popping up in this day and age, and in the founder of the Spartacan progressive party, to boot.' He added for Sue's benefit, 'I don't say I agree with it, but it does confirm my view of history as a process of eternal recurrence.'

'You're just a rotten fence-sitter, Tom,' Bill said.

'You'd have thought we'd have advanced a bit in three hundred years,' Susan said.

Bruce kept chuckling throughout this, particularly when Susan scored a point. He seemed to be enjoying his excursion into what must figure for him as a bohemian and rather fantastic world of idea-play and word-play. Susan appeared to be quite at ease in this world, and quite different from the woman I had met in the country, when she was an indulgent bystander to her husband's and brother-in-law's droll jocosity. I recalled that when I had approached Paul about the use of the cottage he had said that Brian was using it, which I had thought odd at the time, but had not drawn the implication that the marriage had foundered. Recalling again the episode in the garden, I wondered whether Bruce had become her lover. Observing them throughout that evening, I saw no signs that he had. He was courteous and attentive to her and always quick on the draw with his lighter whenever she took out one of her little cigars, but there were no significant looks exchanged, no clandestine little touches or caresses.

It was a custom among us at the house to greet and take leave of female visitors with a kiss on the cheek. When Sue and Bruce left for Sussex that night it seemed to me that Sue turned her cheek to receive my peck rather more coquettishly than she had to Tom and Bill, and that she accompanied it with a little inclination of her body towards me, which made me sharply aware of parts of her as exquisitely moulded as but more fully fleshed than the high and gently curved cheekbone just below which I placed my kiss, and at the same time she gave me a look that maddened me, for I was at a loss whether to construe it as complicity in the desire she aroused or mockery of it.

Sue and Bruce paid several visits to the house over the next few weeks. Generally they were quite brief visits, as they were going on somewhere, to a theatre, a party or, on one occasion, a ball. On the latter occasion Susan turned up dressed in an ivory chiffon strapless gown with a matching bolero revealing a décolletage where there lodged, suspended from a thin gold chain, an intricate little filigree pendant studded with garnets and seed pearls which riveted my attention, not so much for itself as for the swelling flesh that entrapped it. She had had her long dark hair drawn back and piled high, revealing a long, slender neck and throwing into relief those planes and high contours that brought to her features a touch of the delicacy of oriental beauty. I was enchanted, and admired the entirely natural way she bore herself, the nonchalance of her beauty and the infectious excitement she expressed at the evening's prospect. Her leave-taking was as tenderly-teasing as before, and this time in addition to the ambiguous look of complicity or mockery and the little inclination of the body there was a fragrance that clung and lingered, a perfume that perhaps in origin was floral but was redolent of something dark and erotic and most devilishly distilled. That may be a somewhat extravagant way of putting it, but it expresses the plain fact that I was falling in love again.

But Susan Rowland was a luminary in too remote a constellation really to be the focus of my amatory aspirations. The reality was that she was a married woman; she had a child, lived in Sussex, and never appeared in my orbit except briefly and in the company of an immaculate smiling tailor's dummy who whisked her in and then out again in a ridiculous white Jaguar. And my reality was such that it was beyond belief preposterous to think of falling in love again.

An antidote to my inappropriate infatuation presented itself in the possibility of a resumption of my affair with Carole-Ann. We met by chance late one afternoon in the Charing Cross Road, and when I suggested a drink together for old times' sake she readily accepted. We went to the French pub in Soho, which at that hour was not too crowded. When I asked her about her marriage to her opera singer, whom I had mentally cast as a Don Giovanni, she launched into a description that was suggestive of no role in the entire operatic repertoire except that of Falstaff. He had turned out to be a loud-mouthed egotist, a crude lover, fat, and generally a cowardly man given to fits of violence when he could direct them at someone ill-equipped to retaliate. She had, she said, taking my hand across the bar table, often regretted that afternoon when she had left me for him. The gesture was enough to make unnecessary the spelling out of the invitation. I arranged to pick her up at the theatre after the show that night.

We slipped back easily and immediately into the pattern of our earlier affair. I would pick her up at the theatre or be at the flat by the time Mike Flanders dropped her off. She would make a meal, which she sometimes shared with me and sometimes not, as she was on a diet. On those occasions I was given a private floorshow as she prepared for, took and emerged from her bath. London flats in those days could be wonderfully eccentric in the deployment of their amenities, and in this one the bathroom was just off the kitchen. It was an inconvenient arrangement on the whole, but in these circumstances quite an appropriate one, for it meant that I could simultaneously gratify one appetite and stimulate another. Carole-Ann undressed, bathed and dried herself with a series of little movements that were calculatedly erotic, and by the time she emerged my primary appetite was manifest and without more ado we fell to it on the bed.

One morning when I returned early from Putney to Chepstow Road Tom caught me on the stairs and in urgent dumb-show urged me to join him in his room. I was at first mystified, but when I heard his news I was dismayed. Susan was sleeping in my room! She had turned up the previous evening, this time without Bruce, had stayed talking until late and missed her last train, and as the spare room was at the time occupied by John Braine and I was clearly not going to return that night, Tom had suggested that she slept in my bed. He hoped I didn't mind. I didn't, but the news dismayed me nevertheless, for it set going a chain of wild conjectures. What would have happened if I had been there? Had she deliberately given her 'escort' the slip and come to the house prepared to resolve for me once and for all and deliciously the ambiguity of those looks she gave me whenever we met or parted? More mundanely and practically, what would she have thought of me, considering the state I had left the room in?

When she appeared in Tom's room, shortly after my arrival, her main concern was to get back to Sussex as soon as possible. She phoned her mother to check that all was well with the baby and to say that she would be home before lunch. I offered to accompany her to Charing Cross, on the pretext that I had some business to attend to in town.

On the bus she protested when I insisted on paying her fare. I said that I might not be able to run to the luxury of a white Jaguar but a bus fare wouldn't break me, and I would be offended if she refused. She smiled and I felt, absurdly, that my disbursement of a shilling, with tuppence change, on her behalf put our relationship on a new footing. That she had joined me in my world, on the top deck of a London bus, afforded an opportunity that was not to be missed. The last time I had seen her, dressed for the ball, she had seemed unattainable, but this morning she was quite ordinary. Her hair fell untidily about her shoulders, she was wearing neither make-up nor perfume, and her clothes, a longish skirt and a white blouse, were not only unspectacular but also a bit crumpled after her overnight stay. But she could have dressed like a slut and still retain, for me, a special aura.

There had not yet been any explanation as to how she had come to spend the night in my room. It turned out that she had come to London for a late in the day appointment with a solicitor to discuss getting a divorce from Brian. Afterwards she had met Brian and told him what the solicitor had proposed as the simplest procedure, which would involve his giving her grounds for a claim of adultery by arranging for a private detective to ostensibly catch him in a compromising situation with another woman. It was the common way for divorces by mutual consent to be secured at the time, and, as I told Susan, my divorce from Anne had been so arranged. Brian, however, had not been willing to go along with the subterfuge, in fact had not wanted to divorce at all, and she was so distressed when she left him that she had thought to call in at Chepstow Road, as it was nearby. She had gone to the house to take her mind off her problem, expecting maybe some light relief, but had found Tom alone. He had been, she said, a sympathetic listener and quite helpful because he had been through the divorce charade himself.

'I'm sorry I wasn't there,' I said.

'Maybe it was just as well,' she said. I would puzzle over the ambiguity of that for days to come.

I seized the opportunity to probe. I said, 'You seem to have been spending quite a bit of time in town recently.'

'Yes, I've missed London these last two years, she said. 'Brian and I lived in Kensington when we were first married, and before that I was a student here, so it's like coming home. I went to Sussex to have the baby, then Brian fell ill and wasn't able to work, so we stayed there because the living was cheaper.'

'Are you thinking of moving back now?'

'Perhaps, but not yet. I'm going to Germany in a few weeks' time to spend a couple of months with my sister. Her husband is serving in the army there.'

'I spent three months in Germany some time ago,' I told her. 'In Bavaria, Munich. I too was getting out of my marriage at the time.'

She said, 'It's been arranged for months,' implying that it was nothing to do with her marriage. 'I'm going to a place called Paderborn. I've never been to Germany before.'

At Charing Cross she had to rush for her train, so there was no time for an elaborate leave-taking. I had hoped to find out if she would treat me to such a subtly provocative farewell when we were alone as when there were others present, but when we got off the bus there was barely a minute before the train left, so all I got was a quick peck on the cheek and a smile and a wave as she climbed into a carriage.

My alleged 'business in town' had been merely an excuse to be with Susan alone for a while, and when she had gone I immediately got the tube back to

Notting Hill. When I arrived back at the house John Braine was there in Tom's room. If Colin tended to hit London like a hurricane, the meteorological metaphor for John's visits would be an anticyclone, a benign and sunny presence that guaranteed some days of settled weather. Although some media pundits and literary critics had tried to yoke him into the ranks of the 'angry young men', John didn't have or profess common cause with any other contemporary writers, and as he was thirty-five when *Room at the Top* was published he wasn't exactly young. His sharing the rent of the spare room had come about through a chance meeting with Colin at a literary launch party a couple of years before, and was a matter of mutual convenience rather than the literary giant camaraderie that Colin and Bill professed. To me John had always been rather avuncularly encouraging and concerned, partly I think because we were both Yorkshiremen, and from Bradford, or in his case nearby Bingley. Some time back I had attended a family funeral in Bradford, and our party had foregathered for lunch in the Great Northern Hotel. John was at another table with his wife, and was astonished when I detached myself from the dour group that he said he had thought must be 'some kind of Russian trade delegation' and went over to chat to him. I spent an evening with him at his home on that occasion, incurring the disapproval of my Methodist grandmother, whom I was staying with, on account of my late and palpably inebriated return, though she was somewhat mollified by the fact that she had seen in the *Yorkshire Post* that John was being hailed as the successor to J. B. Priestley. At the time I didn't have an acquired tolerance of alcohol, but the evening had established between me and John a degree of friendly familiarity.

John played up to the role of the no-nonsense Yorkshireman, with a covert dry sense of humour and sometimes outrageously contrarian assertiveness, as when he declared that he chain-smoked *Capstan Full Strength* for the good of his health. Wherever he was, he was a Presence, his physical corpulence complemented by a tendency to deliver weighty, indeed immovable opinions on whatever was being discussed, though often with a mischievous twinkle in the eyes behind his pebble glasses. His humour was enigmatic, as you could never be sure whether he was being gently mocking, even when he was talking about himself. He was in characteristic mode when I went into Tom's room, talking about a television interview he'd done the day before. The film version of *Room at the Top* had recently been released and had had an enthusiastic critical reception, and John was, as he said, doing his bit for the publicity offensive, with the emphasis on the word offensive when he had uppity interviewers like the one yesterday.

'Some of these lads seem to think that if you talk with a Yorkshire accent you must be uncouth,' he was saying. 'Well, I like to show 'em we can be quite couth up north. So this one goes on with a clever-clogs spiel about how most first novels are autobiographical.' John spoke slowly, giving emphasis to his words, pausing for effect. 'He says that *Room at the Top* obviously isn't autobiographical, so how did I get the idea for the story? And I tell him I plagiarised it.' He paused, staring at me as if I were the interviewer, then resumed: 'Well, that threw him a bit. "You mean you took the idea from another author," he said, I suppose in case the audience didn't understand what plagiarised meant. I said that's right, I plagiarised the plot from Maupassant's *Bel Ami* reckoning that most English critics would be too illiterate to spot the fact.'

Tom and I laughed, but John's look said that he hadn't intended it as a laughing matter. He had a disconcerting manner of following his statements with a prolonged direct stare which, depending on the context, you could take as interrogative or challenging. He did it again some time later, when he addressed me with his accustomed Yorkshire bluntness, saying, 'Well, our Stuart, what's this I hear about you getting a lass in the family way?'

The fond and familial 'our' didn't mitigate the challenge of the stare. I said, 'Yes, Joan's pregnant, and she's determined to go through with it.'

'You mean to say that you proposed an abortion?'

I recalled that John was a Catholic, a 'cradle Catholic' moreover, he always insisted, as if he considered converts to be somehow Catholics of a lower ilk. I reciprocated the stare.

'I told her I knew people who could help if she wanted one, but she didn't.'

'Good for her. You should be grateful she saved you from mortal sin. So what now? Are you getting wed?'

The Yorkshire manner of speech suggested a possible degree of play-acting on John's part, but the stare was constant and I couldn't be sure that he wasn't in earnest.

I said, 'Her father called me an alley-cat when I told him I saw no point in marrying if you knew it wouldn't last and you weren't in love.'

The stare became a twinkle and he laughed. 'An alley-cat, eh? But seriously, I don't think it makes much difference whether you marry for love or marry the girl next door. Whichever way, as Socrates said, you'll either end up happy or you'll become a philosopher.' He stared again. I smiled but didn't reply. He went on, 'But of course you're something of a philosopher already. Thanks for the copy of *Flight and Pursuit* by the way. I can't say I went along with the chapters on religion. A bit too much on the mystical side for me, but then you're a God-obsessed man, whereas I prefer my relations with the Almighty to go through the official channels.'

'I wouldn't say I was God-obsessed,' I protested. 'In fact, since writing those chapters I've hardly given a thought to the subject.'

'Of course, you've had more down to earth matters on your mind.' He puffed out a cloud of cigarette smoke. 'Well, I don't want to sound like her dad, but mark my words, you could do worse than marrying the lass and getting on with your work. I speak from experience.'

The stare was long and searching, but I just nodded and didn't respond.

I spent that night and several following with Carole-Ann and put Susan out of my mind. But then events developed a momentum of their own that swept me along in a manner and to an end that I could never have planned.

I got a call from the American 'file thirteen' merchant whom Colin had introduced me to and he offered me three hundred dollars for some manuscript material I had given him to look through. Then Joan's play came to the end of its run in Oxford, without the prospect of a London transfer, so she returned to Chepstow Road. This meant that I had to conduct my affair with Carole-Ann more discreetly, which was an irritation, and also that I had to face the prospect of spending five months with Joan sharing my room, which now seemed intolerable. If my thoughts had been drifting towards some kind of accommodation before she went to Oxford, my experiences since had quite reversed the trend. I had to get away. I phoned Paul at the prep school where he was teaching in Hertfordshire, and he said I would be welcome to use the cottage until the summer holidays, when he would be going there himself.

That gave me about six weeks. When I told Joan she remained composed at first, as if it came as no surprise. Only when I raised the subject of money did she become animated. I proposed to give her half of what I had in my account, which was a respectable sum with the American money included.

'Oh no, I'm not going to give you that kind of satisfaction,' she said.

'What satisfaction?'

'Of being able to salve your conscience by paying out some money.'

'I'm offering to help you, to make things easier for you,' I said with heavy patience. 'It has nothing to do with my conscience.'

'Oh, hasn't it?' she said, knowing better. 'Perhaps you believe that, but I don't.'

'So you're going to refuse the money, hoping that it will make me feel all the more guilty?'

'I don't know what you'll feel. I can't concern myself with your feelings. I've got enough to do coping with my own. I refuse the money because I don't want charity; it's the last thing I need.'

Charity, caritas, love: it was the one thing she needed, I thought, and the one thing I was incapable of giving her. I kept my pedantry to myself, and merely said, 'But it's not charity. I want to help.'

'You have to face it. You can't help. And I have to face the fact that I'm on my own.'

'We don't have to be at loggerheads,' I protested. 'You talk of facing things, and as I see it what we both have to face is the situation as it is. I know too well that I can't help in the way that you need help. But you can't deny that having money would make things a bit easier. You seem bent on making a martyr of yourself. It's not necessary. Be reasonable, Joan.'

'Not necessary! Reasonable!' she repeated with a scornful inflection. 'I tell you, your conscience is your own concern. Why don't you just behave in character? Get on with your life and leave me to get on with mine. It's what you really want, isn't it? So why don't you stop dithering and have the courage of your lack of convictions.'

She threw out the final phrase with a fine triumphant flourish. When she spoke like this, I didn't know whether her words represented what she really and deeply felt or were patchwork passions made up from bits remembered from old plays and films. I didn't know if she really meant it when she urged me to get out of her life. But I said:

'Alright, I'll go now. There's no point in prolonging the agony for us both.'

I dragged my rucksack down from the top of the wardrobe and proceeded to stuff my few clothes and some books and manuscripts into it. I banged about, left drawers open, cursed when I couldn't find things. I wanted her to know that this was a gesture, a direct response to her unreasonableness. I was calling her bluff, and I half expected her any moment to call mine, to dissolve into tears or climb down at least to the extent of saying that I could leave her some money. But she just watched me and said nothing. Her eyes followed my every movement, and I couldn't read the expression in them. Was it mockery, triumph, reproach? Was she awed at what she had done, or gratified that she had forced my hand, made me act, as she said, 'in character', and finally reduced the situation to the simple martyr-versus-villain pattern that she seemed to favour? Doubt as to what was in her mind, and presently fear that at the last moment she would say or do something that would turn the tables on me again, speeded my packing, for now I wanted nothing more than to get away. Soon I was ready. I hitched my rucksack onto my shoulder, picked up my portable typewriter and went to the door. Still she didn't move or say anything. She remained sitting in the frayed armchair by the grimy window with her legs curled under her. She continued staring steadily at me, but now I fancied that I caught in those wide eyes an expression of incredulity and appeal. I nodded, said briskly, 'See you, then,' and left the room. As I went down the stairs I heard a wail of despair or fury, and she burst out of the room and, leaning over the banisters, shouted down the stairwell, 'And don't come creeping back with that puny little conscience of yours, because I don't want you or it. I'm glad you've gone. Goodbye and good riddance!'

At Charing Cross I had second thoughts and went into a phone box, but I checked the impulse. After all, she had forced the issue, and perhaps she was right, perhaps it really was kinder to leave her to work out her own life when there was so little I could do for her. I reckoned she had been stupidly obdurate about the money, though.

His Dear Time's Waste - Stuart Holroyd

5

We had had a succession of still, cloudless days since April. This was 1959, the summer that broke all records, and Harold Macmillan the Prime Minister, with a General Election coming up in the autumn, beamed confidently and told the nation that they had 'never had it so good', as if the long-standing liaison between the Tory Party and the Church of England gave him personal access to the ear of the Almighty and had enabled him to fix up this freak summer for election year.

In London the heat and the stillness were stifling, oppressive and enervating. The fact added a little to my sense of guilt at leaving Joan, but only a little and not for long. Bustling, noisy London, and all the emotional turbulence it had recently come to represent, now seemed so far away. While there, I had quite forgotten the sense of affinity I had with this place and the satisfactions it afforded. Except for the climbing roses and the honeysuckle around the walls, the cottage itself was unchanged from when I had been there in the autumn. Inside, the distinctive cottage smell of wood smoke and paraffin fumes still lingered. But outside much had changed. Late autumn starkness had given way to summer lushness. The foliage in the woods that covered the gently rising hills on two sides of the cottage was dense. Bird life was loud and multitudinous. Despite the long drought the nearby stream, which came from a prolific spring, still flowed strongly, and its incessant rush and chatter was the only sound to be heard in the still night after the loud rooks in the copse at the top of the hill had finally settled.

The only problem was work. Initially I tried to get on with *The Dialectics of Despair*, but found that I had lost the certainties that underlay this ambitious project. Perhaps Bill had been right when he said I had lost my nerve. I had lost even the certainty that despair could be tackled as a 'problem'. It seemed rather that it was an inalienable condition of mature human life, that its forms and causes were too many and too personal to yield a solution to analysis and precept, that each of us had to find our own solution, had to 'work out our salvation with diligence'. It was, perhaps, a gain in maturity, but what, I wondered, was the use of maturity if it brought with it a loss of ability to do any work in the world? Better to have illusions and still be creative than be disillusioned and sterile.

That thought suggested an alternative theme. I turned it over in my mind and came up with a title: *Method in His Madness: an essay on Contemporary Man*. It would be a study of the manifold and ingenious ways in which men deceive themselves into believing that they live purposefully, a study of political, religious and personal delusion, done with a sort of Swiftian irony. The epigraph for the essay could be taken from Swift's *Tale of a Tub*: 'happiness is the perpetual possession of being well deceived.'

The irony would hinge on the fact that the essay would be a justification of self-deception. It would confound the sombre Sartrean indictment of 'bad faith' by showing that in order to keep faith with life one often had to break with the principles of intellectual consistency and order that the philosopher held so dear. Who had said that the existentialists wrote philosophy in the manner of a thriller? Well, I would write it in the manner of a comedy. Sartre and Camus had not had the last word; they might yet have to cede their laurels. But when I pondered the matter further I realised that my theme was not very different from Tom's philosophy of 'the Necessary Illusion', so I put that project too on the back burner and turned my attention to the theatre again.

The play that I had been researching when I was last at the cottage, with a role for Joan as the wife of revolutionary hero and martyr in an east European country, had become an abandoned project, but the research I had done into the Hungarian revolution of 1956 had suggested a background for another play. The physician and writer Kenneth Walker, who at the request of his and my publisher Victor Gollancz had read my first book and written favourably about it, had told me that in Paris during the German occupation the spiritual teacher Gurdjieff had entertained both members of the French resistance and German officers, though of course not at the same time, and had exacted tribute from the Germans, in food and alcohol, with which he would then regale the French. I took that situation and transferred it to a contemporary setting in an East European country in the midst of a revolutionary uprising and its suppression, using the Hungarian revolution research and even retaining the wife of the revolutionary hero/martyr as a character, though in a minor role as one of the disciples of the guru figure. The play, too, would be a comedy, though dealing with profound and important Existentialist themes. This, I resolved, would be the first work I would devote myself to during my summer sequestration.

During my first week at the cottage I resisted the inclination to go and call on Susan. But the thought that she was just six miles away was constantly on my mind, and one afternoon I caught the bus into Battle.

A shaggy and exuberant Welsh collie announced my arrival. It kept ahead of me, barking, all the way up the winding, overgrown path to the bungalow. Susan answered the door. She had on a short blue kimono with a sash knotted at the waist. She greeted me cordially, with unaffected pleasure and no hint of embarrassment.

'We're sunbathing in the garden,' she said. 'Do come through.'

The bungalow was shabby; not shabby-genteel as one might have expected of the home of former colonials fallen on hard times, but unrepentantly shabby. The furniture was cheap and just about functional, the carpets worn and the walls and paintwork throughout obviously hadn't been refreshed for years. The garden was even more of a jungle than it had been the last time I had visited, the accessible part of it consisting of a small clearing of rough grass outside the back door. A collapsed greenhouse was just visible beyond banks of nettles and brambles.

'This is our sun-trap,' she said. 'Fetch one of those wicker chairs from the sitting room. You're just in time for tea.' When she learned that I had come down the previous weekend she said with mock reproach, 'You mean to say you've been at the cottage all this time and didn't come to see us?' The 'us' associated her mother, who was sitting in a deck chair shaded by a large parasol, with the alleged slight. I didn't know whether to feel flattered or disconcerted to be regarded as a friend of the family. From the start she had me off balance.

'I've been working hard,' I lied. In fact I had resolved not to rush over to see Susan earlier because I didn't want to give anyone, even myself, grounds to suspect that her being around had anything to do with my decision to come back to the cottage. I wouldn't go so far as to claim that I had renounced philandering, but I had certainly learned to be more cautious and less opportunistic in affairs of the heart.

Susan, too, was cautious. On her visits to London she had been quite flirtatious, but not so now, no doubt because the context was quite different.

Her mother, whom I was asked to address as 'Daphina', was a grey-haired woman of about fifty, who had retained a youthful figure and good looks. Susan had clearly inherited the fineness of her facial bone structure from her. She had a fey, not-quite-of-this-world manner, and she talked about life in India before Partition. This summer weather, she said, took her back. That had been the good life; with servants, sumptuous clubs, tennis tournaments, splendid balls, an ayah to look after the children. 'You never saw anything so gross as a dirty nappy,' she laughed. 'And now look what I've come down to. At my age!'

The laugh took the self-pity out of it, made it a quite jolly reflection on one of life's little ironies.

'Go on,' Susan said, 'you had it so good for so long, it's only right you should have a taste of life's harsh realities.

You know' – she turned to me – 'we hardly ever saw our mother. She was a glamorous creature in a ball gown who came to kiss us goodnight after we'd been put to bed by the ayah and then floated out on a perfumed cloud. It probably has something to do with why we get on so well now.'

She had taken off the kimono she had put on to answer the door and had now resumed her sunbathing in a bikini. While she lay on her rug, her child, Christopher, who had just reached the perilous biped stage, made heavy work of foraging for daisy and dandelion heads with which to adorn her hair. Susan was a capable but unfussy mother. She attended to Christopher's needs, comforted him when he got stung by a nettle, and bore his crude attempts at floral decoration with easy insouciance.

Both these relationships, between mother and daughter and mother and child, were a revelation to me. Such naturalness and ease, such a sense of having effortlessly got the priorities right, I had never witnessed in familial relationships, which in my experience were generally marred by possessiveness or censoriousness on the one hand and resentment on the other.

After a while her mother went into the kitchen to make some fresh tea and drop-scones. I left my chair, took off my shirt and went and sat beside Susan on her rug. She smelled of sun oil, and the brown skin of her midriff, legs, shoulders and neck gleamed with it. When she moved, a sharp line of white where the sun-tan ended just showed under her bra-top. I wondered how she would react if I were to follow my impulse to take her in my arms.

Soon after I had sat beside her on the rug, she turned over on her stomach and reached for a book that lay open and face-down nearby.

'I'm reading *Wuthering Heights*,' she said, flicking through the pages. Her long hair fell forward, hiding her face. I surveyed the length of her. She had two large brown moles just below the level of her bra strap, and dimples at the back of her knees. 'Don't you think it's a great novel?'

I had to confess that I hadn't read it.

'And you a literary man!' she mocked. 'Shame on you! I suppose because it's by a woman.'

The return of her mother with tea and drop-scones put a welcome end to that conversation.

When I left them that first afternoon I was surprised when the mother said, 'Do come again soon, won't you, Stuart? It's so good for Susan to have a friend after all she's been through recently.' I could only assume that the woman either had the naivety of a schoolgirl or the morality of a procuress. The idea that there could be such a thing as a platonic friendship between a man and a woman was novel to me.

I recalled that I had seen a copy of *Wuthering Heights* among Paul's books, and back at the cottage that evening I found it and began to read. I read late into the night and had finished the book when I caught the bus into Battle the following evening. We had arranged that I should pick Susan up after she had put Christopher to bed and then we would take a walk in the country together. She knew the countryside around Battle, all its byways, paths and features intimately, and she led me across meadows, through dense copses, over stiles and fences, until we came to a lake in a wood. As we walked, Susan did most of the talking, following the policy she later confessed to, of keeping me at a distance. She even declined my offers to help her over high gates or fences, saying she had always been something of a tomboy and was quite capable of getting over them herself. She talked about people we knew, Tom and Bill and her 'escort' Bruce, and also about people I didn't know, the sister and brother-in-law in Germany, and the owners of the land where we were walking, the Websters of the Battle Abbey estate, who were wildly eccentric and quite impoverished. Her talk was exuberant and unaffected; people and events came vividly to life in her narration. She didn't rigidly demarcate small-talk and big-talk, and could effect the transition from the one to the other with an ease that implied that life was all one to her and in all its aspects worthy of interest and concern. The timbre of her voice, the range of her talk, the natural grace and agility of her movements, her maturity and self-possession, all enchanted me, and on that first walk I fell more hopelessly under her spell.

I tried a bit of spell-weaving myself, spreading my intellectual peacock-feathers by showing off about having read and formulated opinions about *Wuthering Heights* since our meeting the previous day. It was a great book, I said, remarkable because it took the stock characters of the Romantic novel, the passionate doomed heroine and the brooding diabolical hero, and made them something much more, gave them a mythical dimension.

'I thought its appeal was that it's a great love story,' Susan said.

'It is that,' I conceded, 'but the love story as such ends half way through the novel, with the death of Cathy. Heathcliff is more than the type of the Byronic hero. His precursors are Milton's Lucifer, the fallen angel, and Bunyan's Pilgrim. If you get to the mythical dimension of the novel, you appreciate that it develops the great themes of a fall, followed by a pilgrimage and ultimately the regaining of Paradise.

That's what makes it so powerful. It's one of the great mythical themes that resonates in the subconscious.'

'I haven't finished reading it yet,' Susan said, 'but I'll try to bear that in mind when I do.'

It wasn't exactly an admonition, but neither was it the sought-for response to my display, so I discreetly folded back my feathers and dropped the subject. This woman had a mind of her own and was not going to be swept away by my flights of intellectual fancy.

Our walk brought us at length back to Battle. We went into the pub, The Chequers, where we had spent time with Brian and Paul the year before, and while they entertained one another, had exchanged looks charged with promise and mutual desire, or so I had thought. The landlord, a short dapper man with a ginger handlebar moustache and a high-pitched affected voice, greeted Susan with enthusiasm and solicitously inquired after her mother, her father, Brian and Christopher, before acknowledging my existence and asking what we would have to drink.

'What a creep!' I said when we had got our drinks and I had led Susan to seats in a corner far from the bar.

She laughed. 'Perry was a great buddy of Brian's,' she explained.

'And what a bloody silly name,' I said.

'It's short for Peregrine.'

'That's even sillier. Who ever heard of a barman called Peregrine?'

'Do you always fall into a Yorkshire accent when you're angry?' she laughed.

'It's a good accent for grumbling in,' I said.

'You're quite right of course, he should be more civil to his customers. I think he was particularly fond of Brian because he used to hold the floor and keep people drinking.'

'I noticed you were non-committal when he asked about Brian,' I said.

'It's none of his business. People can think what they like. I don't see why I should pander to their curiosity.'

'Does that go for me too?'

'She smiled. 'Of course not. There's no secret. We've split up. That's all.'

'Mutual agreement?'

'No. He wanted to stay, but there could have been no future in it. I made the mistake of marrying a man much older than myself. As a teenager I was very serious and intolerant. And I regarded most people of my own age as mindless fools. Brian was thirty-nine, gay, intelligent, easy-going, knowledgeable. I was bowled over. But it didn't last; it couldn't with that age gap. It was all over between us before Christopher was born. I'd had left then, but suddenly he fell ill. They suspected T.B. When they told me the treatment and convalescence might last two years I wept for days. I couldn't walk out on him then, when he was at his lowest and needed me, but also I couldn't bear the thought of two more years out of my life. I'm not the martyr type. I couldn't spend my life paying for a wrong decision I'd made at twenty. But with Christopher on the way I didn't have much choice. And now I want to do something to make up for those wasted years.'

'I know how you feel,' I said. 'I made a wrong marriage, to my first girlfriend, when I was twenty, and only finally got out of it a few months ago.'

'I know,' she said, and the way she said it made me wonder how much else she knew. Neither of us had mentioned Joan, though Susan had met her on at least one of her visits to Chepstow Road.

Susan's recent dilemma, I felt, paralleled my present one, in that she too had refused to mortgage her future to pay for a mistake and had been capable of a certain ruthlessness. But the difference was that she had stuck by her sick husband for eighteen months after it was all over with them. On that account alone, I felt, her sympathy might have very strict limits; and then there was the fact that as a woman, and one who herself had a child, her sympathies might extend equally, if not more, to Joan.

With this undertow of doubt and uncertainty in my mind, I felt safer when our talk was of Susan's life rather than my own.

'So how are you going to set about doing something with your life?' I said.

'I shan't set about doing anything. I'll just have fun. I've some catching up to do in the matter of just living.'

That was promising. I knew what I had meant when I had proposed a similar programme for myself after the break-up of my own marriage. But the balloon of my anticipation was pricked by what she said next.

'Germany should be fun.' Of course, I recalled that she would shortly be going to spend the summer holiday with her sister and brother-in-law. I thought my expression must have betrayed my feelings of dismay, for she reached across the table and took my hand. It was her first gesture that might have admitted a degree of intimacy that went beyond mere friendship. But it was ambiguous, because she accompanied it by saying: 'Your last bus goes in half an hour. If you're going to take me home first we'd better go now.'

I walked her home. At the gate she kept her distance, thanked me for 'a very enjoyable evening.' I said, 'We must do it again soon,' and she said, 'Yes, I'd like that. Give me a ring when you're next coming in,' and without more ado dashed into the house.

I resolved after that to spend some days at the cottage and work on the play. My resolve was strengthened by the fact that the next day I received a letter from Joan. It was a reply to a brief note I had sent her soon after my arrival, enclosing a cheque for thirty pounds, curious to see whether she would accept it. She did, saying that she would set the money aside until nearer her confinement or until the baby was born. For the present she could support herself quite well, as she had got a job as a waitress. Her letter was brief and showed no trace of the proud and bitter mood I had left her in. She offered me my room back, saying that she realised I had gone to the country because I couldn't work with her sharing the room, and if I wanted it back she could move in with a friend she had made at work. She signed off, 'With love always, Joan.'

I wrote a brief reply to the effect that I was deeply involved with the play and would therefore stay at the cottage until Paul came for the summer holidays, so there was no hurry to vacate the room. I signed off simply, 'Love and best wishes, Stuart.'

Actually, I did make quite good progress with the first act of the play. After a couple of days I phoned Sue to say that I had to go into Battle for the post office and to do some shopping, and proposed that we should take a walk again in the evening. She said she would love to do that and also she would like me to meet her father, who had just come over from Germany to spend a couple of weeks before accompanying them to Paderborn.

I was a bit apprehensive about that, particularly after my experience with Joan's father. I had a stereotypical image of the retired colonial military man, formulated originally on the Powell and Pressburger film *The Life and Death of Colonel Blimp*, and consolidated by the scenes in John Osborne's *Look Back in Anger* where Alison's father, a retired Indian Army officer, is represented as a blustering and preposterous relic of Britain's imperial past and a fitting target for Jimmy Porter's scorching invective. I hoped that Susan's father would not be like Osborne's caricature, and was relieved to find that he was quite the opposite, not at all loud, assertive and Blimpish, but rather a quiet man, friendly, unassuming and open-minded, with features that would have looked rugged and outdoor had they not been so hollow and gaunt. Richard Bennett, or Dick as he preferred to be called, was about sixty, but illness had made him look considerably older. I don't know what prior image he might have formulated of me, particularly if he knew about the 'angry young man' association, for he scrutinised me curiously when we were introduced, but then smiled a welcome and invited me to join them in the garden for 'sundowners'.

Even the problem of what to talk about with the father, which had exercised my mind quite a bit since Susan had proposed the meeting, turned out to be an unnecessary worry. That summer the England cricket team was comprehensively trouncing the visiting Indians, and I was able to share with Dick the minor pleasure of celebrating the achievements of Fred Trueman, Ken Barrington and Colin Cowdrey. When he learned that I had from my youth been a keen cricketer and had attended two of the 1948 England versus Australia tests, in which the great Don Bradman had excelled in his last U.K. Ashes appearance, I felt that any reservations Dick might have had about this particular angry young man were allayed.

'You have hidden depths,' Susan said later. 'I think Pa quite approved.'

'Don't you mean hidden superficialities?' I said.

'Is cricket superficial? I always thought it was deadly serious.'

'Oh, it is. In fact some very serious people are fans. I learnt recently that Samuel Becket is one, which isn't really surprising, because the game has much in common with absurdist theatre. It has its own arcane language and a game can go on for five days without any result, rather like *Waiting for Godot*.'

We didn't go for our proposed walk on this occasion because Dick and Daphina had had a call in the afternoon from Daphina's sister, who lived in Heathfield, asking them over for the evening, so there was no one to baby-sit. Susan busied herself for a while getting Christopher to bed and preparing a snack for us to have later, then proposed that we should have a whisky.

There was a certain awkwardness between us. Walking in the country or sitting in a pub we could keep up the act of being just good friends, but alone in the house it was more difficult.

'If you're sure your father wouldn't mind,' I said.

'I'm sure he'd mind if I didn't offer you a drink,' Susan said, and as she prepared the drinks went on: 'Pa encouraged us to drink quite young. I remember him saying to me when I was about sixteen, "You must learn to take your drink like a gentleman." He didn't seem to have noticed that I was a girl.'

Laughter eased the tension, and no doubt the whisky did too. Susan told me that before she was married she had been halfway through training as an occupational therapist and had worked for some months in a mental hospital. She had had to give it up because she felt she was herself heading for a breakdown. The work, she said, was both physically and emotionally strenuous. 'And when you're nineteen and fresh out of college armed only with book learning, and you have to deal with people who are mentally disturbed and can be violent, it's a very taxing job, particularly if you tend to identify too much with the patients and kick against the system.' She was thinking, though, that she might go back to complete her training, now that she was older and a bit tougher.

'I can't but feel that you'd be wasted in a mental hospital,' I said.

She pounced on it. 'Why wasted? You mean you think women should just be decorative and not work?'

'Well, there are very few who are decorative,' I said, deliberately provocative. 'Doesn't the parable of the talents tell us that we should make the most of our gifts?'

'And what do you think my gifts would equip me to be?' she challenged.

'Oh, a femme fatale, what else?'

'You're being facetious now. I was serious about thinking of going back to work.'

'I'm sorry.' I play-acted contrite. 'Of course I realise you were serious.'

She took up the note of levity. 'The idea has its attractions. But how does one go about being a femme fatale?'

'If it's a gift it comes naturally,' I said. 'But if you want a bit of practice you can try it on me.'

'But surely the point of being a femme fatale is that you leave a trail of ruined and broken-hearted men behind you. Are you sure you'd survive?'

'No, but I'd take the risk.'

'Live dangerously, eh?'

'Why not?'

'Then we'll have another drink.'

I was standing by the fireplace when she brought me the whisky. Instead of giving it to me she reached over my shoulder and put the glass on the mantel-shelf. Her eyes held mine and I felt her now free hand on the back of my neck. She rose on her toes and gently drew my head down to meet hers. It was a long and tender kiss, searching and intimate.

'Well, that's got that over,' she said when we came out of it. But her eyes had depths that belied the flippancy of the remark.

'Is that what you call living dangerously?'

'Very dangerously.'

The second time I kissed her hard, voraciously, pressing her body tight against mine so that I could feel the swell of her breasts. She struggled at first, succumbed for a while, then tore herself free.

'Too dangerously,' she said. 'I must get my drink.' She went over to the sideboard and I followed her and put my arms around her from behind, my hands on her panting rib-cage, ready to move them up at a sign of encouragement.

'Please', she said, 'let me compose myself. That was more than I bargained for.' She turned her head and kissed me lightly on the cheek.

I had to compose myself too. I retrieved my drink and sat down.

'Didn't your father also warn you about that when you were a young girl?'

'No, nobody told me about people like you. Are there many of you up in Yorkshire?' She was herself again, humorous and slightly mocking. 'I must say nobody has kissed me quite like that before. It was rather a shock.'

'But you've been married.'

'Brian wasn't a very passionate man, except sometimes when he was drunk, but in that state I found him revolting.'

'And Bruce?'

'As I told you before, he's a gentleman.'

'Well surely there's such a thing as a passionate gentleman.'

'No doubt, but I think that for people like Bruce there are two kinds of women.'

'Those who do and those who don't', I proposed.

'It's not quite so crude and simple. Say rather those who might, and so are fair game, and those you wouldn't dream of asking to, unless your intentions were serious and honourable.'

Her inflection put the last two words in quotation marks. It seemed to indicate that for her this gentlemen's code was as anachronistic as I regarded it. It pleased me to think that I had gained by brazen Yorkshire directness what Bruce and other 'escorts' or 'admirers', inhibited by the scruples of their class, had failed to gain by pussyfooting around their idol. But what exactly had I gained? Susan now looked so composed, sitting with her legs drawn up under her in an armchair. I wanted to elicit from her an admission that what had happened was irreversible and signalled the beginning of a new stage in our relationship. I put down my drink, crossed to where she was sitting and bent over her.

'Kiss me again,' I said, taking her head in my hands and bending lower.

'Not now. I must check on Christopher. I thought I heard him awake.

I hadn't heard anything, and when she came back wearing a big jersey over her shirt I guessed she hadn't either.

'You've changed,' I observed.

'I felt it was getting chilly.'

'Is that why you changed?'

'Yes, but also because I feel safer in this.'

'I thought you were going to kiss me again.'

'I didn't promise. And anyway I don't think it's wise. It disturbs my hormone balance.'

'It disturbs mine too. Do you know what I prescribe for readjusting the balance.'

'I can guess what you'd prescribe. But you've no physiological training, and I have, and what I prescribe is distance,' – she pushed me and I fell back into the armchair – 'and conversation. So tell me something interesting.' She sat primly with her hands clasped in her lap and looked at me expectantly.

'You're beautiful.'

'Maybe, but I don't consider that something interesting.'

'I love you.'

'That's interesting, but I don't believe it.'

'Let me prove it to you.'

'You can't. All you can prove is that you find me sexually attractive, but I've known that for a long time.'

'Isn't it a reciprocal feeling?'

'If it were I wouldn't tell you because you'd take it as encouragement, and if it weren't I wouldn't tell you for fear of damaging your masculine pride. I've learnt that masculine pride is a very touchy thing.' She smiled, which took the sting out of the words. I had to admire her resourcefulness, her ability to find the actions and the words to bring a situation round to her own terms. But I had a card to play.

'If you didn't want to give me encouragement, why did you put perfume on before you came back just now?'

She laughed. 'It wasn't intended to encourage you. I suppose I wanted to because it makes me feel feminine, and I find I rather like that.'

'How could you be otherwise? To me you're the quintessence of feminine.'

'I'm sure you mean that as a compliment,' she said, 'but it's a dubious one. I'm not sure that I'd want to be the quintessence of anything. And seriously, don't you think we should remain just good friends? It would be a pity to spoil what is, after all, a rather interesting friendship.'

The mood had changed. We had been engaged in a game, a contest, but now Susan had suddenly raised the stakes. On one level I felt aggrieved at the foundering of my erotic expectations, but on another grateful to her for her lucidity and seriousness.

After that evening it was impossible to return to the level of friendship we had been on before. We had to see one another every day. I would take a bus or thumb a lift into Battle, and after Sue had settled Christopher for the night we would go for our walk. We walked for miles across and around the country, sometimes talking, often in silence, just being together, seeing together, sharing a sense of wonder and delight in the world. The perfect summer continued and seemed to be our private benediction. All that was beautiful or awesome in nature, all growing things and living things, the colours, the movements, the sounds, the scents of summer in the air, were ours. We never tired of watching, listening, being together, pointing out things, telling each other what the world was like. All our senses were awakened and exquisitely sharpened, and the need to be one was not just a need for physical union, though that was always there, but a need also to respond as one, to feel the same feelings, share the same perceptions, to be in every sense and with every sense together in the world. 'Look!' one of us would say, and it might be a splendid sunset or a quicksilver squirrel following an intricate path among high branches. The strange affinity we had with each other was complemented by a shared affinity with the commonplace wonders of the world.

Sometimes we would be like children, racing, hiding or trespassing, and I would leap gates and climb trees and delight in making her worried for my safety. And sometimes I would run ahead of her, sit on the grass and watch her approach, intently watching the way she moved, making her conscious of her movements and her body. My scrutiny embarrassed her and she protested but did not let it discompose her; she just walked steadily on and when she came level kept out of my reach, for the first time I had done it I had suddenly lunged and brought her down on the grass beside me. At other times I dropped behind and watched her walking ahead, but for some reason she objected more to this and when she caught me at it she stopped and waited for me to catch up or came back to me. And when we came to a gate I climbed over first and in helping her down held her close and let her body slide slowly down against mine, and kissed her.

One evening we came to a cornfield. It was getting dark, and the trees around were loud with the twitterings and calls of settling birds. The path we were on led up a steep incline, and at the top a ridge was sharply outlined by a strange brightness beyond. When we reached the ridge we both stopped, breathless, for suddenly we were face to face with an immense harvest moon. It was so low in the sky, so close, so perfectly full and round, so bright and yellow, it was awesome, miraculous, a heavenly visitation consecrating the earth below. Below it, just ahead of us, was this field of tall corn, bright yellow too, rustling and waving. We had shared other wonders and delights, but this surpassed all, stirred a wild joy, made us at first speechless, entranced. Then we both laughed, for it was too perfect, almost like a Hollywood scenario, and hand in hand we ran across the cornfield. I said we should plunge into it, lie there, make love and celebrate the miracle in a thoroughly pagan way, and Sue said it would be terribly prickly and uncomfortable, and I should be romantic and woo her with sweet melodies like Nelson Eddy.

'It's an absolutely ridiculous moon,' I said, and she said did I know that anyone who escaped from a mental hospital and remained at liberty for a full moon-cycle was automatically deemed sane? I said she was beautiful but had a mind full of irrelevant facts, which made her pretend to be indignant and she ran away up the hill, but I didn't chase her because it was marvellous to watch her moving, silhouetted against the sky with the moon so low and so close it seemed she could have run right up to it.

Afterwards we always spoke of the occasion as 'the night of the ridiculous moon'. The incident was typical of the mood of those days. Romantic and impassioned we were, but we both had reasons to make us wary of such feelings, and we sought through mockery of each other and of our situation to maintain balance and a sense of proportion. We both had reasons to feel that this was an inappropriate time to be involved in an idyll.

But I found myself experiencing strange and unprecedented feelings. One evening a young man we had met in a pub and whom Susan knew slightly and addressed as 'Malcolm' offered to drive me back to the cottage. He worked in the City and was down for the weekend staying with his parents, who had a farm nearby. From his voice, manner and dress I judged him to be one of the privileged effete, but Sue seemed to find him amusing and to take pleasure in talking to him about people I'd never heard of. We all went back to the cottage after closing time, and drank half a bottle of whiskey that Malcolm had bought. Then came the time when he had to drive Sue home. I walked up the fields with them to the road and watched until the tail-lights of the car were out of sight, and the throaty roar of its engine, which I thought as affected as its owner's voice, had faded into the night. Back at the cottage I lay awake for hours working myself into a stew imagining what Malcolm might have done on the way back. He was the kind of cowardly runt who would get boozily amorous. And Sue would have been quite helpless. My imagination ran wild, and I saw myself the next morning striding up the drive of the parental farm, demanding to see their 'gentlemanly' son, and there and then giving him such a pasting that he wouldn't be able to show his face in the City for at least a week. I dwelt on the scene with such a sense of savage satisfaction that I eventually alarmed myself with the thought that I was actually wishing for something to have happened so that I could demonstrate to Sue what an ill-bred and passionate man I was.

Whether the linked terms ill-bred and passionate had for her the positive significance that they had for me was not a question that occurred to me. There were enough examples in current literature to support the view that the terms were related, Joe Lampton in *Room at the Top*, Jimmy Porter in *Look Back in Anger*, Jim Dixon in Amis's *Lucky Jim*, not to mention earlier in Lawrence's *Lady Chatterley's Lover*, and of course Emily Bronte's Heathcliff. There was always in this literature an implication that the well-bred were dispassionate if not downright impotent and that in any contest for the favours of a female the passionate plebeian would carry the day. But all that was just literature, and with the one extraordinary exception all written by men, and although it had subtly imbued my views of life and relationships I didn't know whether Susan had been similarly conditioned. Often I was at a loss to understand her reactions or the way she looked at me. As she did one night when we returned to the house late. I had missed the last bus and would have to walk the five or six miles back to the cottage, but would stop by for a coffee to set me on my way. Daphina and Dick had already gone to bed. In the kitchen, as I ground coffee beans in a hand-grinder, I became aware of Susan staring at me. She was standing by the wall opposite to me waiting for the kettle to boil, staring steadily and looking pensive.

'What are you thinking?'

'That you're a strange creature to have suddenly come into my life. I'm not sure that I like it.'

'It?'

'What you do to me.'

'You mean when I kiss you?'

'I mean the strange and alarming sensations you arouse in my body.'

I put down the coffee grinder and went towards her. She watched me with the same solemn expression. I stood in front of her, very close, and looked down into her upturned face. Her eyes seemed to be searching mine for something. I touched her face, gently parted her lips. They remained parted and I kissed them tenderly. I took her head in my hands and sought her tongue with mine. She shuddered, her eyes closed and her arms embraced me and drew me closer. I pressed her hard against the wall, and still held her there when our faces drew a little apart.

'Strange sensations,' she said. 'You have no right to make me feel like this.'

I kissed her again, stretched out her arms along the wall and rolled my body against hers. When I released one of her arms it dropped limply to her side. I caressed her cheek, her long neck, her shoulder, then undid her shirt, pushed her bra strap off her shoulder and held her breast. She rolled her head until she managed to disengage her mouth from mine, and said 'You mustn't do these things to me.' She shook her head vigorously, as if trying to clear it. I stilled it with my free hand and gazed into her eyes, which now had a wild and troubled expression.

'No! no! I won't be bullied,' she suddenly protested, tearing herself free.

'Let's go to your room,' I pressed.

'You're crazy. Christopher's asleep in there.'

'My body aches for you.'

'I want you too,' she said. 'But I'm going to Germany next week and I don't want to take that memory with me. So let's be sensible and have that coffee.'

I submitted to be sensible. We took the coffee into the sitting room. Sue switched on the electric fire, not for heat but because the light from it was more intimate than the glaring overhead light. We sat at a distance from it, on the floor with our backs to the couch. She took my hand and squeezed it so hard that her nails dug into my palm.

'I'm sorry,' she said. 'It's not that I'm a particularly moral girl, if that's what you think.'

'I think you are, in the profoundest sense of the term.'

She shook her head. 'In fact once, not long ago, I offered myself to a man.'

I felt a flush of anger and jealously rise to my face, and my lips involuntarily tightened.

'Does that shock you?'

'It surprises me. Was it Bruce?'

She nodded. 'It was soon after Brian had gone. It had been such a bleak two years. I felt I had some catching up to do. On one of our first trips to London Bruce and I stayed at a hotel. We had adjoining rooms. I told him he could sleep with me if he wanted to.'

'And he didn't?' She shook her head.

'How ungallant,' I said, but inwardly I seethed with anger and a sense of betrayal. Susan looked calm and thoughtful.

'He said I'd hate him afterwards. He said I was unhappy and not myself and he'd rather wait until I'd got over the break up of my marriage. For the time being all he wanted was to take me around and give me a good time.'

'Very gentlemanly,' I said. 'It showed remarkable self control.' I just managed to get the words out before a constriction seized my throat, tears welled into my eyes and my whole body started trembling. I felt intense pangs of anger, jealousy, of tenderness for her, of awe at Bruce's behaviour, and of thankfulness for the outcome. There could be no resolution of such a turbulence of conflicting emotions except in tears. Yet I was as surprised as she was at the vehemence of my passion.

'Whatever is the matter?'

'I... I think I really do love you.'

She laughed and drew my head down and holding it against her breast stroked my brow and cheeks and smiled down at me. 'That's a true philosopher's declaration,' she said.

'I don't know what came over me,' I said. 'I seem to be prone to such strange fits of emotion recently.' And I told her about my feelings on the night when her friend had driven her back from the cottage.

'Malcolm wouldn't lay a finger on me,' she laughed. 'You know, I've never in my life had to, as they say, fight for my honour, except of course with you. It has worried me sometimes. My prospective lovers suddenly turn moral and want to marry me. I don't see myself as a wife type, but others seem to.'

'Maybe you are. When you've had the opportunity to be what we've called the femme fatale type you suddenly back off.'

'That's because I'm not sure who it would be fatal for. The trouble is, I can't do anything with just a part of myself. Some people seem to have the enviable ability to split themselves up and live in different parts of themselves at different times. I just can't do that.'

'And you say you're not moral?'

'It's not a matter of principle. My mind doesn't come into it. I may think I want to do something, like go to bed with you, but somehow... ' She paused, seeking the words.

'The gut rebels,' I suggested.

'Something like that.'

So in fact you're not principled, but just inconveniently saddled with a gut morality. You really knew that Bruce wouldn't take you up on your proposition, didn't you?'

'Perhaps, but I couldn't be sure.'

When I set out to walk back to the cottage that night I felt such vigour in my limbs and such lightness in my head that I could have walked to London. The moon rode high above the sleeping outskirts of Battle and above the fields and farms that I passed. The air was still and the night silent except for the occasional hoot of an owl or a rustling in the hedgerow. I felt a wonderful elation. I thought of Susan sleeping in her room with Christopher in his cot beside her. I would have liked to be there, not to disturb her but just to watch and stand over her and listen to her breathing. I would tell her when we next met, 'I take back my philosopher's caution. I no longer think I love you, I just love you, full stop.' I would say it lightly, but she would know just how much weight it carried. This, I was certain, was my first real love, and by comparison the language of all my other romances seemed plodding and rhetorical. There had been too much earnestly declared, too little left unsaid, altogether too much weight, too great an apprehension of the void beneath the words. And in a way what applied to love applied equally to work. Intellect must be gay, must go directly to its mark. Not for me now the plodding through the arid deserts of modern philosophy with its gloomy dwelling on angst, alienation, doom and despair. Thought must be of the gut, instinctive, precise, direct and inconfutable. Of course, she knew that, yet she had seemed quite serious when she had spoken of the enviable ability of people to split themselves up, to separate head and heart, mind and body. That could be irony, but it could be a failure to recognise what in her was exceptional, what seemed to me unique. In a time that produced part people, divided people, she was miraculously and wonderfully whole. And I would have her whole. This at least I would have in common with gallant, gentlemanly Bruce. I would do her no violence, would do nothing to split her up. But unlike him, I would not let her go.

Yet she was going to Germany in a week's time, and anyway I only had the use of the cottage for another couple of weeks, when Paul was due to begin his summer holiday. And then there was the problem of Joan. I had begun my night walk with a sense of joy and elation, but I ended it with bitter reflections on the perversity and unfairness of life.

When I parted from her that night I had asked Susan to bring Christopher and come and spend the following day with me at the cottage. She had agreed without hesitation and asked me to meet her off the eleven o'clock bus in the morning. I was waiting on the road when the bus drew up and helped her off with her push-chair and carrier bags.

'What's all that? Have you come to stay?' I said.

'Most of it's sordid baby-clutter,' she said, 'but I also brought some food and a bottle of wine. I thought I'd make you a meal.'

'Wonderful, but I'd rather make a meal of you.' I kissed her on the lips by way of greeting, but resisted the urge, inappropriate in the circumstances, to make a meal of it. Her mouth was fresh and cool, she had no make-up on, and her hair, newly washed, was fragrant and fell about her shoulders loosely.

The push-chair was useless over the fields, so I hoisted Christopher onto my shoulders and carried it in my free hand. I knew by the way Susan looked at me and smiled that it gave her pleasure to see me with her child, and I thought how effortless and natural parenthood was and how absurd it was to make heavy work of it.

When we got to the cottage Sue unpacked her carrier bags and immediately set about preparing the meal. I stood by helplessly. Chris followed her about and got under her feet.

'You men are useless in the kitchen,' she said. 'Why don't you go and amuse one another in the garden? I won't be long.'

'I like watching you moving about and doing things,' I said. 'I could stand and watch you for hours.'

'I'm only cooking. Surely there's nothing romantic about that.'

'No, nothing romantic, but something very real and down to earth. You're a real woman.'

'Of course I am,' she laughed. 'Oh dear, you have got it bad, haven't you?' I nodded. 'But do tear yourself away just for a little while. I'll join you in ten minutes.'

I took Christopher out into the garden. We looked through a picture book together for a while, and he happily showed off his monosyllabic knowledge, pointing out 'house', 'bird', 'cow', 'train'. Then he was distracted by a stray black cat that had slunk in through the fence and sat looking up at the bird table.

'Puss!' he said, and advanced towards it. The cat fled. We both crept to where it had disappeared into the bushes and called, 'Puss! Puss!', but the cat wisely wasn't to be inveigled.

I thought I would try to further the child's education and extend his syllabic range. I tried to teach him to respond to the question, 'What kind of puss is Christopher?' with the answer 'An oedipuss'. Oddly, he seemed to find this amusing, and we were still practising it when Susan came out.

'What are you doing corrupting my child?' she said. But she was laughing.

'It's never too early to learn the facts of life,' I said.

'Doubtful facts,' she said. 'Anyway, I'm no fan of Freud. He seems to me as a case of the sick ministering to the sick.'

'And with a flick of her feather duster she demolished the sage of Vienna and toppled the pillars of modern American life and culture,' I declaimed.

She laughed. 'And why not?'

'Why not indeed. The wisdom of the gut is supreme.'

We were sitting on the grass. Susan lay back, raised her face to the sun and closed her eyes. 'It's glorious here on a day like this,' she said.

'Smells good, whatever you're cooking,' I said.

'Curry,' she said, not opening her eyes. 'Hope you like Indian. I've not made it too hot. It'll be ready in about an hour.'

I said, 'You function very well as a woman.'

'Odd thing to say. How else could I function?'

'I mean you carry it all so lightly. My mother used to spend hours in the kitchen to prepare meals. And with Chris you're so easy and natural. You do what's necessary and give him love, but don't make too much of a fuss about it. It's right, it's as it should be, to be so capable and contented, but it's unusual and strange.'

'You think women must be discontented because they're not like men? That "penis envy" stuff of Freud's is another thing I think silly. I'm quite happy to be a woman.'

'And I'm happy that you are, and that I'm a man.'

'Vive la différence,' she said.

'I agree. But it seems that the differences all favour men, and that doesn't seem to worry you. I'm thinking of that time when you so exasperated Bill by saying you weren't concerned with setting the world to rights.'

'Did I? Well, it's true. It's a man's world, and the sexes aren't equal, and I accept that. Some women get all steamed up about it, and political, but I wouldn't want to be a man, and what you call functioning as a woman seems a fine thing to me.'

'It certainly is. But it's a bit of a mystery to me. When I say that the differences all favour men, I mean that men are not so tied as women are to their biological and social functions, to having periods, child-bearing and home-making for instance.'

'It's a bit of an old chestnut, isn't it, that women are governed by their biological cycles, and are therefore intellectually and spiritually inferior to men?'

She was suddenly sharp and steely.

I said, 'That's not what I meant.' Susan stood up and said, 'I must check the curry and put on the rice. Why don't you open the wine? We can have a glass before we eat.'

I stood and barred her way into the house.

'Kiss me,' I said.

'No.'

'The stomach rebels?' I tried to make her reciprocate a smile, but she wouldn't.

'Yes. So will you let me pass?'

I yielded, bleakly aware that I didn't know where her flashpoints lay. I didn't understand how I had so upset her, but suddenly there were deserts between us. This wasn't a matter of provocation and teasing that could be resolved by a bit of horseplay over her entering the cottage. Or was it? I didn't know, but I didn't take the risk. I let her pass and opened the wine.

The strain between us lasted right through the lunch. I felt desolate. The magic had gone out of the day. Yet Susan did nothing that I could reproach her with. She was gay and talkative and acted for all the world as if nothing had happened. It was I who was sulky and uncommunicative. I was aware of that, yet in my heart I blamed her. She had withdrawn part of herself, the part that I most cherished. She busied herself with the food, served it up, spoon-fed Christopher from a tin of baby food, and chatted away just as she might have done to any casual acquaintance. It was a display of social accomplishment, and as such it riled me; but at the same time I was glad of it, because for both of us to have been sulkily silent would have been worse. Yet her aloofness gave me more pain than any recriminations would have done. I resented in her the nonchalance and pride of her class, the ability to put on a superficial and impenetrable mask of calm and normality while the depths bubbled and seethed. In my head I formulated a verbal frontal assault: 'Alright you've made your point, you're an independent and complex human being with a life of your own; now cut out the social chatter and come back to me.' The trouble was that I didn't know that it would be relevant. I wasn't sure that it was merely social chatter, that there were any seething depths, that the mask wasn't the face. Her playacting, if such it was, was consummate. It was just possible that I was imagining it all, that she had already forgotten or dismissed whatever I had said that had offended her. The thought afforded no consolation, however. I still felt desolate and distanced.

'It's always seemed to me a great shame that one half of the human race should be so cut off from the other. It's such a waste.' This was later in the afternoon. Christopher had been put down for a sleep, and we were lying in the garden. The sun blazed high in a clear sky and the only sound was of insects buzzing and humming.

'I don't see why the sexes need to be cut off from one another,' I said.

'Nor do I, but they are in so many ways. It's a sad fact. And I'm not saying that men are wholly to blame. Women can be just as prejudice-ridden and cliquey.'

I interpreted this as her way of making it up. I felt that she had come back within reach. Perhaps it was the effect of the wine, the good meal, the idyllic afternoon. I said, 'Well, you seemed to be blaming me earlier, judging by the way you froze me off.'

'I was just a little disappointed,' she said. 'Brian and Paul used to talk in much the same way, with patronising ideas about women.'

'I'm sorry if I was unoriginal.'

She laughed. 'Oh dear, now you're on your dignity.' Then teasingly, 'Have I injured that masculine pride?'

'No. And pride certainly isn't exclusively masculine.'

'You mean it's a fault of mine too?'

'Not a fault. Let's say sometimes a characteristic. It comes with your class, and your nose.'

'What's wrong with my nose?' She pretended indignation.

'Nothing. I think it's a fine nose, maybe somewhat longer than normal, but a splendid nose for looking down.'

'Cheeky, impertinent man,' she laughed, then suddenly leaned over and kissed me lightly on the lips.

'You have a sensual mouth,' she said, 'but sometimes you hold it too tight. When you relax your lips, they have a soft, sensual line.' She traced it with a finger. 'Sometimes in London I had an impulse to kiss you just to make you relax that grim, set expression.'

'You should have done.'

'There wasn't the opportunity. We were never alone.'

'We are now. Time to make up for lost opportunities.'

But I didn't turn on the pressure as I would have done before. I remembered my resolution to do her no violence, to cherish her wholeness. And I had decided that the time had now come when I must tell her about Joan.

I said, 'There's something I want to tell you.'

She watched me and waited while I racked my brain for the right words. I was nervous. I couldn't imagine how she would react. But it had to be done.

'I didn't tell you before because - well, because I didn't expect things to get so serious. I took her hand and fondled it. 'You see, the thing I want you to know, because it's important to me now that between us there should be nothing hidden, is that Joan: perhaps you remember her at Chepstow Road?' Susan nodded slightly. 'Well, Joan is pregnant, and by me.'

Did she already know? She appeared to receive the information quite calmly. I searched her eyes for signs of anger, jealousy, reproach, but there were none. She just looked solemn and composed. She averted her eyes and said in a soft voice, 'I'm glad you told me. But why did you?'

'I wanted you to know. I couldn't keep it to myself, things being as they are between us.'

'What are you going to do?'

'I don't know. Things were complicated enough, but now to make them more so I find myself in love with you.'

She shook her head. 'You mustn't let that complicate it. Anyway, I shall be gone in a week.'

'But you'll be back.'

'Two months is a long time.'

'But I'll still love you.'

She smiled. 'I'd take odds against that. Anyway, wouldn't it be better for both of us if you didn't?'

'I don't know. I only know that I'm in love with you and I can't bear the thought of it not continuing and developing.'

'It's been an idyll,' she said, 'a summer infatuation. After all, we're both on the rebound. You'll be cured by the time I get back.'

'I don't want to get cured,' I said, 'and I don't regard it as an infatuation.'

'No. Well, we shall see.' Her tone was resigned. 'I think you should try to get cured, anyway. I'd help you, only I'm afraid that just now my stomach wouldn't let me.'

'That wouldn't cure me. It would make it worse.'

'Oh, I don't know.' Now she was crisp and ironical. 'After all, it's only a physical attraction, isn't it?'

'No, it's more than that. It's something different, complex and special.'

She didn't sustain the ironic note. She changed to the rueful: 'Perhaps, but if it is it has come too late, hasn't it?'

And it was in an elegiac mood that we spent our last days together before she went to Germany. She didn't return to the cottage after that day, but we saw each other every evening and went for walks and sat in pubs holding hands. Our mutual physical attraction remained undiminished, though there was no question now of it being consummated. We could scarcely bear to be apart, and when we were together we had to be continually touching, kissing, or simply holding hands. When physical contact was not possible, we held each other with intense looks.

One day when Sue's mother and I were briefly together alone, she said, 'I could boil your head in oil, Stuart, for making Susan fall in love with you. She was just getting over the break up of her marriage and looking forward to the trip to Germany, and now she mopes about and doesn't show any enthusiasm for going.'

Her voice was so light, level and uninflected that I couldn't tell whether her words expressed a genuine reproof or just a tease. I muttered that I was equally stricken myself, and she changed the subject. I cherished the information she had given me, though, for it was more than Sue would ever admit to, and as the time for her departure drew nearer I became hungry for any scrap of evidence that I had a hold on her that would endure. If she was sceptical about my feelings, I was equally so about hers. In Germany she would be back among her type of people, and I did not doubt that her natural exuberance and gaiety would soon reassert themselves. Sue was not the type to brood upon - or let her life be disrupted by - a passion that afforded little hope of a happy issue. Our physical affinity was exciting and extraordinary, an experience without precedent for both of us, but it seemed a slight and unreliable thing to put any hopes on or to match against the process of emotional attrition that could come about through separation and the inevitable impingement of other lives, other responsibilities, other problems. It was too strong a feeling to be denied or suppressed, and during our last days together we gave it rein up to a point, but always there was a melancholy undertow. Not only did two months seem an endless time, but it was impossible for either of us to see what life would be like on the other side of it.

'You should go back to London and Joan,' Sue said.

'I shall see her and try to help,' I said, 'but I shall await your return and still be around when you come back.'

Susan shook her head. 'Why?' she said.

'Because it can't be otherwise. We can't leave it like this.'

We were sitting facing each other in a loud and smoky bar, hands clasped across a wet and littered table and our eyes avidly reading the melancholy and the hope in each other's face. Sue said, 'Stuart, I don't want to be your escape route.'

'It's not that, I promise you.'

'You should go back to Joan.'

'It's impossible. It would be even if there were no chance of our meeting again.'

She seemed to believe me; but she was disinclined to press the point further, except to say, rather wearily, 'Maybe. Poor kid, though. Pregnancy isn't any fun, even at the best of times. You must be kind to her.'

'I will,' I said, poignantly aware at that moment, as in the months that followed, of the sad irony that the promise so solemnly entered into really had nothing to do with Joan, who was to be its beneficiary.

It was through no intervention of Sue's that her father offered me the use of the bungalow while they were away. In fact, the offer came as a surprise both to Susan and to Daphina. Dick was known to them as a taciturn and careful man, not given to spontaneous acts of generosity. Nor did he make the offer in a particularly generous spirit; he just said that it would suit him to have the place occupied instead of standing empty while they were away. I accepted the offer gladly, and on the day of their departure I left the cottage early with my rucksack, hitch-hiked a lift to Battle, and accompanied them to the station. There Sue and I discreetly kissed. I promised to write often and to be faithful to her, and she told me not to make any promises. I said that in two months' time I would be waiting on the other platform just across the line there for her return, but she said she wouldn't depend on it. I told her to enjoy herself, but not too much, and to beware of sneaky subalterns, and she told me to work hard and to be sure to get myself cured as soon as possible. I told her it was heartless of her to leave me with her scepticism and mockery as a last memory, and she made up for it by placing upon my lips a tender kiss with a secret intimate swirl of tongue. The train came and I helped them with Christopher and with their luggage. Susan remained leaning out of the window as the train drew away. The wind blew her hair all over her face and she kept using her hand alternately to push it back and to wave to me until the train rounded a bend and we lost sight of each other.

Two long months, I thought. Well, I would work hard and try to get my life in order. The only work I had done recently was a story titled *'Nostalgia'*, in which I expressed my feelings on the night when Malcolm Fraser, Sue's City friend, had driven her home and I discovered in myself an extraordinary nostalgia for violence. I re-read the story and now it seemed flat and banal. Yet I had written it in a frenzy. It was bewildering that feeling was so delusive and treacherous a guide in matters of art; and it was a chastening thought that the same might apply in life. The same did apply in fact. The affair with Joan had begun with such intense feelings and equally promisingly. I was convinced that with Susan everything was and would be different, but it was a conviction based on feeling. Time would tell, and the months ahead were to be a crucial test.

His Dear Time's Waste - Stuart Holroyd

6

I went to London a few days after Susan had left for Germany, and it soon became clear that news of my life in the country had preceded me. This didn't particularly surprise me. Paul's cottage was one of three on the Brightling Park estate, all of which were occupied that summer by people who were frequent visitors to Chepstow Road. There was Ewan Cameron, an ardent but pacific world-changer, ever ready to espouse a worthy cause and now the most zealous of Spartacans. He rented the old gamekeeper's cottage in the middle of the estate, a few hundred yards from Paul's, where he spent most weekends, being during the week an itinerant house-drawer, an occupation which seemed quite lucrative, for he was able to run a car and maintain a place in London. Then there was Peter Lambert, an earnest young man who was a protégé of Bill's, who had urged him to give up a good job as a patent agent and go to the country to write. After two months in the country, he had told me, he had discovered that he wasn't a writer but just an out of work patent agent. He had a wry sense of humour, and it was he who had put the 'Beware of the Doggerel' warning on Tom's door. I had seen something of both Ewan and Peter during my weeks at the cottage, and it was obviously through them that Bill and the others had learned that I had been spending much of my time with Susan.

There was, as usual, a crowd in Tom's room when I arrived, more than usual in fact, and I didn't recognise everyone. Tom, Bill and Greta were there, and also Colin, in town on one of his brief visits, and among the others a tall young woman with a curled crown of shiny black hair. But there was no sign of Joan.

I walked in on a scene of general and inexplicable hilarity. People were moving about the room and everyone seemed to be laughing. I put down my rucksack near the door and Tom came across to greet me and drew me into the middle of the room. He introduced me to the strangers. The girl was called Amanda. She held out a limp hand and turned her face to be kissed. She had a slender figure, wore a sack-style knee-length dress gathered just below rather small breasts, and high-heeled shoes which emphasised the length and shapeliness of her legs. Her face wore a fixed expression of surprise and naivety with its high pencilled eyebrows and heavily mascara-ed false lashes.

'So you're the backwoodsman Bill has told me about,' she said.

'Bill's been building you up as a latter-day Thoreau,' Tom said.

Then Colin came over to me, broadly smiling, and suddenly stuffed something down my shirtfront. It was alive. I felt the thing struggling to get out and panic seized me lest it should bite or scratch. Everyone laughed delightedly, except Amanda, who tore at my shirt, ripping a button off, and extracted a small, brown, fluffy creature which she clasped to her breast.

'Poor Caesar! You've frightened him,' she admonished Colin.

'I'm sorry, love, I couldn't resist it,' Colin said. 'Here, let me kiss him better.' Pretending to do so, he nuzzled the girl's breast with a boisterous show of lechery. She slapped him on the back of the head and he drew away, laughing.

The creature was a bush-baby. Amanda released it and it leapt from her hand and clung high up on the curtains, an amazing feat for such a small creature. It surveyed the room with a curiously human expression. Amanda said it should be left alone now for a while or it would develop a complex, so everyone sat down and the noise and laughter gradually subsided.

'Been getting much work done down there in the country, Stuart?' Bill said across the room to me, twinkling with covert raillery.

'Quite a bit, Bill,' I countered firmly. 'How's the novel going?'

He ignored the question and said, 'What have you been working on then?'

'A new play. It's coming along quite well. How about your novel?'

Bill screwed up his face in simulation of the agonies of creation. 'Not very well, Stuart old man.' Then with heavy irony: 'It's alright for you, alone in the country, but I keep getting involved with people, and that plays havoc with the work.'

'You should get away to the country yourself,' I said. 'There's no place like it for work.'

'So it seems. Fast work!' He laughed and slapped his thigh.

'Stop bitching, you two,' Tom said. He turned to Amanda. 'Women are supposed to be bitchy, but they've got nothing on writers. They're all egotists, and the most malicious breed on the face of the earth.'

Colin, now slumped in a deep armchair, joined in. 'It's not malice, Tom, it's concern. We've got to keep each other up to the mark creatively. Stuart has a great disadvantage as a writer because he's cursed with romantic good looks and is attractive to women. And he's a randy bugger. For his own sake someone has to keep reminding him that his intellect is the only interesting and important thing about him, and if his friends don't, who will?'

Though this kind of genial slanging was accepted form among us, I knew that Colin meant every word of it, and I felt obscurely that not to argue back would somehow be disloyal to Susan.

'I don't agree, Col,' I said. 'I think that if a man is strong on intellect he should focus on developing other sides of himself to balance it out. Surely the best writing is that which is the expression of the whole man.'

'Remember Browning's *Paracelsus*: "Man is not man as yet"?' Colin said. 'That was written a hundred years ago and it's still true. Quite literally, man does not yet exist. Plenty of whole men in your sense of the term exist. You see them everywhere, contented idiots perfectly adjusted to their environment. These people's lives are so full and they're so self-satisfied and taken up with the business of living fully that they don't stop for a moment to think, to ask "What is man's proper element?" Wells had the answer when he wrote at the beginning of his autobiography that men are striving to become creatures of the mind. That's exactly it. Man's element is the mind. But who are these men who are striving to become pure mind? They're not your so-called whole men, who have developed all sides of themselves so that they can run like a well-oiled machine.'

'They're the fanatics,' Bill put in.

'Yes, in a sense, Bill,' Colin went on, 'but they're not your revolutionary or social-reforming fanatics. I'm sorry, but your fanatic who wants wrongs righted doesn't really interest me. He doesn't count in the evolutionary process, and my point is that evolution alone counts and man's potential for evolution is in the life of the mind. This is so plain and undeniable to me that it astounds me that I seem to be the only man in England today who sees it.'

He stopped, perhaps to see if anyone would rise to the challenge. I said, 'I'm sorry, Col, but for me the very idea of creatures of pure mind is a repugnant one. I suppose it's a temperamental difference.'

Colin shook his head. 'Call it that if you like. It seems to me, though, that Bill's right, and that you've lost your nerve, Stuart. It's lonely work and I could do with some allies.' He gloomily contemplated his lonely vocation for a moment, then suddenly bounded up. He had to go, he said, to pick up Joy somewhere before going on to a literary party at seven o'clock. He suggested I should join them, saying I'd surely have been invited if the host had known I was in town and it should be interesting because it was in honour of the American novelist James Jones. I said I might and noted the Kensington address.

When Colin had gone I asked Tom where Joan was. He was surprised that I didn't know that she had left the week before. She had moved into a flat in Bayswater with a girl she was working with. Tom gave me the address. 'But she doesn't finish work until five,' he said.

It was a quarter to four. I went to my room. Joan had left it neat and tidy and without any trace of her tenancy. There was a musty smell from the old furniture and I opened the windows to disperse it. I had been away only four or five weeks, but it was like visiting a shabby mausoleum scrupulously preserved to the memory of a dead self. There were all my books, carefully shelved and classified, there was my wall montage of press clippings, pictures and letters, my double bed, my portrait in oils done by my artist friend Lionel Miskin in Cornwall. It was all very familiar, but it all belonged to a past too close to evoke nostalgia and too distant to produce a warm glow of homecoming. The place seemed dead and inhospitable.

Presently Bill appeared carrying two mugs of tea and full of inquisitiveness. I held him at bay for a while by asking him about the Spartacan movement. Things were held up at the moment, he said, on account of the printers' strike that had been going on for a month now.

'But tell me about your industrious life in the country,' he said. 'We've heard on the grapevine that you've been seeing a lot of Sue Rowland.'

'Well, I've been making good progress with the Gurdjieff play,' I lied, 'and yes, I've seen quite a bit of Sue.'

Bill nodded. 'A fascinating woman. Can't say I blame you. Are you in love with her?'

That was a point that I wouldn't lie or prevaricate about with anyone, except maybe Joan. I said 'Yes'.

'It's hell, isn't it?' Bill grimaced. 'I must admit I've got a touch of the old delirium myself at the moment.'

The idea of Bill being in love was somehow incongruous.

I blurted out an astonished 'You?'

'Well you needn't look so damned incredulous,' he said, piqued.

'But who?'

'Amanda. She's a model; top of the profession; an original mind too. But I tell you, Stuart, this love thing is a trap for the creative man. It's a delightful state to be in. Don't I know it! But it plays hell with your work.'

'Do you know it? I wonder.' I suspected that Bill's confession was a stratagem for drawing me out. I didn't resent it, but I wanted him to know I saw through it.

'I tell you, through these last weeks I've been through the whole gamut, the ecstasies of possession, the agonies of separation, the gnawing irrational jealousies. I'm an exhausted man.'

'You don't look it.'

'I mean emotionally and spiritually exhausted. That's what it does to you. I haven't done a stroke. There was nothing left to put into my work. It's no good, Stuart, we must conserve our energies. We must renounce love. Remember Kierkegaard, Kafka, Verlaine.'

Stirring clarion calls. Illustrious literary precedents. It was all as familiar and as dead to me as the room we were sitting in. I said, 'We have to live our own lives, not Kierkegaard's, Kafka's or Verlaine's.'

Bill said, 'Ultimately what every woman wants is marriage and children, and Connolly was right that the pram in the hall is the greatest of the enemies of promise. Don't fall into the trap.'

I laughed. The idea of Susan laying a trap deserved only derision.

'You can laugh,' Bill said, 'but you're in mortal danger.'

'Perhaps,' I said, 'but I believe in living dangerously.'

Joan's flat was in a street of tall terraced houses parallel to Queensway on the Paddington side. A card beneath one of the bells indicated that she was on the second floor. Soon after I had pressed the bell her voice crackled through the intercom grille set in the wall.

'Who is it?'

'Stuart.'

'My God! Well, you'd better come up.'

The door buzzed and opened and I mounted a dim staircase. Joan was waiting for me on the second floor landing.

'This is a surprise,' she said. It was a relief that she was neither effusively welcoming nor coldly forbidding. She seemed rather to be waiting to judge my mood. I kissed her on the cheek.

'You look well,' I said. She was considerably plumper than when she was at the cottage, particularly in the face.

'I am well,' she said, 'but I feel a mess at the moment. I've just got back from work. I wasn't expecting any visitors. Come into the flat, but close your eyes to the squalor.'

It wasn't particularly squalid. It was nondescript, like most London flats available for short-term tenancies, with heavy old furniture and discoloured paintwork, but the living room was spacious and there were doors leading off into a separate kitchen and bedroom.

'Nice place,' I said.

'It's alright. I couldn't afford it myself, but with Sheila sharing it's quite reasonable. And the coffee bar where we work is on Queensway, so it's quite convenient.'

'Very.' We were polite strangers, awkward with each other and struggling for things to say. I felt superfluous and that my conscientious visit was pointless. She had her life in order.

'Did you get my letter?' she said. 'I wrote to you a couple of days ago.'

'I've been away from the cottage.'

'Oh-h.' She drew it out, and her expression – elongated face, sucked-in cheeks, a slight inclination of the head – was the standard theatrical mime for a swift mental readjustment to an unforeseen turn of events. 'That explains it,' she said.

'Explains what?'

'Your coming. I wrote to say – well, it's complicated to go into now, you'll see when you get my letter. But now you're here I suppose I'd better offer you tea.'

'Didn't you want me to come?'

'Yes and no; it depends what your motives are.'

'Well, I wanted to see you, and to see if there's anything I can do.'

'Such as?'

'I don't know. Anything.'

'I don't think there is anything. As you see, I've got my life pretty well organised for the present. Thanks again for the money, by the way.'

'I'll send you some more when I can.'

'Don't put yourself out.'

'Why not? I mean, you've been pretty drastically put out by this. It's the least I can do.'

This seemed to stir in Joan an emotion which she found difficult to control. She said, 'I'll just go and put the kettle on,' and went into the kitchen.

It was fully five minutes before she returned, carrying a tray of tea-things. Her manner declared that she had got under control whatever emotion had possessed her and was determined now to be gay and inscrutable.

'Yes, it's turned out rather well,' she said, putting the tray down in front of the couch where I was sitting. 'Sheila's a marvellous person to share with, and she's terribly excited about the baby. The way she talks about it and makes plans, you'd think she was the one who was going to have it. It's marvellous for my morale. I'm in my fifth month now. They say it's the time when you feel at your best, and it's true. A month or two ago I'd never have dreamed I could feel as well as this. I was feeling very low before you went away to the country, and I'm afraid I dragged you down with me, you poor man. I'm sorry.'

'You needn't be. It's a relief to me to see you so well.'

'Bill and Tom were very kind,' Joan said as she poured the tea. But I felt it was an embarrassment for them to have a pregnant woman about. It's such a bachelor establishment. I began to feel out of place, particularly in that room with all your things around.' She laughed. 'I got odd urges to change the curtains and paint the walls. It must be a sort of nest-making instinct. And also I got so tired of all that interminable talk. It suddenly seemed so unimportant. I'm sure it's me, and that it's all terribly important really, but you see why I couldn't go on living there? But for Sheila, I think I'd have felt like crawling into a hole far away from anybody and just waiting for the whole business to be over. Pregnancy brings about such extraordinary changes, not only in your body but also in your thinking and the way you see things. I can understand people going temporarily insane when they're pregnant. I could have done, living in that house. Isn't it the Indian Brahmins who send their women back to their mothers to go through their pregnancy and confinement? It's probably the best way. A woman needs other women at such a time, and once they've done their bit men are quite irrelevant. Bill and Tom were the soul of sweetness, but I knew I embarrassed them and would do more and more as I got fatter. It's not really fair to ask men to understand. When you think of it, it's odd even for another woman to if she hasn't been through it herself. But I suppose coming from a large family helps. Sheila has six brothers and sisters.'

It was as if she was wound up and couldn't stop the flow of talk. I detected beneath the flow a hardening edge to her voice, a slight change to a shriller key. I sought words to pacify her, to conciliate her suppressed desperation, but could find none, and I was just wondering what I could do if she suddenly burst into tears when I heard a door open. Joan jumped to her feet.

'Sheila, darling! Come and join us. I've made some tea. Come and meet Stuart.'

Sheila was a tall thin girl with short black hair artificially streaked with silver. She had sharp features and her eyes were brown like Joan's but even bigger. She was no beauty, but by dressing colourfully and using make-up she had done her best to acquire by art what she was denied by nature, and the effect was a little outlandish but not unattractive.

'So this is Stuart.' The voice was throaty and theatrical, and the eyes were cool and appraising. 'I must admit I've been madly curious.' She thrust out an arm and flopped her hand from the wrist as if offering it to be kissed. I shook it.

'Isn't she looking marvellous? Don't you think pregnancy does wonders for a woman? I think I'll get pregnant myself when Joan has had hers, and then we'll have a cosy little ménage à quatre. Unless of course you've come to whip her away and make a respectable woman of her.'

Joan laughed. 'Sheila, don't tease. Stuart's just come on a visit.'

'Oh, well that's alright then,' Sheila said. 'Just a social call, eh? Taking tea with the ladies? Well, I'm sorry, but this particular lady has to dash. I have a date, and I must have a bath and change.' She swept into the bedroom.

'She's quite a character,' Joan said affectionately after she had gone. 'So you see' – she waved both arms in a gesture that was perhaps intended to indicate a sweeping away of all the past – 'all's well that ends well.'

I could have left then, but I felt sorry for Joan because her friend was going out and she would be left alone, so I suggested that she should go with me to the party. At first she protested that she was tired after working all day, but then she agreed that a change of scene and a couple of drinks would soon take care of that. Then she objected that she had nothing suitable to wear, but I convinced her that even if she went looking scruffy and unkempt she'd just be taken as a best-selling young novelist. She was easily persuaded, and asked me to wait ten minutes while she got ready.

While she was gone, Sheila came out. She made a noisy to-do about finding a black evening bag, which she finally located under a cushion on the couch where I was sitting. She was dressed in a smart black jersey-wool suit with a white shirt with a frilly front and sleeves, and wore ear-rings made of match-thin sticks of jet that tinkled as she moved. As she struggled to stuff into the small evening bag a powder compact, a lipstick, a cigarette-rolling machine and a packet of tobacco she said to me, sotto-voce:

'Joan is immensely bucked that you're taking her out. It'll probably do her good, but, you know, she's just about got herself mentally adjusted and she is still prone to the occasional bout of depression. So take care. You know what I mean?' With contracted brow, wrinkled nose and two or three short sharp nods of the head she emphasised the urgency of her plea on her friend's behalf. I said I understood and would take care not to upset Joan. Satisfied, Sheila called out a cheery, 'Bye then, enjoy yourself,' to Joan and left the flat.

When Joan appeared, in a loose-fitting dress that made her bulge almost unnoticeable, and with her hair drawn back from her face and gathered with clips into a chignon, she looked a different woman and I experienced a flashback insight into what had originally drawn me to her.

'You look magnificent,' I said 'not at all the scruffy angry young woman.'

'Thank you, sir!' she said, smiling happily.

I wondered what Susan would have felt if she could have seen us. She could hardly mind, as she was probably going to lots of parties in Germany with a host of panting subalterns in tow, and anyway I was acting on her behest to be kind to Joan.

The taxi took us to a large Georgian house in a crescent in Kensington, and we were admitted by a uniformed maid, who directed us upstairs. The party was in full swing. There must have been about fifty people in the elegant, high-ceilinged room, and they all seemed to be talking at once. Waiters moved among them with trays of drinks, and I stopped one and took a couple of glasses. We skirted around the fringes of the party and found Colin at the other side of the room. He was talking to a man I recognised as a well-known professor of philosophy, a short, saurian man with quick eyes with heavy pouches under them.

'Come and support me, Stuart,' he said. I'm trying to persuade Professor Ayer to introduce a course on Whitehead into the curriculum at his university, but he takes the view that his work is metaphysical nonsense and not worth reading.'

'Now that's naughty!' the professor admonished, wagging a finger. 'You misrepresent me. What I said was that after his collaboration with Russell on the *Principia Mathematica*, Whitehead stopped doing philosophy. *Science and the Modern World* is an interesting book, but it's a contribution to the history of ideas, not to philosophy. Most of Russell's later work, too, is non-philosophical. Let's be clear about this, I've no objection to a man writing whatever he pleases, providing he doesn't call it philosophy when it palpably isn't.' He spoke with a light, crisp voice, and when he had finished he beamed.

'What about *Process and Reality*?' I said, responding to Colin's request to support him. An enthusiasm for Whitehead's philosophy was something I unconditionally shared with him. 'You can't claim that that isn't philosophy.'

'I haven't read it,' Ayer said, still beaming.

'Well, I think that's a deplorable admission for a philosopher to make,' Colin said.

Ayer was unruffled. 'Why? For my non-professional reading I prefer French and Russian novels, and if I occasionally have a taste for a bit of poetry I prefer to take it straight and not masquerading as philosophy. But you must excuse me.'

This last was not an apology, but a signal for the termination of the discussion. A tall man with thick grey hair and distinguished features had joined us. He apologised for the interruption and took the professor away to meet 'a German *confrère*' who had been longing to meet him.

'All logical positivists ought to be shot,' Colin spat out vindictively when he had gone. 'I suppose they'll sink back into the slime they came out of and nobody will have heard of them in fifty years, but it irks me to see a man like Ayer occupying a chair of philosophy and snootily dismissing Whitehead.'

The man with grey hair returned and apologised again for taking Professor Ayer away. Colin fulminated to him about the reputation of English philosophy depending on 'the antics of a troop of performing monkeys', and then introduced me to the man who turned out to be our host, John Lehmann, editor of *The London Magazine*.

'You should get Stuart to write something for you, John,' Colin said, and then turned away to talk to someone who had just approached him.

By this time Joy and Joan, no doubt bored by the philosophical wrangle, had moved away and were talking to a stocky man with a battered pugilist's features and greying hair who was standing by the fireplace. Also across the room I noticed Michael Hastings and my ex-wife Anne.

'I enjoyed your last book,' John Lehmann said. 'Pity you didn't let me see a proof. I should have liked to publish an extract before it came out. But perhaps you'll make up for it by contributing to our feature "A Writer's Prospect".'

'Yes, I'd like to do that,' I said. In the circumstances any commission that might bring in a bit was welcome.

'Good, perhaps we can arrange lunch and chat about it,' he said. Then: 'Tell me, Stuart, are you homosexual or heterosexual?' The tone was conversational. He might have been asking if I preferred coffee or tea. But the corners of the mouth lifted just a little in the ghost of a smile, and obsidian eyes fixed mine.

I was caught off guard and utterly discomposed. Words deserted me. I wasn't even sure that 'heterosexual' didn't define some sort of deviancy. To be on the safe side I answered, 'Well, er... normal, I suppose.'

The mouth tightened, the eyes narrowed, and Lehmann said, in a voice flinty with disapproval, 'You mean heterosexual.'

'Well, yes,' I agreed, feeling a warm flush suffuse my cheeks. That's me written off, I thought.

I was rescued from my embarrassment when a couple who were leaving came to thank John for his hospitality and he escorted them to the door. I crossed the room to where Michael and Anne were in conversation with a man I recognised as Michael's agent. Michael was looking prosperous in a dark tailor-made suit and with flashing cuff-links and tie-pin. I had heard that he had a job with BBC television now. Anne, too, had dressed for the occasion, and looked pretty and pert in a silver calf-length dress with a décolletage. She turned to me.

'We haven't seen you for months. Have you been avoiding us?' She pouted reproachfully.

'No, but life's been a bit complicated,' I said.

'I know. We've heard all about your woman troubles. I'm disappointed in you. You promised you wouldn't get seriously involved with another woman for at least five years. You were going to write lots of marvellous books and things. Then you go and get a girl pregnant.'

'Yes, it's a mess,' I conceded, 'but things will sort themselves out.'

'Are you going to marry her?'

'No.'

That clearly pleased her. She said, 'Bloody fool she is anyway. Why did she let herself get pregnant? Why didn't you make her protect herself, as you always made me?'

'Look, love, this is hardly cocktail party conversation, is it?' I said. Oddly, I didn't resent her interrogation. We had known each other since we were adolescents and had not yet been apart long enough for the protective crust of deference and social inhibition to harden between us. It wasn't her questions that embarrassed me, but the fact that we might be overheard.

'Well, you never come and see us,' she said. 'What other chance do I get to talk to you?'

'I've been spending a lot of time in the country.' Then, rashly, and half regretting it as I said it, but glad to be able to change the subject, I said, 'Why don't you and Mike come down some time? There's plenty of room in the place where I'm staying for the next couple of months.'

'We'd love to – if you really mean it,' she said.

'Of course I mean it.' To prove it I wrote the address and phone number on a piece of paper and gave it to her. She put it away carefully in a handbag. 'So now we can talk trivia,' I said. 'I must say, my dear, that you're looking absolutely resplendent this evening.' I lisped the 's'es and gave it camp inflections. Anne laughed.

'You sound just like Jon Rose,' she said.

That led into my telling her about the recent visit to Jon and Sandy's with Colin and Bill and the two girls, which drew Michael into the conversation, his agent having gone off to talk to another of his clients. When I eventually went to rejoin Joan she was still standing by the fireplace with Joy and the man with the pugilist's face. Closer up he looked older than I had first thought, about forty I judged from the lines on his brow and around his eyes and mouth. But his expression, gentle and humorous, gave him a more youthful look. Joy introduced us.

'But this party is in your honour,' I said when I learned that he was James Jones, author of the novel *From Here to Eternity*, which I had read and admired. I suppose my surprise that a writer of such celebrity should have spent so long talking to two women who themselves had no claim to fame must have shown, for he said, in a soft American voice, 'Well, I seem to have been forgotten. But that suits me, as I'm being charmingly entertained by these two young ladies, and to tell the truth, most of these people terrify me. Joy here has been giving me a very interesting run-down on some of rivalries and bitchings going on here. It's just like New York, only in New York I no longer go to cocktail parties.'

'What brings you to this one then?' I said.

'My publisher fixed it up, but he seems to have disappeared, probably trying to poach some other firm's best-selling author. They certainly work for their money, these guys; they're never off duty.'

John Lehmann had suddenly become aware of his stranded celebrity, perhaps because he saw him talking to me, for he came over and swept him away to meet 'a lady who was particularly keen to talk to him'.

'What a wonderful man,' Joan said. 'I bet he writes marvellous novels. I must read some.'

When we left the party, Joan didn't want to go back to the house with Bill and Colin, as was proposed. It was a warm evening and still light, so we walked up Exhibition Road and across Hyde Park. Other young couples were walking hand in hand or with arms around one another, and it may have been the sight of them that changed Joan's mood to rather sombre after we had talked a bit about the admirable James Jones. We walked in silence for a long way, for I felt that any topic I considered raising would only draw attention to the gaping chasm between us by trying pathetically to bridge it.

At last she broke the silence. 'If you want to go and join Bill and Colin, don't let me stop you.'

'I'll see you home first.'

She laughed. 'Isn't that a rather unnecessary touch of gallantry in the circumstances?'

'It's the least I can do.'

She stopped walking, turned and looked me in the eyes. 'That's becoming a favourite expression of yours, isn't it? Perhaps sometime you'll try doing the most you can do for a change.'

'We can do without sarcasm, Joan,' I said. 'It doesn't help.'

'Oh, but it does,' she flashed back. 'It helps me. But what doesn't help me, what I positively hate, is being on the receiving end of your pity and your "least I can do" charity.'

'It's not that,' I protested, but as I said it I remembered Susan's 'be kind to her'.

'It is,' Joan insisted, 'and it's humiliating.'

Tears came to her eyes. I took her elbow and started her walking again. She walked with her head down, watching her steps, which were measured and deliberate. 'And what is all the more humiliating,' she went on, 'is that you expect me to be the wronged woman nursing her resentment and hatred, you expect me to be all wrapped up in my little tragedy. You don't give me credit for any other feelings, you imagine that all the guilt and the pity are on your side. You may feel rotten about the mess you've made of my life, but doesn't it occur to you that I too might feel guilty as hell about what I've done to you?'

These words, which Joan spoke in a low voice and without raising her head and in a tone as deliberate and measured as her steps, produced in me a feeling of having totally lost my grip on the situation. My predominant feeling was of dismay, for I saw that the future was not going to be simply a matter of doing right by Joan in order to get off on the right foot with Susan. Joan was going to figure much larger in the situation than such a glib estimate of it allowed for. Exactly how she would figure in it I couldn't begin to predict, but the fact that she now stood revealed as a person and not a mere figure representing a wrong to be atoned for, and that she was capable of complex and for me inscrutable emotions which would have to be taken into account, put quite a different complexion on the whole situation. All this flashed through my mind as she finished speaking, but none of it came out in my reply.

I said, 'But I do think that for you to feel guilty about me is putting a bit of a fine point on it. After all, you're the one who's pregnant, who has to go through all the discomfort and pain, and who is finally going to be saddled with the child.'

'But don't you see, none of that is bad?' she said. 'I'm happy to be having your baby, I really am. The experience isn't going to damage me. I can come out the other side a better and stronger and probably happier person. But what about you?'

'I'll come out all right,' I said. I didn't entirely trust this turn-about. The positive note was just a bit too strident, the buoyancy too emphatic. I didn't think she was playacting or doubt that every word was in earnest, but I suspected that among the mass of conflicting attitudes and emotions she had temporarily fixed on and emphasised those of brave independence and magnanimous concern.

'But will you? Will you come out all right?'

'Yes,' I said firmly.

'You're shut in on yourself. I can't begin to guess what goes on in your mind. I was quite prepared to go through all this without ever seeing you again. I was content to regard you as the loser in the whole affair and to leave it at that. But now - well, seeing you makes it different. I feel... '

'Sorry for me?' I suggested.

'Not exactly, but sorry that you apparently aren't going to gain anything from the experience. And, poor man' - she gave a little laugh - 'you're paying dearly for it, so you're entitled to gain something.' She became wistfully reflective. 'It must be a wonderful thing to go through with someone you love and who loves you.'

'Yes, I suppose so,' I said. We walked on in silence, came to and crossed Bayswater Road and turned into Queensway. Joan pointed out the place where she worked, a glorified coffee-bar with chianti bottles in raffia baskets strung across the big plate-glass window. I suggested we should go in for a meal, but she didn't want to. We reached her front door and I was glad when she said, 'I'd rather you didn't come up if you don't mind. When you get back to the cottage you'll get my letter. It still applies.'

I told her I was no longer at the cottage and gave her my new address. She showed no curiosity about the change.

The next morning I was alone with Colin for a while and after chatting about the party we got on to what he called 'the Joan business' and he suddenly said, 'Why don't you marry her?'

I was staggered. This seemed downright treachery.

'I thought you didn't like her', I said feebly.

'I wouldn't be marrying her, would I?' he said. 'No, the way I see it, Stuart, is that one has to have a woman and it doesn't matter much who she is, provided she's suitably adoring and doesn't get under your feet. I sometimes feel that you and Bill waste too much time getting involved with all sorts of people and schemes and having affairs. I honestly feel that your best plan would be to get a woman, move into the country somewhere and really get stuck into work.'

'The trouble is I'm no longer in love with Joan.'

Colin was unimpressed. 'I don't think it matters. As I say, you have to have a woman. The "in love" situation is always short-lived anyway. Woman is the warrior's rest, his relaxation after the battle. It's as true for the crusader of the intellect as it was for the warriors of old. And that's what we've got to be, Stuart,' he said with rising emphasis. 'We have to be intellectual crusaders.'

He said he was sorry if he had been a bit abrupt the previous evening, but he was genuinely disappointed that I seemed to have lost, if not my nerve, at least my enthusiasm for 'our cause'. We had made a breakthrough, in a comparatively short time established ourselves as a literary group that was talked about and had to be taken into account, and now was the time to consolidate, produce more work and confound our critics. I had said something about our temperamental differences, but of course there were temperamental differences and that was our strength. Also, he conceded, we all had our faults. He tended to be too intolerant and impetuous, Bill too careless and imprecise in expressing his ideas, and I was too diffident. Working side by side, criticising each others' work, we could iron out these faults. We had to bring out the best work in one another. Eliot might say that nothing is achieved by literary groups and that a man produces his best work alone, but hadn't he submitted *The Waste Land* to Ezra Pound and accepted his re-write of it? That was the kind of cooperation he had in mind. In a sense he was himself very much a loner. He'd always assumed that he'd end up as a sort of Tolstoy figure, occasionally uttering gloomy roars from 'Mevapolanya' and distributing bits of his garments to pilgrims, but really he hated the idea of being a guru-figure. He didn't want followers because they were always a trap. But he did, as he'd said, need allies, exchange of ideas and criticism, the sense of working not entirely alone. My emotional life was my own business. Though he personally didn't take to opinionated women, it didn't really concern him whether I finally settled for Joan or for Susan. What did concern him was that we should go on working and supporting each other and that we should really consolidate ourselves as a powerful literary bloc in England.

It was both an appeal and an exhortation, and I was both moved and enthused. I assured Colin that there was no question of my deserting or giving up writing, and I was making progress with the Gurdjieff-in-Paris play. But I felt that I needed to be out of London, just as he did, and to have a space to get my life in order and revise some of my thinking. The only thing I lacked enthusiasm for was Bill's political aspirations. Colin said he knew what I meant, but on the other hand he thought Bill was right in believing that we should extend ourselves and make an impact on as many fronts as possible, and we ought to support him if only out of loyalty.

That afternoon I went to the offices of the magazines *Time and Tide* and *John O'London's Weekly*, which I had written regularly for before the recently terminated printers' strike, and picked up some books for review. In the evening I took the train back to Sussex full of zest for work.

When I got back to the bungalow I found a card lying on the mat inside the front door. The picture side showed a *gemütlich* German tavern scene, and on the back were the words:

Just to let you know we arrived safely. This place is as uninspiring as it looks, but my sister's husband John has three weeks' leave and we're off next week for a camping holiday in France, which should be fun. Hope all is going well and that you're doing lots of work and making progress with your cure.

Ever, Sue.'

Evidently she had decided to send a card because it enforced brevity. There was nothing to read between the lines, and the way she signed off was entirely non-committal and nicely ambiguous. It could stand as an abbreviation for 'yours ever' or as an assertion that Sue would ever be Sue, which was a thing I didn't doubt but that in the circumstances gave scant comfort.

I went to bed that night rather gloomy and disgruntled, but woke the following morning in a room – Susan's room – glowing with sunlight through the thin yellow curtains, which quite dispersed the gloom. I resolved to teach her to try to disenchant me with cool postcards. I would write her, if not exactly a love letter, at least an unashamed lover's letter. I took a cup of coffee into the garden and wrote, and when I had finished I read the letter through with satisfaction, enjoying imagining the expressions that might cross Susan's face as she read it. There were parts of it that might provoke a frown of disapproval:

No, my love, I am not yet cured, nor do I see any prospect of being so. But at least I am no longer a drooling, knocked-aback infatuate with starry eyes and no faculty for concentration. Take warning that I shall never forgive you for reducing me to that state of idiocy during the weeks before you went to join the army.

Were they weeks? or days, or... Until I think back to details it seems they could have been only hours even, or minutes. We were so prodigal with time, we burned it up, and now all our times together make up one moment of sublime incandescence, and that moment still burns.

I could see her, perhaps, taking her lower lip between her teeth the way she did when my importunities discomposed her and came near to breaking through her wall of sense and principle. Then I saw her smile as she read on:

I told myself before I began this that I wouldn't write a love letter. No adolescent nonsense, I said, above all nothing sentimental or high-flown. Tell her that you went to London yesterday, had a bush-baby pushed down your shirt-front by Colin, endured a predictable ribbing from Bill, who had got word of us through the bush telegraph, got propositioned by a prominent homosexual at a literary party, and fled precipitately back here to the sanity and solace of memories of you.

After pondering for some time over the signing off, I made it simply 'ever yours, Stuart.' The letter, I thought, captured the mood of our times together and might have the intended effect of setting her back in her own 'cure'.

The morning postal delivery brought another letter, forwarded by Paul from the cottage. It was Joan's, and most of it was in the vein I had expected. She gave her reasons for moving out of my room, enthused about her set-up with Sheila, explained how she had become not only reconciled to but even happy about having the baby. On the subject of my part in the affair, however, she was more explicit than she had been when we met. She said she didn't want, by selfishly insisting on marriage or nothing, to deprive me of my rights or the baby of the advantage of having a father. She had sorted herself out and had decided to keep the baby whatever happened. If I wanted nothing more to do with them ('You see, I'm already thinking in the plural') she would accept that and get used to it, but she'd rather make a clean break now than later. But if I wanted to play some part, however small, in their lives, she promised me a reasonable and unemotional reception any time I felt like going up to talk about it. If she didn't hear in the next couple of weeks, she said, she would get the message.

So when I had turned up at the flat she must have thought at first that I had received the letter and had gone up immediately to talk about it. That explained a lot. And now she would still be awaiting my response. She had said of the letter, 'It still applies'.

The two weeks passed and I did nothing about it. I couldn't see what Joan expected of me. It was clearly too soon to discuss which school the child should go to or which of us he or she should spend the holidays with, as divorced parents did, but beyond such practical issues I couldn't see what paternity could count for. Joan had written about the advantage of the child having a father. Probably she had in mind something about giving the child emotional security. But I failed to see how it was possible for a father to be involved in his child's life without being fairly intimately involved in the mother's. And the most telling fact of the situation was that as yet there was no child. For the present there was only Joan, and I didn't entirely trust her declaration of independence and was wary of involving myself in any way lest I should disturb the possible precarious balance of her present life. So indecision led to inaction and the weeks passed.

They were weeks of productive work. I enjoyed writing the play, which I had now given the working title *The Prophet*, and exploiting the comedic and dramatic potentials of the subject of Gurdjieff in wartime Paris while engaging with such questions as whether the essential change was political or spiritual. The play was conceived and written in the manner of the literary Shavian theatre, which at the time was being superseded by social realist, expressionist and absurdist drama, but I was blissfully unaware at the time that I was labouring in an exhausted mineshaft.

One weekend Anne and Michael arrived unannounced. They turned up in an enormous Daimler and brought with them a great loping dog that they said was a lurcher, a breed prized by gypsies as a hunter. Suddenly my quiet retreat was filled with noise and life. Anne and Michael shared a passion for spontaneously doing things and going places, and for acquiring expensive, fashionable or eccentric accessories to their lives, that she and I had never had, and it was typical of them to turn up with such éclat. I didn't mind. I welcomed them warmly and admired their new toy, the Daimler, with appropriate enthusiasm.

'The BBC job must be paying well,' I said.

'Pretty well,' Michael said, 'and I've got a couple of other irons in the fire. The BBC thing is just a six month contract. They've got a special budget to recruit writers for a stint in the drama department to get practical experience of working in TV. You get a free rein, an office in the TV centre, a project to work on, and only have to attend a couple of script conferences a week. It's a cinch. You ought to apply.'

'I'm pretty tied up at present,' I said.

We went through the bungalow and out into the back garden.

'So what are you doing in this run-down, overgrown backwater, you bloody hermit?' Mike said.

'Writing,' I said.

'Escaping from Joan,' Anne said.

'But it's great, marvellous. Who does it belong to?'

'Friends of mine.'

It was characteristic of Mike to find almost everything amusing. He had a range of laughs, from a rich throaty chuckle to a hearty guffaw, which gave the impression that he had a prodigious faculty for enjoying life.

He chuckled at my prevarication. 'You're a damned dark horse. What friends?'

'An ex-Indian army colonel,' I said, enjoying the mystification of such an improbability. But Anne was sharp. She had been taking everything in and she picked up a framed photo of Susan from the mantelpiece.

'Is this the friend?' she asked, putting heavy emphasis on the last word.

'That's the colonel's daughter.'

'Aha! the dark horse is unmasked,' Mike chuckled gleefully.

'She's pretty,' Anne said. 'Really, Stuart, one can't keep up with your love life.'

'It'll be easier from now on,' I said.

Anne frowned. 'Do you mean you've met your match?'

'You could put it that way,' I said.

'Come on, let's explore the estate,' Mike said. We all went into the garden and he fought his way through the undergrowth, followed by the boisterous dog. Anne, daunted by the brambles and nettles, refused to follow him and I remained behind with her. Presently he shouted from behind the bushes, 'Look out!' and I looked up just in time to see an object like a ball descending towards us. It landed nearby and smashed to pieces. It was an apple.

'There's a fabulous orchard over here,' Mike called. 'Catch.' More apples came over in quick succession, some of which I managed to catch.

'He's such a boy still,' Anne said. He's in his element here, leaping about with that bloody silly dog. Hateful beast! Would you believe, it cost us thirty guineas from Harrods? I could have got a new dress for the price. Well, actually, I did get a new dress. It was the condition on which I let him have the dog.'

I laughed and said, 'You know, I could never have kept you in the style to which you wanted to become accustomed.'

Anne shrugged. 'I don't really need all these things, but Mike's earning good money at present and we spend it. Now there's something I want to ask you. Do you think I should marry Mike? He wants me to. He wants to have a big splash of a wedding with a reception at the Café Royal. Do you think I should?'

'I suppose the answer to that must be: if in doubt, don't,' I said.

'Well, we are virtually married,' she said, 'and not being officially so does create some difficulties and put one in awkward situations sometimes. And I do love him. We have rows and fights sometimes, but I can't imagine that I'll ever get on as well with anyone else.'

'Then go ahead,' I said. 'It's not my advice you want, is it? It's my blessing.'

'Yes, do you give it?'

'Certainly. I think you're probably very well matched.'

'I must tell Mike you approve,' she said. 'He'll be pleased.'

He was. Oddly enough, they both tended to regard me as a kind of older brother. And, indeed, I felt like one. I couldn't quite take them seriously. Their way of life, their enthusiasms, their problems, were so different from mine. Mike was obviously in love with Anne, but I couldn't conceive that his passion was anything like mine for Susan or that there could be between them any of the tensions, the subtle nuances or even the powerful sensuality of our affair. It seemed to me that they were just playing at life and love; but on the other hand I had to concede that they had got their lives in much better order than I had mine.

It turned out that the visit was not as spontaneous and unscheduled as it had at first appeared. The next morning Mike announced that he had a surprise for us. After he had spent some time studying a road map, we all set off in the Daimler, Anne driving and Mike directing her, at the same time chuckling with pleasure at our mystification. Eventually we arrived at an imposing Tudor manor house with tall chimneys situated in park land with a splendid view over miles of the Sussex Weald. The bell-pull set up an appalling clangour, which brought to the door a stern-looking maid, who apparently was expecting us, for we were ushered into an oak-panelled drawing room and asked to wait while she informed Her Ladyship of our arrival.

'You can't keep us in suspense any longer,' Anne said. 'I'll feel such a fool meeting someone and not knowing what it's all about.'

'You'll soon find out,' Mike said. He was pacing around the room looking at the pictures on the walls. He pointed to a large pastoral painting. 'That's a genuine Cuyp,' he said. 'It's amazing what treasures the impoverished English aristocracy have stowed away.'

The door opened and Her Ladyship appeared. She was a woman in her mid-forties, tall, slender and still attractive.

'Mr Hastings, delighted to meet you,' she said, coming towards me with outstretched hand. Mike intervened, corrected her mistake and introduced me and Anne. 'Then you are the one I want to speak to,' she said. 'Come over here and tell me how you're going to make me lots of lovely money.' She took him by the arm and led him firmly across the room to an alcove. 'Your friend can pour us all a drink. There are bottles on the sideboard. I'll have a gin and tonic.'

The mystery was soon explained. The house was a possible location for the filming of a television play. Mike told her all about the play and she interrupted his account with frequent exclamations of: 'How thrilling!', 'Delightful', 'Absolutely marvellous'. Then she gave us a conducted tour of the house and grounds with a commentary on the history of the place and her recommendations of several 'ideal film locations', and took us to meet Mrs. Macfarlane, the stern maid who had answered the door, to discuss arrangements for accommodating the film crew and actors. Although Mike kept insisting that he had only come to see the place and wasn't authorised to make any commitment, Her Ladyship acted as if the interview finalised every detail and proposed a fee which Mike told us afterwards was more than half the budget for the entire production. 'The woman's quite mad,' he said, but I wasn't so sure that she was, because before she mentioned any figure she had managed to sell him two ten-guinea tickets for a charity ball at the Dorchester.

Life was never uneventful when Mike and Anne were around. Later that day, back at the bungalow, while we were relaxing in the garden reading the Sunday papers, suddenly Scruff, the dog, came out of the undergrowth with a wildly flapping hen held firmly by the neck. He presented it to Mike, who made him drop it. Anne screamed as the badly mauled creature flapped about on the ground, saying 'You must put it out of its misery.' Mike grabbed it and tried to break its neck, but eventually had to decapitate it with a chopper that I fetched from the garden shed. Scruff barked and bounded about while the headless bird continued to flap and seemingly try to get to its feet, which made Anne scream again in revulsion. Eventually it became still and we discussed the fine moral dilemma of whether the owner should be found and compensated or the whole incident be hushed up. Mike said that we should first pluck the bird, as he had heard or read somewhere that this should be done while the flesh is still warm, so he and I set about the task while Anne berated us as thieves and murderers and said that she wasn't going to cook it if that was what we thought. While we were plucking and surrounded by feathers Anne answered a ring at the door and, either out of malice or a sense of the comedy of the situation, brought the bewildered owner of the bird through to the garden. He listened to Mike's account of the 'accident' with an expressionless face, and when asked how much he wanted by way of compensation replied promptly 'ten shillings'. Anne gave him the money and he went away without another word and apparently well satisfied, as well he might have been because Anne did eventually consent to casserole the bird and even after cooking for over two hours it was unappetisingly sinewy and tasteless.

These incidents gave me something to write to Susan about, which I did the next day, after Anne and Mike had gone back to London. We were now into September, and Susan must be back from the camping holiday. All I had received during these weeks was a handful of postcards from Montelimar, Aix and Perpignan. None of them mentioned my letter, and the last one began, 'In case you're still at the bungalow', as if she expected me to have left and gone about my own life by then. So I wrote another letter, eloquently passionate in parts but relieved by anecdotes, to let her know that I was awaiting her return and was still, as I had told her in my first letter by no means 'cured'.

This was certainly true. I had during these weeks thought a great deal about her and about the marvellous times we had spent together before she went away. But sometimes there were doubts and questions too. She had once, during those last days, asked what I wanted of her, and I hadn't been able to answer. Nor could I now. I just wanted to offer her a totally committed and enduring love. I was certain that I could do so. But had I the right to involve her in the mess that was my life? And wasn't it just possible that my feelings for her were heightened and exaggerated by a residual guilt at not having been able to feel enough for Joan? I didn't believe that this was the case, but the thought was there. I remembered Bill's recommending a flight from love and citing illustrious exemplars; and there were moments when I suspected that perhaps he was right, that love could be a refuge from life's intractable problems. I remembered Susan's saying 'I don't want to be your escape route', and I was resolved that she should not be, that I would give her up rather than make use of her. But the thought of giving her up, or of losing her through my own folly, struck a cold panic into me.

I had already arranged with Paul to be able to return to the cottage when Susan and Daphina came back from Germany. When I had moved out early in July I had left Paul a note thanking him for the use of the cottage and telling him where I was. He turned up at the bungalow one afternoon some time before Mike and Anne's visit, saying he had been doing some shopping in Battle and thought he might call in for tea. I was at first a little apprehensive about our meeting, since he was Susan's brother-in-law, but he accepted without question my explanation that Dick had asked me to look after the bungalow while they were away. He stayed on chatting after tea and then suggested that we should have a beer at the Chequers before he caught his bus back to Brightling. There he was greeted with professional bonhomie by the preposterous Peregrine, and gradually attracted an audience for his characteristic tales and opinions, in which were wedded the dire forebodings of apocalypse and a kind of Goldsmithian lament that 'rural mirth and manners are no more', although his quaint anecdotes and exaggerated bucolic accents assured his audience that apocalypse was still far off and rural mirth very much still with us. He obviously enjoyed the evening, and when I later asked him if I could have the use of the cottage again when he returned to his teaching job he said he would be only too pleased to have it occupied and wouldn't be needing it himself until the Christmas holidays.

Towards the end of September another postcard of telegraphic brevity arrived: 'Returning October 5th, about midday, Sue.' Paul had already gone back to the school, so I would be able to get re-settled in the cottage before their return.

Two days later I received another letter from Joan. It was bad news. Sheila had got married the previous week and gone to live in Putney, so she was on her own again. She had got the message of my deafening silence since we met and she didn't expect me to do anything, she said, but she didn't see why I should be able to take comfort in the thought that she was lying on a bed of roses when in fact she was 'bloody miserable and sometimes desperately terrified'. It was the nearest thing, allowing for her pride, to a cry for help. I doubted that in fact I could really help, and feared that any attempt to do so now could only lead us into a thicket of tangled emotions, misunderstandings, recriminations and pain. But there was no alternative. My fate and Joan's were now inseparable. I would have to do something, and soon, before Susan got back. So I phoned Joan and persuaded her to come down the following weekend.

I took a taxi to the station to meet her. She was now quite heavily pregnant and had given up any attempt to conceal the fact. She walked with her weight thrown back on her spine. But she seemed in excellent health, with a clear complexion and bright eyes, and her manner was almost gay. In the taxi she talked about Sheila's marriage. It had come as a tremendous surprise, she said, but it was the best thing that could have happened for Sheila, and she would make a marvellous wife and mother. The husband had a well-paid job in advertising and had been a regular customer in the coffee-bar where they both worked. It had taken him weeks to work up the courage to ask Sheila to go out with him, and no one had dreamt that the only reason he had been coming in was to see her. It was all so romantic and she was so happy for Sheila's sake, though of course she was going to miss having her around. And the flat was a bit big and expensive for her to occupy alone, but then Sheila had paid her share for the next month and wouldn't hear of having it back, and with the money I had sent her she would be able to keep the flat on at least until she had had the baby, then she would have to look for something smaller and cheaper.

Joan said all this quite cheerfully. It was difficult to reconcile her manner with the desperate tone of her letter.

I had anticipated her being curious about how I came to be occupying the bungalow, and before she started asking questions or jumping to assumptions as Anne had done when she saw Sue's photo, which I had now put away in a drawer, I told her that it belonged to friends of Paul Rowland who were away on holiday and would be back soon.

'What will you do then?' she asked.

'Go back to the cottage. Paul is back at school now and it's empty.'

I knew from the way she had asked the question and the way she nodded at my reply that she had hoped for a different answer. But the time was not yet come for an opening of hearts and minds. Joan enthused about the bungalow and the wild garden and said it must be a marvellously peaceful place for work. It told her about the work I had been doing, and about Mike and Anne's visit, and she listened with interest. She clearly wanted to please. Later, while I did some writing in the sitting-room, she spent a long time in the kitchen preparing a meal.

In the evening we went for a walk around Battle. In those days, before it became a National Trust property, you could walk freely around the grounds of the Abbey that William the Conqueror had built on the site of his victory at the Battle of Hastings. I showed Joan all the sites of historical interest, the spot where King Harold had fallen with the arrow in his eye, the ruined scriptorium of the Abbey, the ramparts promenade. Afterwards we had a drink at the Abbey pub, and throughout Joan was interested, gay and convivial. The first tentative sounding of the deeper issues that we had both been deliberately and delicately side-stepping came as we were walking back home from the pub.

'You certainly seem to have got a new life cut out for yourself down here,' Joan said.'

'Yes, it's a good place to work.'

'Why did you ask me down?'

'To give you a break.'

'Ha!' It was a sharp and derisory exclamation. 'I'm sorry, but it does seem a rather improbable reason after weeks of silence.'

'Well, in your letter you sounded pretty desperate.'

'Oh yes, I'm desperate all right, but a couple of days' break in the country isn't going to make me any less so. It seems you only wanted to get me down to show me how settled and how satisfied with your life you are.'

'That wasn't the reason at all,' I said softly. I felt that it was not the time or place to go into it. There were other people around and the night was so still and silent that voices carried. Also, Joan was getting breathless with the uphill walk. We walked on in silence, but for the sound of Joan's heavy, regular breathing. I felt guilty even about the lightness of my step, but as we passed the village recreation ground I had an urge to vault the low fence, run across the football pitch and disappear into the darkness beyond, where I would seek out the cornfield, which by now would have been harvested but would still bring back poignant memories of the night of the ridiculous moon. But I did nothing so wild. I adjusted my pace to Joan's slower one and felt ill at ease with my body. There was no ridiculous moon on this night, but the stars stood out bright and clear.

I thought of interstellar space and Pascal's terror of it. It was surely an academic, a mathematician's, terror. There were spaces as infinite and as terrible between people.

Back at the house, I reopened the conversation. I said, 'I just couldn't ignore your letter. It was rather a cry for help, wasn't it?'

'No, just a cry.'

'I would help if I knew how to,' I said, 'but you're so changeable, sometimes full of the joys of motherhood, confidently independent, and at other times, as you said in your letter, miserable and terrified.'

'Poor Stuart,' she said, 'can't you accept that that's exactly how it is? It's quite normal, I assure you. I'm no freak. Other pregnant women go through the same ups and downs of mood. I'm not being deliberately perverse just to make things difficult for you, I promise you.'

Yes, I thought, and other women had husbands to give them moral support. Sue had said, 'Pregnancy isn't any fun, even at the best of times.' It was, I realised, unreasonable of me to expect Joan to be all of a piece, consistently happy and capable and in need of help, just to make it easy for me to decide what to do about her.

'You have to tell me what I can do to help,' I said. 'You must have had something in mind when you wrote and when you agreed to come down.'

She shook her head slowly. 'Just hope,' she said. Her eyes were tearful. 'No schemes to spring on you. Just a rather desperate hope.'

'But for what?' I insisted.

'I can't tell you. It must come from you.' She began to cry. Big tears overflowed and ran down her face. I sat rigidly in my chair, paralysed by a conflict between pity for her and reluctance to be drawn into a scene.

'You humiliate me so,' she sobbed. 'You probably don't mean to or even know you're doing it, but it is humiliating to be put in the position of having to ask for favours. Can't you understand that?' She looked up suddenly and threw back her hair. A look that mingled pride and appeal flashed across her eyes.

'Yes, I understand that,' I said, 'and I'm sorry I put you in that position.' But what, in lieu of love, had I to offer her? I recalled her first letter, in which she had urged me to face up to being a father. I said, 'The reason I didn't reply to your letter was simply that I didn't know what to say. How does a man fulfil or even acknowledge his responsibilities to an unborn child? I didn't know, and I still don't.'

Joan shook her head vigorously. 'It's not that now. I was being brave and trying to be a modern woman when I wrote to you, but really I'm not at all brave or modern. Frankly, I'm terrified; more and more so as the time draws closer.'

'But what is there to be frightened of? Didn't you tell me the doctor said you were a text-book case and that everything was going normally?'

'I'm not a case, I'm me,' she wailed. 'And to me it's not normal. Look.' She stood up and thrust out her belly. 'Is that normal? It's alright for a man. Even if he is a doctor he's never been and is never going to be pregnant. Can you imagine what it must be like to have this happen to you? Put yourself in my place. Men and women aren't all that different. Don't imagine that because I'm a woman I have some special faculty for accepting the discomfort, the ugliness, the unnaturalness of it and to cope with the terror of going through the actual birth. I haven't. This hasn't happened to me before and I know nothing more about it and am no better able to cope than any man. I'm frightened. It isn't the baby that needs your help, it's me.'

'I'll help. I'll do anything you ask.'

'That's a rash promise. Would you come and live at the flat?'

Was she serious? It wasn't put in the manner of an appeal. I was more like a rather weary inquiry, to which she knew in advance that the answer would be 'no'.

'You mean in London?' I had to prevaricate.

She nodded. 'There, I've done it,' she said, becoming tearful again. 'I swore I wouldn't beg any favours and lay myself open to humiliation again, but now I have done. I'm such a fool. I shouldn't have come down in the first place. But do you think I'd ask such a thing of you if I wasn't desperate? It seems to me it's not a very big thing. I'm not asking you to sleep with me, to pretend to love me or anything like that, but just to be there. We needn't even talk much. You could have your own room to work in. Oh, I know you don't want to go back to London, but would it be such a sacrifice just for two months?'

'It wouldn't work,' I said.

'But why not? Only until the baby's born, that's all I ask, then you could go your own way. I won't try to stop you or make any other claim on you.'

For a moment I was tempted to tell her all, to say: 'the reason I can't, Joan, is that I'm desperately in love with Sue Rowland. I couldn't bear to be separated from her for two months, and I know that if I lived with you out of a sense of duty or pity I would treat you abominably for sheer frustration, or even revenge.' But to say that would be wilfully cruel and crushing. I said, 'No, it wouldn't work. You speak as if it would be a simple, clear and practical arrangement. But it wouldn't, would it? There would be emotions involved, and all sorts of underlying tensions.'

'Oh, you're so scared of emotions,' she said. 'It's pitiful.'

'That's not true,' I said. 'I just want to avoid getting involved in an emotional mess that won't benefit anyone.'

'You kid yourself,' she said. 'What you want to avoid is life. You don't want to move an inch out of your ivory tower. Let's face it, you don't want to help me, you just want to make some gesture to satisfy your own conscience.'

'I do want to help you,' I said, 'but I know I wouldn't be any help to you living at the flat. Quite the opposite.'

'Is there another woman?'

It was a natural assumption to make, but the question took me by surprise. The way she said it, though, with a suggestion of a sneer, made me decide not to tell her the truth. I didn't want Susan sneered at.

'No, that's not the reason either. You just have to accept that I can't live at the flat. I can come up sometimes, and you can come and spend days at the cottage. And I expect to be able to help with a bit more money soon. Also perhaps I can find a cheaper flat where you can live afterwards. What do you say? Aren't there lots of ways I can help without moving into the flat, which I'm sure would be a big mistake.'

'What can I say? I haven't any choice, have I?' Joan said resignedly. 'Having thrown myself on your mercy, I have to accept what you hand out, even if it is a kick in the teeth.'

'It won't be,' I promised.

'We'll see,' she said.

His Dear Time's Waste - Stuart Holroyd

7

September passed serenely into October and the benign Indian Summer weather seemed set to continue until at least election day on the ninth, when all the polls were predicting that Harold Macmillan's Tories would be returned with an increased majority, expressing the electorate's grateful concurrence with the Prime Minister's assurance that Britons had 'never had it so good'. The critical day on my calendar, however, was the fifth, and in the final days before Susan's return I became increasingly apprehensive. The closer the moment of our reunion came, the fainter became my memories and the more confused my thoughts of her. Her beauty and something of her character I could recover from a sheet of photos that I had found in a drawer, but these gave me no insight into her mind, and it was her mind that I was apprehensive about. Joan was unpredictable, but at least she was so in a predictable way, a way that I could categorise as feminine and emotional. But Susan, I felt, was capable of sustaining a coolly rational truculence in matters of principle; she was capable even of putting principle before passion or self-interest. She had had over two months to accomplish her avowed intention of getting 'cured', and it was quite possible that she had succeeded, that those marvellous weeks in July had by now been pigeon-holed in her memory as a 'romantic episode', and that she would find my still being at the bungalow when she returned an embarrassment. At the height of our passion I had respected her wholeness and resolved to do nothing to break it up, but now that I was prey to doubts and uncertainties I saw her wholeness from a different angle. I failed to see what, being whole, she could possibly gain from me.

With such thoughts and apprehensions I built up a mental image of Susan that immediately clashed with the reality when, early in the afternoon of October 5th, she returned.

They arrived by taxi. I heard their voices and the slamming of car doors in the lane and went out to meet them. It was a hot day and Susan was dressed as she had been in mid-summer, in a skirt and blouse and sandals. She was very sun-tanned and her hair had grown longer. Daphina was nearest to the gate when I came out, so I greeted her first with a kiss on the cheek. Then Christopher toddled up to me and I had to give some attention to his latest treasure, a friction-driven toy car.

'He's grown amazingly in two months,' was the first thing I said to Sue. I must have spent hours thinking about what I would say to her at this moment.

'Yes,' she said, 'he had a wonderfully healthy holiday, dashing about on the beach all day and living on bread and olives and all those marvellous French fruits and vegetables.'

I tried to greet her with a kiss on the mouth but she turned her cheek to meet my lips.

'You've shrunk,' I said.

'I have not shrunk.' She pretended to be insulted but her eyes were laughing.

'Are you pleased to find me still here?' I kept my hands on her waist and looked into her eyes, and there I read the answer that I wanted.

I helped them get their luggage into the bungalow. Both Sue and her mother were impressed by the tidy state the place was in. I didn't mention that Joan had cleaned it up a couple of days before.

I had packed my things in readiness to return to the cottage – there was a bus soon – but Daphina suggested I stay. 'With all this duty-free whisky we ought to have a little homecoming celebration,' she said.

'We don't want to interrupt the flow of some work of genius,' Sue said.

I said, 'I think I can afford time off to celebrate your return.'

'Is it a thing to celebrate?'

'Oh yes, quite definitely.' The novel thought occurred to me that Sue might have been as apprehensive about our meeting again as I had been. Daphina was in the kitchen. I crossed the room to where Sue was standing and kissed her softly on the mouth.

'You don't want to hang about all day while we have baths and unpack and such things,' she said. 'Why don't you get settled in at the cottage and come back in the evening? I'll cook you a meal.' She squeezed both my hands.

There was so much to rediscover. The mental image I had formed of her had been a fond caricature, insubstantial, a creation that was not so much Susan as a congeries of my own hopes, fears, longings, doubts. If just once during those weeks of separation I could have heard her voice, touched her hand, looked into her eyes, she would instantly have ceased to be a figure in a situation, my situation, and would have become what she was to me now, a unique, complex, mysterious person with whom I had a strange affinity at a depth that had nothing to do with my situation.

I turned her curiously rough palms upwards and kissed them. 'These hands,' I said, 'those eyes, that voice, those lips, that funny long nose for looking down.' A familiar nervous look came into her eyes. 'You make me feel strange,' she said. 'What about them?'

'I'd forgotten what they could do to me.'

She looked down for a moment, then quickly up again. 'I'll cook you a curry. Would you like that?'

A curry. That day at the cottage before she went to Germany. Life knitting itself together again, like the cells and tissues of a healing wound.

I arrived at the bus stop just as the bus was drawing up. Leaving my rucksack and typewriter in the luggage space under the stairs, I took a seat on the upper deck. I had not been to the cottage since the end of July, and I fondly dwelt on the familiar scenes and landmarks of the route. The fields had been harvested and ploughed and the lush greens of summer were turning to autumnal brown and gold. I remembered my night walks along these roads.

'You make me feel strange,' she had just said. 'Strange, strange sensations,' she had murmured, in the kitchen at the bungalow all those weeks, those months ago. And there would be other times, other summers, other autumns. There was so much to rediscover, and much, much more yet to discover. We had time. We would take love easy, let it have its seasons, let it put down roots, grow at its own pace, become strong and rich.

The familiar smell of paraffin and wood-smoke met me as I entered the cottage. On the table was a welcoming note from Paul. I had a momentary pang of guilt at making him an unwitting accomplice to the break-up of his brother's marriage, but negated it by recalling his merriment on our recent night at the Chequers.

Settling into the cottage didn't take long. I made up a bed, put my few clothes into drawers and arranged my work and books on the table in the small upstairs room where I wrote. I made and drank tea, washed a pair of socks, got in two buckets of water from the stream and laid a fire. There were still three hours to get through before the bus was due. I couldn't concentrate on reading or writing, so there was nothing for it but to walk the time away.

I could have saved a bus fare and walked back to Battle, but it would have meant trudging the roads and I'd have arrived prematurely anyway. So I set off through the woods and up the hill through the estate to Brightling village. The then owner of the estate, a Major Grissell, had no objection to his metropolitan tenants roaming over his lands, provided we didn't leave gates open. I had met him once, in the summer, when he had accosted me on horseback, and when I identified myself as Paul's friend he said, 'Ah, the writer fellow,' in a way that suggested an attitude of amused condescension. When I told Paul about the meeting he confessed that he had lent the landlord his copy of *Flight and Pursuit*, which had been returned to him with the remark, 'reads like the fellow could do with a good dose of salts', which of course I construed as a typical expression of the philistinism of the squirearchy rather than as a considered literary criticism. But then a man who looked out from his bedroom over several hundred acres of his own Wealden park-and farm-land, and on a clear day could survey a vista down to Pevensey Marshes and the Channel, was not likely to be perturbed by Existentialist angst or aspersions upon his 'inauthentic existence' or for that matter much exercised by philosophico-religious doubts and speculations. Nor, in fact, was I, at this time. 'Authentic existence' was here and now, in the sights, sounds and musty autumnal smells of these woods, in the vigour of my stride and the joy of my anticipation of the evening.

Beyond the wood I passed Ewan Cameron's 'Keeper's Cottage', then the famed Greek Temple folly that the 18th Century squire Jack Fuller had had built. I eventually reached the village, passed the pyramidal tomb in the churchyard where 'Mad Jack' himself, or rather by now his skeleton, was said to be buried seated at a table with a meal and a bottle of wine to hand, and descended the Robertsbridge Road to the 'Fuller's Arms' pub. I had had a beer there with Paul on my first visit to the area, when he had regaled me with anecdotes about the eccentricities of Jack Fuller, and also urged me to read his copy of Hilaire Belloc's *Four Good Men*, an engaging account of a walk from East to West Sussex starting from the George Inn in Robertsbridge, which evoked an Edwardian age idyll of rural life. Much no doubt had changed since Belloc and his companions walked this way, but I too had acquired a fondness for and affinity with the area and had even looked at houses and cottages for sale, fondly dreaming of a life there with Susan, although there was no way I could foresee of ever being able to raise the money to buy one. Beyond the Fuller's Arms there was a magnificent view over the Darwell Reservoir before I entered the woods again to complete the round trip back to the cottage. The walk had taken over two hours, so there remained only a short time to kill before the bus would be due.

When at last I got back to the bungalow Susan had already put Christopher to bed and she and her mother were quaffing their first 'sundowner' in the sitting room. The rich, exotic smell of cooking spices permeated the place. It was odd to be back as a guest after having spent so long alone there.

Daphina did most of the talking at first. Their holiday had been full of incidents, and she took evident pleasure in recalling them. Susan and I sat on the low couch holding hands and Sue contributed the odd detail while her mother relived their adventures. She did so in a tone of merry insouciance, and many of her anecdotes were innocent enough, but some featured Susan in relation to some 'admirer' and suggested beneath the merriment a mischievous subtext. An officer in the Lancers had sent Sue a side of venison because she had mentioned at a party that she had never tasted the meat. She hadn't known how to cook it, but another young officer had taken the problem in hand and organised a barbecue party for her. In France a Minister's son had serenaded her outside her tent and had offered to take her for a trip in his private plane. And how many proposals of marriage had she had? Was it three or four? – including one from an heir to a peerage who was very wealthy and would make a perfect match if he hadn't got such a big nose. One could perhaps accept him if he agreed to have plastic surgery. It was all very well Susan saying she wouldn't want him even if he had a perfectly normal nose, but one had to be practical in life. The sensible thing would be to have someone like his prospective Lordship as a husband and then take Stuart as a lover.

Yes, she was mischievous, but it gratified me immensely that I should be, as it seemed, parentally accepted and approved as Susan's lover.

'Do you think that would be a good idea?' Susan asked me.

'I can't really see you in the role,' I said. 'I think you'd find it difficult to live a double life.'

Susan smiled and squeezed my hand. Daphina said, 'Nonsense. It's only a question of controlling your feelings. History has been made by people who controlled their feelings.'

She was being mischievous again, but I had to contest that one. I said, 'That might apply to the history of the British Empire, but I can't think of any great revolutionary noted for his stiff upper lip.'

'Revolutions never changed anything,' Daphina said with a shrug.

'Well, in any revolution you care to name yours would have been one of the first heads to roll,' Susan said.

'I don't see why, dear,' her mother said mildly. 'I'm really rather a socialist, you know. I think Mr Attlee was a dear little man with all the right ideas. I'm not sure that I trust this Mr Gaitskell, though. He does seem to promise the earth.'

We had more anecdotes over the meal, which was a chicken curry. Perhaps prompted by the hot spiciness, Daphina's anecdotes looked back to her time in India and focused particularly on a banquet hosted by a Maharajah where the curry was so hot, Susan said, that it blistered her mouth for a couple of days afterwards. 'He probably used his curries as a political weapon,' she said. 'Didn't that ever occur to you, Daphina?'

'Oh no,' her mother said, 'he was a perfect gentleman. And he played an absolutely cracking game of tennis.'

Susan's smile said that with her mother such inconsequentiality was a norm.

After the meal we went back into the sitting room, drank coffee and looked at holiday photographs. It soon got to be quarter past ten. My last bus was at half past. When I mentioned the fact Daphina suggested that I should stay on and spend the night in the spare room. I looked at Susan. She gave a scarcely perceptible nod and I accepted the offer.

'I'm going to read myself to sleep,' Daphina said shortly afterwards. 'I'm almost dropping in my tracks after that overnight journey. Susan must be too, so don't keep her up too late or she'll be bug-eyed and foul-tempered in the morning and I'll have to cope with Christopher.'

'I won't,' I promised, and she went off to bed with her book.

'You're in favour,' Susan said. 'First Pa offers you the house, and now Daphina puts you up for the night.' I should beware, she said, because Daphina's next favourite game after bridge was matchmaking and she could be quite unscrupulous about it. A product of overbreeding herself, she believed that what the family needed was some new blood, a more robust strain. She had probably marked me down for Judy, Susan's youngest cousin, who was studying in America at present but would be back for Christmas. Judy was very pretty. She had a photograph somewhere. She went over to the writing desk and looked for it in a drawer.

'Stop playing the fool, Sue,' I said. 'I've seen enough photographs.'

But she had found it. A studio portrait of a strikingly pretty girl. She had Susan's high cheek bones, but the eyes were smaller and the nose retroussé.

'Isn't she pretty?'

'Very,' I said, 'but it's you I love.' I turned her round and kissed her. She dropped the photograph back in the drawer, put her arms around my neck and reciprocated the kiss.

'I suppose you do,' she said resignedly, 'but it's very inconvenient.'

She asked how many women I had 'entertained' at the bungalow while she was away. I told her that Joan had been down for a couple of days but there had been nobody else. I had been working hard and had lived a celibate life for four months now. She found that hard to believe. I said I wouldn't have believed myself capable of it some time ago, but it was true. 'I don't want anyone else,' I said. 'There's only you.'

'But you can't have me.'

'Can't I?'

She shook her head solemnly.

'Then I shall remain an embittered, frustrated man.'

'I don't believe that either.'

'Nor do I. At least, I can't see myself living like that. But on the other hand, I don't see any alternative if I can't have you.'

'That's emotional blackmail.'

'I know, but you should know by now that I'm unscrupulous. I'll use any means.'

'To get me to bed?'

'To get you. Full stop.'

She shuddered. 'You frighten me. I don't want to be taken over. I want my own life. I came back fully intending, if you were still here, to speak to you very severely. I had all sorts of sensible reasons and arguments lined up.'

'You think we should part?'

'I don't think we should be together. You should have gone back to London before I returned.'

'And lived with Joan? That's what she wants. She asked me to live with her until the baby's born.'

'You should.'

'Do you want me to?'

'We're not talking about what I want. I should get my life in order too.' And when we had both got our lives in order, she said, we might find that we no longer felt the same. I might find that I didn't want her any more. I said it was more likely to be the other way round. I'd come back with a nice shining clean slate, only to find that I'd lost her.

'It's a risk we both take,' she said.

I said, 'It's a risk I'm not prepared to take.'

She asked about Joan. I told her that she was well, still working, seemed to be looking forward to being a mother but sometimes to be frightened at the thought of the actual birth. Sue said she remembered the time she'd had with Christopher, the depressions during her pregnancy, the sense of being completely alone, the terror of dying or of the child's dying or being malformed. She said, 'The trouble is I'm not sure how I'll react over a long period in a situation that goes against the grain.'

'You mean the famous stomach might rebel?'

She smiled. 'You could put it that way. It does seem to be a rather special thing we've got. I don't know why it is. I don't really understand it at all. It's like a tender shoot that could grow into a great big tree, but is in danger of being crushed or blighted before it gets a chance.'

'We'll put a big fence around our tender shoot,' I said, and put Keep Out notices on all sides.' But that wouldn't help, she replied, because we were both inside the fence and were quite likely to tread on it by accident.

She told me that in Germany she had allowed a young officer to fall in love with her, which had been a bit unkind, but it had all been linked, she said, with her imagining my having girl friends at the bungalow.

I said, 'I see I shall have to lock you away, if only to protect other innocent and vulnerable young men.'

'I don't want to be locked away,' she said. 'The trouble with you men is that you assume the right to claim a woman body and soul. And what do you offer in return?'

I said, 'Body and soul.'

'In that order,' she said, 'and with a big gap between.'

'My love for you is without any gaps between.'

'So what do we do now?' she said,

'Muddle through.'

'To what?'

'I don't know. I only know that I can't let you go.'

Susan was abstracted and thoughtful for a while. I had to cajole her to tell me what was on her mind. It was that Brian had written to her while she was in Germany. He didn't accept that it was all over between them. He considered that now he had got a job and sorted himself out they ought to try again to make the marriage work.

'You must tell him,' I said.

She shook her head. 'He's coming down next week. I don't want him to get the idea that I'm leaving him for someone else.'

'Why not?'

'Because I'm not. That isn't the reason. It was over with us before you came on the scene.'

Brian had a holiday. He would stay for a few days, perhaps the whole week. 'And you want me to keep out of the way?' I asked.

'I don't want you to,' she said, 'but on the other hand I don't want him to know. You see how difficult it is, this muddling through?'

While they were away I had slept in Susan's room, but that night I slept in the neighbouring spare room. I expected to be racked with frustration after my months of celibacy and with her so close. When we kissed goodnight she said, 'Think of our tender shoot.' She left the doors of both rooms open and was soon asleep herself and I found the sound of her regular breathing and the sense of her proximity strangely quieting and didn't suffer the expected pangs. It was enough for the present to have had my anxieties allayed. The cool truculence I had feared, the sacrifice of passion to principle, had not been in evidence. She had confessed to jealousy, weakness, need, an acceptance of muddling through. In her absence I had exaggerated her self-possession, her control, her good sense. These were certainly aspects of her. But she had shown others tonight, revealed herself as a woman caught up in life, perplexed, passionate, vulnerable, nervous and apprehensive, and moreover with problems in her own life quite as difficult as mine with Joan. What if Brian should persuade her to try again to make the marriage work? It was as unthinkable as the idea that I should marry Joan now, but unthinkable or not it was a thought, and a recurrent, nagging one. Joan's situation in this whole affair was not unique. Love had made more than one conquest, life claimed more than one victim.

I had to go to London later that week to look up some material at the Hulton Picture Library for a television programme commissioned by BBC Religious Broadcasting as a result of the producer's reading my book, *Flight and Pursuit*. Susan came with me. Since her return we had spent every evening together, but I had managed to do some work at the cottage during the days. As we were now set in for a long period of 'muddling through', it seemed essential to establish and pursue some routine of work, so we had resolved not to meet in the days except at weekends. The trip to London was an exception, an opportunity to be together. From the station we phoned Tom, who, spontaneously welcoming as ever, invited Sue to go over to Chepstow Road while I was at the library so that I could pick her up there later in the afternoon.

I got through my picture research quite quickly, so I decided to call in on Joan on my way over to Chepstow Road. She wasn't at her flat, so I went round to the coffee-bar in Queensway. She was working in the kitchen, but as it was a quiet time of day she was able to come out, sit at a table and have a coffee with me. I thought she was looking tired and asked why she didn't pack in the job and live on the money I had sent her, but she said she hadn't much longer to go before she qualified for maternity benefit and it would be a pity to forfeit that now.

'Well then, come down to the cottage for a few days' break next week,' I said. 'Can you get time off?'

That wasn't any problem, she said. But what was the point? Her last visit hadn't exactly been a relaxing break. I told her we might spend a day or two looking for a flat for her. I had been thinking about it, and it seemed that life would be a lot easier and cheaper for her, and healthier for the baby, if she moved out of London, perhaps to Hastings or Eastbourne. Flats could be found for about a third of London prices in Hastings.

It was true that I had been thinking about it and had come to this conclusion, and had also talked over the idea with Susan, but of course the proposal wasn't entirely altruistic. Brian was going to be down the following week.

'It's an idea,' Joan said, meaning the suggestion she should take a seaside flat. 'I'll think about it.'

'Well, come down anyway,' I said. 'Come on Sunday and meanwhile think it over.'

'You're a strange man,' she said. 'Talk about me being changeable! You want something of me but I can't make out what it is.'

'All I want is for things to turn out as best they can for you.'

'There's more to it than that,' she said.

That was shrewd of her, I reflected afterwards as I walked along Westbourne Grove on my way to Tom's, to say that I wanted something of her. I hadn't thought of it that way. I had thought of her at different times as the victim, the martyr, the passive recipient of charity, the beneficiary of the overflow of my love for Sue; but that she had an active role, that she could give something that I needed, was a new angle on the situation. What did I want of her? Not exactly forgiveness, but something akin. An honourable release, perhaps. If in my private drama she had been cast as the victim, I in hers must have been cast as the heartless tyrant, and what I wanted was to be released from this role. But how? Perhaps by letting her know about Susan, so that she would see me not as a tyrant but as a man forlornly in love? Was this selfish? I thought not. It would surely be less humiliating to her to know that I was not so much repelled by her as attracted by another. She was bound to find out sooner or later, and when she did she might very well reproach me with having deceived her, having treated her with misconceived kindness when it would have been better to have given her credit for being able to face up to the whole truth. To let her know about Sue would be to give her an opportunity to play more than a passive, receiving role in the situation. And if she really was concerned about how I was going to come out of it, and felt guilty about what she had done to me, as she had claimed during our walk through Hyde Park some weeks before, then it was only fair to tell the truth, for knowing it she would no longer have to feel guilty.

All this seemed very plausible, and I might have turned back and made my confession there and then had it not occurred to me that by doing so I would be involving Sue more than I had any right to, and it might affect her problem with Brian. The ethics of the whole business were really too bewildering.

Sue was with Bill and Tom when I got to the house. Bill rose and greeted me with his usual manic bonhomie, but I detected behind it a flinty edge of hostility. He remained standing and said pointedly that he couldn't waste any more time talking because he had a pile of work waiting for him upstairs.

'How's Amanda?' I asked.

'I had to break it off,' he said with a smile that didn't reach his eyes. 'I've got too much to do, no time for love affairs.'

'I hail the superhuman,' Tom declaimed dramatically. 'I call it death-in-life and life-in-death.'

'I wish you did, Tom,' Bill said, shaking his head regretfully.

'I gave up Yeatsian aspirations long, long ago,' Tom said, 'I prefer to go for life in life and play safe.'

Bill sighed his mock condolence. 'I know, Tom, I know. Most people prefer to play safe.'

'Go on, off to your mountain top, Zarathustra', Tom said.

'Oh, I nearly forgot, Stuart,' Bill said. 'Message from Colin: if you don't write to him soon about the Hero book he'll not sign his letters to you in future so you won't be able to sell them when you're old and needy.' He raised his hands in a gesture of benediction, said 'Bless you, my children,' and left the room.

'You rattled him, Sue,' Tom said. 'Bill always gets most insufferably godlike when he's really rattled.'

'What happened?' I said.

'I resent being expected to sit here and have my life and character dissected,' Susan said. 'I thought I'd do a bit of dissecting back.'

'The trouble with supermen is that they're not good subjects for dissection,' Tom said. 'They secrete a fatty substance, like blubber, that coagulates around the incision, so you can't get at 'em.'

'Not blubber,' Sue said, 'but blather.'

'Good, good,' Tom laughed, 'but we mustn't be too hard on our superhuman friends. If my experience of the condition is anything to go by, they must have a very tough time of it living among us lesser mortals.'

'Your experience?' I said. 'We know you've been around for centuries, but I can't imagine you were ever godlike.'

'It was, I suppose, what you'd call a mystical experience,' Tom said. 'I woke up in the middle of the night with a strange sensation. I could breathe in very deeply, but I couldn't breathe out. I felt as if I was growing with every breath. It wasn't at all painful. I felt wonderful. I could have run ten times round the Serpentine. I've never felt so energetic and full of health in my life.'

I laughed. This was Tom at his most whimsical, mocking the cult of mystical experience.

'You can laugh, Stuart,' he said quite seriously, 'but I didn't find it funny. I thought that this might be how people feel before having a heart attack. I felt as if something might snap if I breathed a little deeper. But at the same time I wanted to. I wanted the luxurious feeling of deeper and deeper draughts of life. As you know, I'm disposed to be a bit of a cynic, and I thought: this is just the sort of trick the fates might play on you – give you a taste of how wonderful life could have been, then the next moment snuff you out. I rang up Paddington hospital and explained my symptoms, saying I wasn't worried but just wanted to know if what I was undergoing was like anything in the book. They asked me to go round, which I did and got a student doctor who obviously thought I was some kind of crank. He asked, "What seems to be the matter?" I said, "I feel like a god and it's bloody uncomfortable." He asked me to breathe in and out to his count. He counted up to ten, saying "in-out, in-out" ten times, but when he got to ten I was still breathing in. He fobbed me off with some pills, which I took when I got home, but without any immediate effect. The feeling took hours to wear off, and when at last I slept again I was out for a good twelve hours, but was very relieved when I woke to find that I felt my old ungodlike self.'

'I don't know that it would qualify as a mystical experience, Tom,' I said. 'It sounds as if you were under the influence of some drug.'

'You're right,' he said, 'that's just what it was like. But the point is I wasn't drugged, hadn't taken anything. There I was, sleeping placidly after the evening's work, and I woke up feeling like a god. Someone else might have taken the experience as a call, or a vision of ultimate truth, but I don't know, I'm not in the business of proposing explanations. I'm just a journalist.'

'Well,' Sue said, 'you certainly fit my idea of a super man much more than you know who.'

'Thank you,' Tom said. 'But enough about me. I have important news for you, Stuart. The house is going to be sold. The rumour is that the police are turning up the heat on Rachman's operations and he's selling up while he still can. So we're all going to have to find somewhere else.'

'I'll just have to arrange for my books and things to be moved,' I said. 'And wherever you move to, we must keep in touch.'

'Of course,' Tom said, 'and we'll have a big splash of a party before we go. You must both come up for it.' He shook his head. 'I'd never have guessed that you two would get together. Yet it seems quite right. I'm sure it will work out for you. As our friend would say, "Bless you, my children".' He placed a hand on each of our heads and smiled as benignly as was possible with a cigarette holder clenched between his teeth.

'Tom was on good form today,' I said to Sue later, on the way back to Sussex. 'But Bill was in a lousy mood. What had happened before I arrived?'

'Oh, he gave me a lecture on the unreliability of genius, the duties of women and other related topics. I had to shut him up eventually with sarcasm. Poor Bill! I hope he turns out to really be a genius, because he's not equipped to be anything else.'

Love, Bill had told Sue, is a trap for the creative man. A writer needed a docile, background woman, one who made few demands on life for herself and was content to be an appendage, a martyr to the man's work. He didn't think she was cut out for such a role, and he could only see two possible outcomes to our relationship: either my work would suffer or I would give her a hell of a life. She had asked Bill why he had so little confidence in himself that he had to be so concerned about other people's lives. That was the thing that had rattled him, though he had laughed at the preposterousness of the idea. But still, what he had said had sunk in and it echoed some of her own private doubts and worries. She could never settle for being an appendage, she said. When she had separated from Brian she had resolved that in future she would live her own life, in her own world.

'I want our life, our world,' I said.

'But what would that be like?' she asked. I couldn't answer that. We'd see. And what about the great works? Perhaps Bill was right, and it was deprivation, frustration and desperation that brought out the best.

I said the great works would take care of themselves. They'd find their way out in time if they were really there.

But would they? she insisted. They might not. They might have to be forced out. It was a thought.

It was a cliché, this image of the artist as martyr, as the great sufferer, the self-denier. But was there not a germ of truth in it? 'What have we to do with happiness? We have a duty to our genius,' Bill often said, misquoting Byron. His was a dramatic view of life, but it was possible that to hold and act on a dramatic view was the only alternative to making of life an undistinguished compromise, to succumbing to all life's complexities and perplexities and becoming a pawn of circumstances. Yeats had written that one had to choose 'perfection of the life or of the work', but it was dubious whether perfection could be realised in either area. The stirring imperatives and admonitions of poets really were treacherous guides in real life situations.

When I told Susan that I had invited Joan down for the week when Brian would be with her, she confessed to mixed feelings. Of course I was right to ask her down, she said, but she didn't exactly relish the idea of my having another woman at the cottage.

'We'll sleep in separate rooms,' I said, 'as surely will you and Brian.'

'Of course. And a week isn't long. Think of the two months when I was in Germany.'

'We've grown closer since then.'

'I know. And I have, most inconveniently, grown to love you.'

'It's the first time you've said it in so many words,' I said. 'The memory will see me through the week.'

I had a shock when I met Joan at the station, for she had suddenly turned blonde. She looked rather shamefaced about it.

'Don't say anything,' she said. 'I know it looks horrible.'

'It doesn't,' I said, 'but why did you do it?'

'God knows. I felt so dowdy. I suppose it was pregnancy blues. I got fed up with being myself. And all I succeeded in doing was make myself conspicuous and horrible. I feel everyone's looking at me.'

'Well, you'll be able to relax at the cottage,' I said. 'There'll be nobody to look at you there.'

'Except you,' she said, 'and of course you don't count, since you find me horrible anyway. You needn't deny it. It's a fact I've learnt to live with.'

When we arrived at the cottage she cooed over it. 'It's just the sort of place I could settle for,' she said. 'A hideaway, a hole to crawl into, that's what I want. Shall I move in? Shall I write a letter giving my notice and just stay on here?'

She put the suggestion teasingly. Since she had got off the train she had been in this peculiar mood, superficially gay and animated, but with bitterness showing through. I asked her what the hell had got into her.

'Oh, I'm fed up to the eyeballs with being the good little martyr that everyone tramples over,' she said. 'I've decided from now on to be myself.'

'If that means being embittered, I think you'd do better as a martyr,' I said.

'You think,' she said. 'Oh yes, it's much more comfortable for you if I bravely suffer in silence. But I'm not concerned with making it comfortable for you; not any more. From now on it's me that counts. You've stood by me, as I suppose you'd call it, in such a lame and half-hearted sort of way. Am I supposed to be grateful? Are you really so godlike that to be admitted into the Presence once in a while should count as a great favour? I'm inclined to believe that is how you see yourself, because no other explanation of how you carry on makes sense.'

Of course, there was an explanation that made very good sense, and again I was strongly disposed to tell her everything, but I didn't, and she probably interpreted my silence as further evidence of my magisterial indifference.

'You're so insufferably smug,' she went on. 'I thought you wanted something of me, that that was why you kept up this half-cocked relationship. But I don't think you need anything from anybody.'

'You're so wrong,' I said.

'Did I catch a note of real feeling?' she said. 'Well, if you want anything of me you'd better spell it out because I'm no good at guessing games. And if you don't, if all you want is to square things with your own conscience, then you'll have to put up with all my moods and tantrums and demands, won't you? Or else of course throw me out. But as long as you keep me around, or keep on extending the helping hand of charity to the poor maiden in distress, I shall be myself and say and do exactly what I want.'

These were fighting words and they seemed to announce a real change in her attitudes and conduct. But rage did not come easily to Joan; she was capable of occasional rather theatrical fits of it, but it was soon dissipated. Throughout her stay she busied herself about the cottage quite happily on the days when I worked. She cooked, cleaned, went to the local shop, and took long walks from which she returned sometimes with bags of mushrooms or late blackberries. We spent two days flat-hunting in Hastings and Bexhill. She agreed that it might be a good idea to move out of London when the baby was born, but on these trips we didn't find a flat that appealed to her. I said I would buy the local papers and keep looking during the coming weeks.

One afternoon I was sitting upstairs at my work table in front of one of the windows when I saw a car pull up on the grass verge beside the road and three people get out. Joan was blackberrying in the middle field between the cottage and the road and couldn't see the visitors at first because of the high hedgerows. Not until they were approaching the middle field could I make out quite clearly that the woman with the two men was Susan. I watched as the two women in my life greeted each other and walked down towards the cottage together with the two men behind. Afterwards Susan told me that Joan was so welcoming, friendly and unsuspecting that it made her feel terribly guilty.

I left my work and went out to meet them. One of the men, of course, was Brian, and the other was the pub landlord called Peregrine, the one with the handlebar moustache and the affected voice whom I had taken an instant dislike to months before.

'Hello Stuart, how nice to meet you again,' Brian said. 'We're not invading you, don't get alarmed. I've just come to pick up some things that I need.' He was, like his brother Paul, effusively genial. He laughed when he spoke, even when what he said was quite ordinary. He introduced me to Perry, saying, 'But of course you must have met our distinguished landlord, who for this occasion has turned chauffeur, bless him.'

'No trouble at all,' Perry said. 'I enjoy a spin in the country on a day like this.' He shook my hand and smiled. I wondered what he made of the situation. We hadn't been in his pub often, but he had seen Sue and me around Battle sometimes and now here we were forced to behave like strangers in the presence of her husband and a girl whose condition announced no mere casual acquaintance with me.

Sue gave nothing away. She was cool and cordial. Later she told me she was terrified. She hadn't been able to object to their coming because she had no reasonable grounds to do so and might have aroused Brian's suspicions. When I greeted her with a kiss on the cheek I felt her stiffen as if she feared I would suddenly wrap her in my arms and give everything away.

'Won't you all stay for a cup of tea?' I said.

'If we're not interrupting your work, we'd be delighted to,' Brian said. 'Wouldn't we, Susie?'

Susie! I thought of the song, 'If you knew Susie like I know Susie,' and inwardly smiled.

Susan wasn't smiling. Unenthusiastically, she said, 'If you like.'

I went into the cottage to fetch some chairs. There was also a wooden garden bench, on which Brian and Perry sat when Sue insisted on sitting on the grass.

'Many a happy hour I've spent in this garden, bashing away at the old typewriter,' Brian said, and talked about the time, ten or fifteen years ago, when he and Paul had lived at the cottage together, addressing Perry much of the time, which gave me an opportunity to watch Sue, who avoided my eyes. Then Brian turned to me, with a typically jocular question.

'So how are you getting on with the problems of the universe, Stuart?'

'Oh, I think they're yielding gradually to patience and steady work,' I said, looking at Susan and trying to make it a message for her.

'I read your last book,' Brian said. 'Remarkable stuff for a man of your age. Mind you, there are things in it that I would quarrel with.'

'There are things in it that I would quarrel with,' I said. 'I wrote it over a year ago, and there have been some fundamental changes since then.' Sue's eyes said, 'Message received, but please stop it.'

'Of course, one's ideas change and develop all the time,' Brian said. 'I think it's a brave man who commits himself to print on any question of a philosophical nature.'

'I don't know,' I said, 'I think there comes a point where you have to commit yourself and face the consequences, when you say, "Here I stand, I cannot do otherwise".' I was quite enjoying the game of declaring my love to Sue while ostensibly talking quite seriously to her husband.

'There's no water for tea, Stuart,' Joan said, appearing from out of the cottage with an empty bucket. 'Will you get some, darling?'

Sue acted quickly, saying she had to go to the loo, and disappeared round the side of the cottage.

The lavatory was a wooden hut at the bottom of the garden behind the cottage. The path led on past it and round the bend in the stream to the point where we got our water. We always went out of the front gate, however, to get water, because the path was wider and not so overgrown. So Sue and I went in different directions, and when I got down to the stream she was already there waiting for me.

We kissed greedily.

'I've missed you so,' she whispered.

'Me too. I think of you all the time.'

'I didn't want to come, but I had no choice.'

'I'm glad you did.'

'So am I, now. But it's dangerous. You mustn't look at me in that way. And the things you say!'

'We're talking philosophically.'

'You can be too clever and too confident. It makes me nervous.'

'Have you told him it's all over?'

'Yes, but he won't accept it. He wants us to go and live with him in London.'

'You can't. You're mine.'

'Oh yes, I want to be.'

'I'll tell him if you won't.'
'Don't worry, I certainly won't go to London. But what about Joan?'
'She's queer and moody, but I can cope with it. Everything's going to work out.'
'You must go back now, or they'll wonder.'

I straddled the stream and dipped the bucket into the deep part in the middle. Sue watched me and when I was steady on the bank again she kissed me, briefly and tenderly, then disappeared up the path. I took the water straight through the cottage into the kitchen, then took my time pumping and lighting the primus stove. When I rejoined everyone in the garden Susan was sitting on the grass where she had been before and Brian was telling a story about an artist friend who had accepted a cranky old lady's commission to draw her cat, but every time he went to the house the cat had 'just gone out' and 'was sure to be back in a minute' and he had to sit and drink gallons of tea and be regaled by the old lady's reminiscences. I laughed with the others, but inside I seethed with anger that this clown should have the presumption to imagine he had anything to give Susan or the audacity to claim anything of her.

After we had had tea and endured more droll anecdotes, Sue suddenly cut Brian off and said they had to get back for Christopher's bedtime.

'Didn't she used to come to Chepstow Road with the man in the white Jaguar?' Joan said when they had left. 'And I remember Brian was around occasionally. I got the impression that they were separated.'

'Perhaps they've got back together,' I said indifferently.

'They didn't look very together. She sat there as if she was thoroughly bored.'

'Perhaps she's heard all the stories before,' I said. 'Marriage to a man like that must be rather boring after the first fine careless rapture; if ever there was one, which I think extremely unlikely.'

Joan raised an eyebrow. It was one of the subtler and more eloquent of her theatrical 'takes'. It made me realise that I had slipped up, had shown a sharpness, a bitchiness even, that was out of character. I didn't know what she would make of it, whether she would see it as a sign of jealousy and resentment or put it down as a lapse from my accustomed indifference, but I knew she noticed it.

I said I had better get back to work and went upstairs.

Work wasn't going particularly well. It wasn't only that I was distracted by anxiety and frustration, but also I had engaged myself to do work that I now had little enthusiasm for. The BBC Religious Broadcasting programme I had been commissioned to write and present was a television essay explaining why my generation rejected political and religious orthodoxies. It wasn't so much the subject that troubled me as the idea of setting myself up as a spokesman for my generation. The producer wanted all this background graphic material on the war, the atom bomb, the depression of the 'thirties, the Russian and Hungarian revolutions, to give viewers a picture of the world I had grown up in and been influenced by. The idea was that because we had been disillusioned by our elders' failure to match their actions to their ideals, and because we had this great threat of nuclear annihilation hanging over us, we felt that the old orthodoxies, party politics and the religion of the churches, were no longer relevant to our condition. I could argue the case competently enough. It had a grain of truth in it, but it was only a partial truth, even for me, and whether it was at all true for my generation as a whole I had no idea. The war, the Bomb, our elders' failures, were problems that had been very remote from my thoughts and life recently, and I would feel something of a fraud sitting before the television cameras pretending that these had been the great formative influences of my life. Susan had meant more to me and done more to shape my attitudes than Hitler, Stalin, Franco and all the other monsters and martinets of modern history, but I could hardly put that to an audience of millions as a statement representative of the views of my generation.

So I had no enthusiasm for the work. On the other hand, it had to be done now that the BBC had paid me half my fee in advance and spent money on filming and gathering material, so I sat upstairs and laboured at the wretched project throughout the evening, breaking off only to go down to light a fire, get in some logs and to join Joan for the supper she had prepared. She raised no objection to my absorption in my work, and when I eventually went down again about eleven o'clock, she looked up from her knitting and her book, smiled and said, 'Done a good day's work?'

'I don't know about good,' I said, 'but I've finished the thing.' I sat in the armchair on the other side of the fire and looked through my manuscript.

Joan said, 'Good,' and went on knitting and reading. I thought, What a cosy, domestic scene: the woman in full bloom of pregnancy, happily knitting, the man, just returned from an exhausting foray in the realm of ideas to the comforts of hearth and home! It's the common, the consecrated pattern, and perhaps it's folly to demand more of life.

'Do you think you're a woman representative of your generation?' I asked her.

She laughed. 'What a funny question. Why?'

I said that as I was supposed to be speaking for our generation I'd welcome her reaction, at least to the ending of my piece, which I read out to her:

'We believe that we are attending at the birth of a new world, and we express our belief in it by saying No to the old. No! to the specious freedom that is offered us on a plate. No! to the big empty words, political slogans and rallying-calls. No! to tyranny (pictures of Hitler and Stalin on the screen). No! to hypocrisy. No! to prejudice (a picture illustrating racial discrimination). No! to all those vast, impersonal things that make men feel insignificant beside them (picture of a rocket on its pad). And it is at this point that our No becomes a Yes. It becomes an affirmation of our belief in man's power to change his world. It becomes an assertion of our independence; yes, of our resolute freedom. So at the last moment we discover that we have a cause to fight for. We cannot fight for it on the barricades. Its battles must be fought in the loneliness of our own minds and hearts. But the cause is the same cause all the great wars and revolutions in history have been fought in the name of: the cause of freedom. Freedom today begins in understanding. We can't score for freedom by putting a cross on a ballot paper or joining a church. We serve it best by standing outside the clash of ideologies, interest and factions, and promoting among people an understanding of themselves and their world. If this understanding makes them say No to the present order of things, we are prepared to face the consequences of this. And with this No on our lips we will endure, steadily working towards the light and patiently waiting for the dawn of a new era.'

I stopped and looked at Joan. 'Would you say that that has the authentic ring of the voice of our generation?'

'I don't know,' she said. 'It certainly has a ring.'

'You mean that to you it's just me making noises? Don't protest. You'd be right to think that. But that's what the television people want.'

'I think it will go down very well,' Joan said.

I laughed. This time the theatrical term was apt. 'Yes, it will go down,' I said, 'though not in history; into oblivion rather, but at least I'll get paid for it.'

It was a day fit for a funeral, with a leaden sky, early morning rain still dripping from the trees, and muddy patches around the field gates, when I took Joan to Battle to catch the London train. Paul had a stock of pairs of galoshes for such conditions, and we were grateful for them as we plodded up the field to wait for the bus. Joan was panting and breathless when we reached the road and changed into our shoes, leaving the galoshes in an upturned wooden box that was there for the purpose. On the bus and at the station we talked about practical matters, particularly the flats we had seen and the reasons why they were unsuitable, and I promised again that I would continue the search. I kissed her formally on the cheek when I saw her onto the train, and waved a perfunctory farewell as it pulled out of the station.

A quarter of an hour later I was kissing Susan on the cheek, also rather dispassionately as she was busy with some domestic chores and had not been expecting me. She said she had had a harrowing week, and there were signs of strain and nervous tension around her eyes and mouth. Daphina's greeting, too, was less cheery than usual, and I was relieved when she said that she was just going into the village to place her daily bet at the bookies' and do a bit of shopping. Brian had left the day before, Susan said, and both she and Daphina were taking time to get over the ordeal of having him at the house, even though he had spent most lunch times and evenings at the pub. Not that he had been particularly difficult or unreasonable, but he had at first wanted her and Christopher to go and live with him in London, and it had taken hours of discussion to persuade him that there was no future for them together. He had even agreed to give her grounds for divorce. But it had been an ordeal for her, having to persuade him and discussing what part he was going to play in Christopher's upbringing.

Chris had been difficult all week, too, fractious and tending to hang on to her skirts all the time. And she had missed me, and wondered what was happening between me and Joan.

'Nothing is happening,' I said, and told her about our fruitless flat hunting, my work on the TV programme and my dissatisfaction with it.

'I'd like to read it,' she said.

That gave me the opportunity to put a proposal that I had been contemplating for the last few days.

'Of course, but you'll have to come out to the cottage to do so. In fact I think what we both need after the past week is to spend some time together,' I said. 'Why don't you come tomorrow and spend a day or two?'

It was the first time she had smiled since I arrived. 'I'd love to,' she said, 'but I don't know about the "or two". I could ask Daphina to look after Chris for the day, but I couldn't really ask her to stand in for me the next morning.'

'Why not?'

'It would be making her complicit, wouldn't it?'

'With your spending the night with me?'

'Of course.'

'But she was suggesting the other day that you should marry into the nobility and take me as a lover.'

'That was in fun. In reality I wouldn't want to involve her, or to put her on a spot. But I'd really love to come for the day.'

'Good. Then I'll come in to pick you up on the nine-thirty bus. We'll do some shopping for meals and have a lovely day.'

'I'm already looking forward to it.'

And I too looked forward, ruminating on what she had said, thinking she had implied that her reluctance to compromise Daphina was now the only obstacle to her spending the night with me, to our at last becoming lovers in the full and true sense of the word.

Susan had certainly read, though she had never commented on, the chapter titled Sex and Love in the book of mine that Major Grissell had so pithily disparaged, and I had sometimes wondered whether what she had read had strengthened her resolve to resist my sexual overtures up to now. I had re-read the chapter, as if through her eyes. She would certainly not have recognised it as an essay in the Sartrian Existentialist mode on the exercise of 'the look' in the erotic context. It had been through looks, hers as well as mine, that we had flirted the first time we met and often subsequently. I had written of the look as an act of 'appropriation' of a woman as 'a world of otherness distinct from me but respondent to me', I imagined this would have raised a frown of repugnance or of puzzlement, in her. The sub-text here, and in the rest of the chapter, was the widely-held 1950s' view that a woman had to be prevailed upon, by fair means or foul, to yield to a man's sexual importunings, that the 'favours' that she had to bestow were to be gained either robustly by conquest or subtly by seduction. It was all a nonsense, of course, particularly in its ignorance of the reality of female sexuality, but it was a potent and pervasive nonsense, both in literature and in life. The discussion in the chapter went on to repudiate the Sartian nihilist view and to positively distinguish lust from love, but in such abstract terms that any reader experienced in life and love would regard it as a rather laboured statement of the obvious, or a banality obfuscated by philosophical verbiage, which I suppose was what Major Grissell implied with his 'fellow could do with a dose of salts' comment. Whether Susan had so regarded it I didn't know, but I did know that she would have found no passion in the writing, and might have had doubts about someone who could write about love with such unfeeling philosophical bravura.

Perhaps when I had tearfully blurted out, 'I think I love you', and she had laughed and said, 'That's a true philosopher's declaration', she had had the Sex and Love chapter in mind, and there had been in her statement a gently indulgent touch of mockery of philosophical doubt and equivocation. Well, I had surely by now demonstrated my feelings and my intentions in a quite unequivocal way, and she too had explicitly declared her love, and with her kiss and her words down by the stream had shown the strength and the urgency of her feelings. So why now, I thought, should we not really become lovers? Our summer romps in fields and woods, over gates and fences, when I had discomposed her with my frankly sexually appraising looks and manifestly ardent embraces, had been playful, but since her return from Germany our kissing and caressing had become more serious, desperate, urgent and erotic.

The fact that we didn't, on arrival at the cottage, fall so avidly upon each other as we had at the stream suggested a certain nervousness on her part, a holding back from the momentous consummation that could change everything. Besides, we had practical things to attend to, unpacking the shopping, getting the log fire going, preparing the paraffin lamp and the candles for the evening, and making basic preparations for the meal. We had a snack and in the afternoon took a stroll in the woods, where Susan showed a thorough knowledge of edible fungi and we foraged a basket of mushrooms to contribute to our evening meal.

It was getting chilly when we returned to the cottage, so I stoked up the embers of the fire and opened the doors so that the heat would rise to the bedroom.

'So are you going to give me your TV text to read now?' Susan said.

'Ah yes, I'd forgotten.'

'It's what I came over for, isn't it?' Her smile was knowing and teasing, so I played along with it.

'Of course. I can't wait to hear your opinion. It's what I've been longing for for days.'

Susan sat in one of the armchairs in front of the blazing fire and for half an hour focused her attention on my manuscript, reading it right through from the beginning to the peroration I had read to Joan. I watched her read, following the movements of her eyes, admiring how the firelight played in her hair and highlighted the contours of her high cheek bones and well-fleshed lips. Once or twice she looked up and smiled, and when she had finished she put the manuscript down and said, 'I don't think you need to change it. Why are you dissatisfied?'

I shrugged. 'I suppose because I feel it's not really me.'

'You mean you don't believe it?'

'Not exactly that, but I feel that this level of yea-saying and nay-saying is not the level on which real life is lived. It doesn't touch on anything really fundamental; not for me, anyway, not now. Life is much more complex and difficult and the really important things can't be so neatly polarised and tackled within the scope of a half-hour TV programme.'

'But are you supposed to be giving a whole philosophy of life? I thought they just asked you to talk about what people of our generation think about politics and the church.'

'That's just it. Frankly, I haven't a clue what young people think. And for another thing, it's not new.'

'Does a thing have to be new to be worth saying?'

'No, I said, but it should be deeply and personally felt. 'And at the moment I don't think anything is worth saying except "I'm in love with Susan Bennett", and I can't go on the box and say that, can I?'

I thought she would laugh, or at least smile, but she took it seriously. 'It seems as if Bill was right, doesn't it? I do have a bad effect on your work.'

'You don't. It's my being in love with you that has made the difference, and in the long run that can't but have a good effect.'

'Maybe,' she said, 'but what about in the short run? I shouldn't like your friends to say that it has been the ruin of you, that there goes another man fallen a casualty in the war of the sexes, or something of the sort.'

I laughed. 'Who cares what they say?'

'I do. I don't like to see people confirmed in their prejudices.'

'So I'll do the programme,' I said, 'just as it's written. But enough of that now. Remember, we're here to celebrate.'

'Celebrate what?'

'Just our being together after our stressful week.'

'I'm sorry,' she said, 'I'll certainly celebrate that.'

'So come and kiss me, sweet and twenty,' I quoted.

'Twenty-four,' she corrected.

'Still applies,' I said, 'and even rhymes better with 'Life's a thing will not endure'.'

Our kiss this time was passionate, but with perhaps a touch of exaggeration suggesting it was untimely, which was implied too when she said, 'Now I must start to cook the meal.'

It was a simple meal, conceived for the limited amenities of the cottage, of fillet steak, peas and potatoes, garnished with our wild mushrooms, and with fruit and cheese to round it off, all accompanied with a bottle of red wine, and followed by a digestif of brandy by the fire.

Outside it was getting dark now and there was a steady splashing of rain from the gutter into the water butt at the front door.

I put more logs on the fire. Susan shifted to make room for me when I squeezed into the armchair beside her and put my arm around her. We sat a while just enjoying our closeness and the sight and sound of the fire and listening to the rain until eventually I put the question that had loomed over our small talk with increasing insistence, 'Shall we go upstairs?'

'Yes,' she said, 'but can we have another brandy first?'

'Of course. Is the prospect such an ordeal? You know I wouldn't want to go against the wisdom of the gut.'

I poured us each another brandy.

'Well, in this case the gut is saying "Yes, let's do it".'

'But the head says, "Hold on"?'

'No, it says, "What then?" I suppose I'm nervous of putting our "something special" at risk. Also, though it may seem silly for a woman who has a child to say, but I'm afraid I'm not very experienced.'

'I wouldn't particularly want you to be. I just want us to make love. Whatever happens will be good and beautiful.'

'I'm sure it will. And I'm glad you had the foresight to get the brandy. It steadies the nerves.'

Maybe it helped. I, like Susan, felt some trepidation after so long a wait and this had given rise to an anxiety – would the reality be equal to the dream? But our apprehensions were eventually allayed. If anything disappointed that night it was the fact that the rain stopped, dashing my hope that it might serve as a plausible reason for Susan staying the night after all.

So out came the galoshes again, and I had a wry reflection that here was Susan stepping into Joan's shoes as we prepared to plod up the hill to wait for the last bus. It was a wild night, dark but with a half moon riding the wind-rushed clouds above the silent rooks' wood at the top of the hill. The bus driver, obviously not expecting any passengers in mid-country and in these conditions, overshot the stop and had to wait for us to catch up. We were panting and laughing when we boarded, and the conductor reciprocated with a cheery 'Evening all' and a smile that I thought was knowing and complicit, as if he could guess why a young couple sprung out of the bleak autumn night should look so unseasonably sunny and exuberant.

8

Bill had dreamed up a characteristically provocative and impertinent scheme to mark our departure from Chepstow Road. He had got a sculptor friend to make a blue plaque similar to but larger than those that the London County Council fixed to buildings to announce that famous people had lived there. Bill's plaque announced: 'Colin Wilson, John Braine, Bill Hopkins, Stuart Holroyd, Tom Greenwell and Greta Detloff lived here, 1956-59'. He had arranged to have it firmly fixed to the front of the house and to have a ceremonial unveiling, with reports and photographs in the papers. Rachman had no objection, and Bill had looked into the legal aspect and found that there was no law against such self-advertisement, probably because it had never occurred to the official mind that anyone would have the audacity to do it.

Tom thought it was a splendid stunt and an appropriate cock-a-snook ending to the 'angry decade'. It had been a good time, and it was sad to be splitting up and going our separate ways. Still, we would always be welcome at his new place, a big flat located below a nonconformist chapel in Kensington. Bill had found a flat in Paddington, and said he would take my books and other belongings and store them until I needed them. I was in London to help with the move and also for the TV broadcast which was to go out live on a Sunday night.

There was no television set at Chepstow Road, nor did Susan or Joan have access to one, which I was glad of, although the BBC people seemed pleased enough with the broadcast, as did the majority who contributed to the postbag that the BBC sent me the following week. There were critics and cynics among the several dozen people who were moved to write, but most offered plaudits and encouragement, and one, curiously, with a photograph enclosed, made a proposal of marriage.

One person who had a television, and had seen the programme, was John Braine. He had come down from Yorkshire the day after my broadcast to retrieve some of his things from the shared room, and proposed to stay for a few days to attend to business with his agent and publishers. He came into my room while I was packing books into boxes in readiness for the move, and handed me a copy of his recently published second novel, *The Vodi*. I thanked him and he said, 'I hope you'll like it better than most of the critics did.'

He sat in a chair and lit a cigarette. I was pleased to see him, and glad that he clearly intended to stay and chat for a while.

'Saw you on the box the other night,' he said. 'Obviously a bit nervous, but you dealt with the questions well enough.'

'I felt a bit of a Charlie, holding forth like that,' I said, 'but that was what they wanted.'

'Charlie the charlatan, eh?' John smiled. 'Yes, you're not very convincing as an angry young man.

As for giving the buggers what they want, I didn't with *The Vodi* and they trashed it, but they'll get their sequel to *Room at the Top* soon enough. On the other hand, giving them what they want on demand is a sure way to write yourself off, because next month they won't want it any more, there'll be a new fad to follow. All they want is stuff, or stuffing, for their schedules.'

'Well, I don't think I'll be doing any more of it,' I said.

'Maybe you should,' John said. 'As I said, you come across well, and with a bit of practice you'd get more at ease with the cameras. What are you working on now?'

'A play.'

'On commission?'

'Not exactly, but Devine and Richardson at the Court have asked to see something else.'

'You should have a go at a novel,' he said. 'That is, if you can clear your mind of all its philosophical baggage.' He fixed me with his characteristic challenging stare. When I didn't respond he went on, 'Take Tolstoy for instance, he was just mediocre enough as a philosopher to make a great novelist. You need a mind that can't be seduced by ideas.'

'Like Henry James?' I suggested.

'Yes, I suppose,' he conceded, 'though personally I don't get on with the way he huffs and puffs around a subject before getting to the point.'

I had to put in a defence of one of my literary heroes. I said, 'But he does get to the point, and I think that what you call the huffing and puffing illuminates it.

'Maybe, but it doesn't work for me,' John said, and to change the subject gestured towards the boxes. 'So where will you be moving to?'

'Bill's going to store my books,' I said. 'I'll still be living down in the country for a while. I'm looking for a flat for Joan in Hastings.'

Outside, in Chepstow Road, an indeterminate rumbling sound that had been getting louder for some time resolved itself into the music of a Caribbean steel band. John rose and went to the window, where I joined him to watch the motley procession of musicians, equipped with an assortment of commonplace implements, pots and pans, dustbin lids, washboards, bottles and glasses, from which they collectively elicited a captivating syncopated melody which had attracted a crowd of laughing, shouting and dancing followers.

John was clearly not captivated, however. 'Prancing niggers,' he said, and observing my probably rather nonplussed reaction smiled and explained: 'It's the title of one of Ronald Firbank's stories, but in the circumstances I think quite apt.'

He returned to his chair and went on: 'Someone said that the British acquired an empire in a fit of absence of mind. Well, I'd say that they're giving it up in a fit of mindless stupidity. It was lunacy for the Labour government to give eight hundred million people worldwide the right to come and live in Britain. If we don't put a stop to mass immigration we'll have a revolution in thirty or forty years' time. It's getting so bad in Bradford already that Pat and I have decided to move down south. I'm viewing a couple of places in Woking tomorrow.'

'Woking?'

John resumed his chair and laughed at my surprise. 'Yes, suburban Woking, Surrey. Just half an hour from Waterloo. Reasonably priced property, and some decent schooling. Ah'm a family man, you know.' He exaggerated the Yorkshire accent, self-mockingly. 'Speaking of which, how is Joan getting on? When is she expecting?'

I couldn't help frowning at the implication of the question prompted by his 'family man' reference, and I think he noticed it. 'She's fine,' I said. 'I gather it'll be in about six weeks.'

'And this place you say you're getting for her in Hastings: will you be moving in there too?'

'No, I'll still be at the cottage, at least until Christmas, when Paul will want to use it. Joan understands and accepts that there couldn't be any future for us.'

'On account of this other woman?'

'Susan, yes.' I began to suspect that John had been talking to Bill and Tom.

'Hasn't she got a kid of her own?'

'Yes.'

He didn't need to say what he was clearly thinking, that it would be a queer sort of thing for me to take on someone else's child and reject one of my own. But what he said was:

'I married the girl next door, so to speak. It was no great romance, but I liked Pat well enough, and I didn't kid myself that I was a great catch, a short-sighted librarian with a paunch. On the whole it's worked out, we have a good life and I'm free to spend the necessary time in my study and get on with the work, a thousand words a day on average. I can recommend it: marrying the girl next door, that is.'

I laughed. 'You did recommend it, the last time we talked, if you remember.'

'Sure I remember. It was the day after she'd spent the night in your room while you were away bedding someone else. I didn't know at the time that you were involved with her.'

'It was the beginning then,' I said. 'Things have developed since, and I'm not going to do a Joe Lampton and marry for convenience.'

John nodded. 'Ah, so she's your Alice, is she?' referring to the woman his fictional hero in *Room at the Top* really loved but cravenly and fatally ditched.

'Yes, in fact she's more to me than Alice was to Joe. Bill has been telling Sue that she's not cut out to be a writer's woman, not self-effacing enough,' I said. 'He too seems to be proposing the girl next door option. As does Colin. There seems to be a conspiracy among my friends.'

'We've talked,' John admitted. He leaned forward and levelled his searching look at me again through his pebble glasses. 'I understand her folks have been pretty friendly and favourable to you, lending the house while they were away and such. Has it occurred to you that there might be a bit of a conspiracy going on there too? You are, after all, a man in the news, someone with apparent great potential, and Susan is a divorcee with a kid to bring up.'

'What you're suggesting is preposterous,' I said, laughing with incredulity. 'I can only think Bill has been putting these ideas in your head.'

'Put it down to my imagination,' John said, reclining back in his chair and smiling. 'My novelist's imagination: indigent former colonials, people with charm and a touch of class but no prospects, seek suitably promising match for needy daughter. It's not quite *Pride and Prejudice*, but allowing for the time lapse there are similarities. Have I heard aright, that Susan's family name is Bennett?'

'Yes, it is.'

'Coincidence,' he said.

'Well, I haven't got Mr Darcy's ten thousand a year, I haven't even got a thousand a year in today's money,' I said, 'and there's no chance of a country estate.'

'At twenty-five, with a couple of books to your name and a reputation of sorts, you could be looked on as a fair bet,' John said.

I said, 'Well, I don't know at what odds. Her mother's fond of her daily flutter on the horses, but I don't think she'd go for a fifty-to-one shot.'

'You underestimate yourself,' John said, 'I'd put you at ten or fifteen to one. But it's a rough do, this literary handicap. That's why you need to settle yourself with a good woman and get stuck into your work.'

'That's what I intend,' I said.

In *Room at the Top* John had written a scene in which Joe Lampton had taken Alice to a country cottage and they had made love passionately before he broke the news to her that Susan was pregnant and he was going to marry her. The correspondences with recent events in my life were striking, notwithstanding the obvious and pertinent differences. If anything made a nonsense of the idea that I was a 'catch' for Susan and that her parents had been complicit in netting me, it was my memory of the night at the cottage. I had dwelt on the specifics constantly and achingly in the days thereafter, and on one thing in particular which I felt decisively negated John's suggestion. It was Sue's saying, 'Don't put me on a pedestal. It's not very comfortable up there.' That was surely not the kind of statement that a self-seeking and scheming woman would come up with.

I had re-run the scene repeatedly since the night at the cottage, remembering how, as I had led her up the narrow, dark wooden staircase, her hand squeezed mine in little convulsions. The heater I had put on earlier in the bedroom had taken the chill off and also afforded us some subdued light. I lit a couple of candles to augment it.

We kissed and caressed. Susan took off the woollen sweater that she was still wearing. I unbuttoned her blouse, unclipped and removed her bra, stood up from the bed briefly to take off my own clothes, and soon we were under the sheets and blankets, both naked and in a close embrace. I thrilled to the pressure of her breasts against my chest and to the tentative push of her pubis against my erection. I said, 'Just a moment, my love,' and disengaged briefly to slip on a condom. The candlelight flickered over her body and I drew back a little to appreciate the wonder of it, the breasts with their dark nipples and areolae, the darker pubis, the flat belly, which she covered with her hands, saying, 'I have ugly stretch marks.' I said, 'They're not ugly,' and kissed them, then drew my lips back, over her pubis, and with my fingers sought the soft labia that would soon part for me. My excitement was becoming scarcely containable, and I moved back to kissing her on the lips and breasts. Firmly she took my erection in her hand and guided it. 'Come inside,' she whispered. 'Oh yes', I said, and thrust hard and deeply, once, twice, three or four times, and then exclaimed 'Oh' again, but now with dismay, for the old familiar welling up from the depths was suddenly uncontrollable, though I at first tried to hold it back, which was probably why I filled the bulb of the condom abundantly enough but without an accompanying sense of exultation or joy.

The last thing I would have imagined saying on this occasion, this longed for consummation, was 'I'm sorry.'

'Don't be sorry,' Susan said. 'It's been a long time. You were pent up.'

'I suppose so.'

It was then that she said, 'Don't put me on a pedestal. It's not very comfortable up there.'

'What do you mean?'

'The way you were looking at me, the way you often look at me in fact, as if I were a goddess or something, rather than just a woman like many another.'

'But to me you're not like any other,' I said, 'to me you are special, and very beautiful. Even if you have got stretch marks.'

'What I mean,' she said, 'is that in your eyes, and in your arms, I want to be a woman, your woman, and not some idealised figure of your imagination.'

I knew that what she was implying was that I had come prematurely because there was in my love a factor of adoration that distanced her, that made of her an icon too exquisite to be sullied by the grossness of my lust. And I supposed that there was some truth in that, but the fact that I had been, as she said, 'pent up' after the months of anticipation had to be taken into account as well.

I said, 'I want nothing more than for you to be my woman, and I think that what you just said was the most wonderful declaration of love. So you're coming down from that pedestal and I'm going to make love to you again as just a woman.'

'And this time,' she said, 'you don't need to wear one of those things. It's safe, my period's due in a couple of days.'

It was this breakthrough conversation, and our subsequent lovemaking, that carried us into the joyous and exuberant mood in which we boarded the Battle bus later that otherwise bleak and gloomy evening.

I began seriously thinking of proposing marriage after this. Also I began seriously thinking about money. My funds were running low, my income from advances and journalism had diminished and my liabilities were very soon to be vastly increased. I still had hopes that *The Prophet* would be taken up by the Royal Court, and had in fact now completed a first draft, which I was on the whole pleased with, thinking that the play effectively exploited the comic possibilities of Gurdjieff's entertaining both members of the occupying forces and of the Resistance, and at the same time explored in dramatic terms the pros and cons of pursuing the spiritual as opposed to the political means of bringing about change in the world. Maybe it was, as Kenneth Tynan had sneeringly said of *The Tenth Chance*, a play in the Shavian manner, but the English Stage Company avowedly afforded a platform for all kinds of theatre and had in fact recently staged a successful run of Shaw's *Major Barbara*. I would soon be able to submit a final draft of *The Prophet*, but even if there was an advance forthcoming it would not be soon, nor would it be substantial, so it seemed that I was going to have to consider getting a job.

I hadn't been interested at the time, but now I recalled what Anne and Michael had told me in the summer about the BBC job Mike was then doing, part of a scheme the drama department was running to give writers with appropriate credentials some practical experience of writing for and working in television. Mike had had a six-month contract and had suggested that I might also apply to participate in the scheme. I phoned him to see how I should go about it. Anne answered the call. 'Darling, we watched you on TV the other night,' she said before I could get a word in. 'You looked so young and so nervous, I wished I could be there and give you a smile and a hug. Michael thought you put it across very well.' When I told her the purpose of my call she enthused about the proposal, saying she was sure the BBC would want to offer me a contract, and as far as she and Mike were concerned it would be lovely to have me back in London again. She passed me over to Michael, who said I should write to Donald Wilson, the Head of Drama, and was also enthusiastic, saying they were keen to get writers with some theatre experience and my connection with the Royal Court would surely get me the job.

And indeed it was as easy as that. I was given an appointment to meet Donald Wilson at the TV Centre in Wood Lane, for an occasion which was not so much an interview as a welcome to the team, and was offered a six-month contract at a monthly salary well beyond my expectations. I would have an office at the TV Centre, sharing with another writer. There were no set office hours, though I would be expected to attend weekly script conferences and to be present in the studio for rehearsals of plays for which I would be nominally 'script editor'. Also, I would have a writing project to complete during the term of my employment, the details of which we would discuss and agree later

Susan was delighted when she heard the news. We were at the cottage, and had made love again, as we had done several times since the first occasion. I told her all that the job would involve, including the fact that I would have to be in London during the week and would need to find a flat or at least a room there. It was going to be hard to be away from her, particularly now, but I could go down to Sussex for the weekends, and perhaps she could sometimes come to London for a day or two during the week. She said she thought it was a wonderful arrangement, at a time that was going to be difficult for all of us, with Joan's confinement and her own divorce from Brian coming up, and it was good that I would be getting on with my career. I was a little put out that she responded to my news with such practical considerations, but had to acknowledge that she was sensible and right.

I continued my search for a flat for Joan, and eventually found one that I thought would be ideal. It was in Hastings Old Town, and comprised the second and third floors of a tall terrace house on the

East Hill overlooking the harbour. Away from the seafront, with its monuments to the banality of human wishes – amusement arcades and makeshift wooden huts that offered summer trippers beach teas, fortune telling, souvenirs, comic postcards, shell fish and ice cream – the old part of Hastings had charm and dignity. There were low, oak-beamed houses, winding streets, surprising passages opening into courtyards, pavements elevated above street level. I thought it wouldn't be a bad place to live.

The flat was spacious and from the windows of the main room there was a magnificent view over rooftops with varied elevations down to the harbour and the sea. It had a shared entrance from the street, with a hall spacious enough to accommodate a pram, that sinister 'enemy of promise' according to Cyril Connolly. The landlady, Mrs Beavis, who was on the ground floor and had an entrance to her apartment from the same hall, had no objection to having an unmarried mother and her child as tenants. In fact, she said, she would welcome them, as she was alone in the house, having recently been widowed. Her late husband had been a bookseller and her rooms were comfortably furnished with packed bookshelves. She had, she said, some wonderful first editions, and reverently put in my hands an autographed copy of *Winnie the Pooh*, a masterpiece that was not at the time within my literary compass. The husband, apparently, had specialised in children's books.

Joan came down the first Saturday in November to see the flat. She quite liked it and got on well with

Mrs Beavis, but she had some reservations about its location, with the steep hill up from the harbour, and with regard to its furnishings and state of decoration. We told the landlady that we'd think about it and be in touch in a few days' time.

Over a fish and chip lunch in a harbour café I told Joan about the BBC job, mentioning also that on the strength of it I had been able to arrange an overdraft with my bank and so would be able to buy the items of furniture that were lacking, like heating appliances, a cooker and a television, and as the job didn't start until the following month I could put in some time decorating the place.

Joan smiled at my proposal and said, 'I didn't know that interior decorating was one of your talents.'

'It isn't particularly, but... '

She interrupted. 'Don't say it. I know, it's the least you can do. But what I don't understand is why you're so keen for me to take the flat.'

'I thought it was obvious. It's cheaper than London, that is to say there's more space for the money, and it's a nicer and healthier place to be, if only for a while.'

'And you're going to be in London?'

'Yes, but that's not to the point.'

'Isn't it? It seems somehow a convenient sort of reversal. But whatever your reasons, I do like the flat, and think I might take you up on the offer.'

That Saturday was Battle Bonfire Night, a celebrated annual event in Sussex, a carnival occasion with big bands, a fancy dress procession, a splendid pyrotechnics display and an immense bonfire on the so-called 'Green', though it was no longer green, but a concrete car park in front of the medieval Abbey. Joan recalled that she had seen posters advertising the event the last time she was down and said she would like to see some of it before getting the train back to London. This was awkward because she had originally said she would get an early train back and I had arranged to take Sue out that evening. When I tried to discourage Joan by pointing out that we had a long wait before eight o'clock when the festivities began, she said. 'Why don't we call on your friends Brian and Susan? They live in Battle, don't they?'

I phoned Sue and told her what had happened. She said she thought it would be alright if we went over for tea, but we would have to be careful and discreet.

We were very discreet. We managed to get away together briefly in the kitchen, where I told Sue about the flat and kissed her and told her that things were working out, but the rest of the time we spent all together in the sitting room, busy with all the fuss and niceties of the English tea ritual. Daphina suavely told stories about their life in India, to which Joan listened and responded with polite interest. Then when Susan put Christopher to bed, Daphina asked Joan about the progress of her pregnancy and the arrangements for her confinement. I thought what a strange woman she was. By now she knew about the whole situation, but not once had she expressed an opinion about it or shown any disapproval of my involvement with Sue. And she didn't seem to feel that having Joan in the house put her in an awkward position. She was neither cool nor excessively solicitous towards her. With Sue's approval she sorted out and gave to Joan a carrier-bag full of baby clothes, saying, 'My dear, they grow out of them so quickly, it's only practical to pass them on to someone else.' I was grateful to her, thinking that her manner would allay any suspicions that Joan might entertain. Already Brian's absence had been explained by the fact that he was looking for work in London.

The meeting seemed so painless and uncomplicated that I saw no reason why we shouldn't all three go out to see the bonfire festivities. When I suggested it I could see from Sue's expression that she didn't want to come with us, but this time I disregarded the wisdom of the gut and pressed her to come. Daphina supported me, said she would be quite happy to baby-sit, and finally Sue agreed to come though I could tell that she was still reluctant.

It was about a ten minute walk to the Green. I walked between Sue and Joan, linking both their arms and holding Sue's hand in her pocket. We could hear the military band in the distance as soon as we left the bungalow. Sue called on her social training to meet the awkwardness of the situation, and chatted about the local bonfire night tradition.

For centuries the area had been noted for the manufacture of high-quality gunpowder, and up to three or four years before the home-made firework known as the 'Battle rouser' had been one of the hazards of bonfire night, but its use had now been forbidden by the police. Even so, one had to have eyes in the back of one's head because there was always a crowd of youths who came for the fun of letting off bangers and jumping-jacks in the crowd. It was best to stand with one's back to a wall. But we ought to get near to see the actual lighting of the fire, which was always done with a royal flourish by Mrs Harboard, the eccentric lady whose family had owned the great estates of the area for centuries and who still behaved as if she was a kind of viceroy.

Joan walked on, looking steadily ahead, without making any sound or gesture to acknowledge that she was listening to what Sue was saying. The stiffness of her arm and the set of her face showed that she was completely absorbed in her own thoughts and feelings. I thought, Yes, she must have guessed. Hell, this isn't how it should have happened.

Sue, too, picked up the atmosphere and stopped being bright and informative. She looked up at me as we walked and her eyes were troubled and said, This is a big mistake. I felt utterly miserable. I thought, This isn't the sort of situation Sue should have to cope with. I've been stupid and insensitive. I wondered if she would ever forgive me.

When we got to the top of the High Street the procession was just beginning. Led by a military band, a disorderly crowd of people apparelled in a motley range of historical costumes danced and clowned, and the rear was brought up by a phalanx of black-robed and hooded figures carrying long flaming torches. It was not possible to walk three abreast. There was a lot of shouting and cheering and people jostled past us rushing to catch up with the band. Occasionally a firework was let off. Pieces of flaming rag dropped from the torches and were kicked into the gutter where they lay smouldering. Mindful of Joan's condition, I tried to stay beside her while Sue walked on a little ahead.

'It's a bit hectic,' I said. 'Are you going to be alright?'

Joan said, 'Yes, I'm quite used to being pushed around.'

We were able to get together again at the Green, where we walked around the enormous bonfire, as yet unlit. On the top, silhouetted against the night sky, was the figure of the Guy tied to an old chair. I wondered if Joan was wishing Sue up there in its place.

A lot of people had accompanied the procession to the other end of the village, where it would turn around and return in about ten minutes for the ceremony of the lighting of the fire, but others had remained in small groups on the Green. The two high towers of the Norman gateway to the Abbey loomed over the scene, and Sue pointed out the little door in the arched wooden gates through which Mrs Harboard would presently sweep to put the first torch to the kindling. Again Joan pointedly ignored her. I tried to elicit from Sue a look to signal that all would be well with us when this ordeal was over, but her eyes met mine only briefly and they were expressionless.

We stood around in silence, watching the crowd, getting well clear of the occasional jumping jacks that came in our direction, while the sound of the returning military band became louder. When the procession returned to the Green the torch bearers formed a three-quarter circle round the bonfire. The music stopped and the crowd became hushed with expectancy.

Sue suddenly said, 'Look, there's Malcolm Fraser and his crowd. I must go and have a word with them.' And before I could say anything she had left us. I watched her thread through the crowd to a group of young people, who greeted her warmly. I recognised Malcolm Fraser as the plummy-voiced City type who had driven Sue home from the cottage one night in the summer.

A cheer went up when Mrs Harboard, dressed in a black cloak and wearing a black broad-brimmed hat, appeared in the Abbey gateway holding a blazing torch at arm's length. She made her way to the bonfire with a long, slow stride like a dancer's, and paused dramatically before plunging her torch into the tinder. Then she stepped back to allow the torch-bearers to make a circle around the fire, whereupon they moved in all at once and hurled their torches onto the pile.

Joan said, 'It's like being back in the Middle Ages. You can imagine what it must have been like to be present at a witch-burning.'

There was a lot of movement in the crowd now, and people were laughing and shouting and more fireworks were going off. I couldn't see Sue anywhere. I said, 'Let's walk around a bit', hoping to find her. But Joan took no notice.

'Oh, look!' she said, as enormous Catherine-wheels started spinning on the towers of the Abbey gatehouse. Then there were rockets, Roman candles, more Catherine-wheels. 'But this is the best place to see the display from,' Joan said when I suggested again that we should walk around.

The display lasted about twenty minutes. When it was over Joan said, 'What happened to your friend?'

'She went to have a word with someone she knew,' I said. 'She's probably lost us by now.'

'We've been in the same place all the time,' Joan rightly observed. Then after a pause: 'Well, if you're so worried, go and look for her.' I was about to say that perhaps I would when she added, 'But I won't be here when you come back.'

'Oh, come on, Joan,' I said. 'Don't be so unreasonable.'

'Unreasonable! Ha! I like that! He expects me to be all pally with his new mistress and he tells me not to be unreasonable.'

The heat from the bonfire was intense, though we were a good thirty yards away from it. Perhaps it was the reflected light from the flames that gave Joan's eyes their unaccustomed brightness.

'Sue is not my mistress,' I said, secretly exculpating the lie by thinking that she was much more to me than merely a mistress.

'Then why did you lie to me about her husband? On the day they came down to the cottage you said that perhaps they were back together, when you must have known they weren't. I suspected it then from the way you looked at her. And again tonight, it was a lie when they said he was in London looking for work, wasn't it?'

'Is that why you suggested we call on them this evening?' I said. 'Are we in fact here because you wanted to check out your suspicions?'

'That may be half the reason,' she said, 'but the other half is your stupidity. Why did you insist on Sue coming with us when she obviously didn't want to? For the satisfaction of having both your women in tow at the same time?'

A firework exploded a few feet away from us, making Joan jump. A small boy laughed and ran away into the crowd.

'We can't talk here,' I said. 'Let's go into the pub.'

'What is there to talk about? You might as well put me on the train to London then go and find your Sue and make it up with her. I suppose she'll forgive you. Everyone always has done. That's your trouble.'

'I need a drink,' I said. 'Let's go across to The Abbey.'

'Poor man,' she said. 'Does he need to drown his sorrows in alcohol?' But she came with me.

I looked out for Sue as we crossed the Green, but there remained only a few knots of people standing gazing into the fire as if in a state of atavistic entrancement. Nor was she in the Abbey bar, as I thought the Malcolm Fraser group might be. I didn't know what I would do or say if I saw her now, but I was desperate for some sign of her. It seemed impossible that all our intimacy, our avowals, all the bright possibilities for a future together that we had glimpsed and cherished, should be cancelled out at a stroke. But I remembered her saying, 'I can't be sure how I'd react in a situation that goes against the grain', and I was worried.

The pub was noisy and crowded, but a young man seated on a stool at the bar glanced at Joan's stomach and courteously surrendered his place to her. We waited in silence for the barman to get round to us. Joan's face was impassive. She didn't look at me. I noticed in the bright lights that the roots of her blonded hair were beginning to revert to their natural colour.

A large, military-looking man with a flabby face and a moustache sitting on the other side of Joan was talking in a loud voice which boomed into the silence between us, telling someone how he had woken up one morning to find the entire lower half of his body paralysed and that what had most worried him at first was that he 'couldn't go for a Jimmy-riddle'. There followed a less than fascinating account of his subsequent hospitalisation and treatment. I didn't know if this absurdity impinged on Joan's awareness as it did on mine, but it was only after he had finished that she broke the silence, saying:

'It's not your having a mistress that hurts. That was only to be expected after all. It's your taking me for such a fool.'

At last the barman got round to us. Joan said she'd have a *Babycham* and I ordered a pint of bitter.

'I tell you, Sue's not my mistress,' I repeated.

'What's it to me?' Joan snapped. 'I gave up being concerned about your sex life ages ago. It's the way I've been treated that concerns me. It's the way you've made use of me and taken me for a fool.'

'Nobody's made use of you.'

'Oh no? Why were you so keen to get me down to the cottage at the same time as Brian was down? And what's this evening been about? All that charade at the house, with both of them pretending he was in London looking for a job. And that creepy mother of hers is in on it too. All of you taking me for a fool. You can tell her to stuff her baby clothes. I don't want your mistress's hand-me-downs.'

There was no point in denying it. I said, 'I'm sorry. I see I underestimated you.'

'And used me,' she put in.

'Yes, I suppose so,' I admitted. 'But if you knew and resented it so, why didn't you say anything?'

'I didn't know. I only suspected until this evening. I saw all I wanted to at the house. Then you went and rubbed it in by insisting that she came with us. What was the idea? To humiliate me?'

'I didn't intend that,' I said. 'I may be stupid and insensitive, but I'm not malicious, and the last thing I want to do is to hurt you unnecessarily.'

'Poor man, you must have gone through agonies deciding just how much hurt was necessary. It's a problem I wouldn't mind having. Though it's just as well I haven't, because if I had I'd turn the screws very, very tight.'

She stood down from her stool. 'Now take me to the station,' she said. 'I don't want to spend the night at that hateful cottage.'

I took a few moments finishing my beer. The booming, military man was saying: 'went for a drive in the country with a couple of them last weekend, young people, stupid people, stupidly happy; they don't know a thing and they don't give a damn; but they're the ones who have all the guts and are lovely.' He turned and watched our progress out of the bar as if we were the people he was talking about.

It was a ten minute walk down to the station. We passed out of the circle of the bonfire's glow into deep darkness. Joan took my arm for support. At first we walked in grim silence, then I ventured to say:

'I want you to know that Sue has all along urged me to do everything possible for you. She's even tried to persuade me to go back to you.'

'Great for her,' Joan said, unmoved.

I said, 'I'm telling you that no one has been callous and calculating or taking pleasure in putting you down or deceiving you, as you seem to imagine. Neither Sue nor I particularly wanted to fall in love, not in this way, not so seriously at this time. But it happened. We found that we were stuck with it, and with each other.'

'Oh, I see, it's a case of "this thing is bigger than both of us".' She ham-acted it.

'If you want to reduce it to a cliché, yes.'

'It is a cliché,' she said, raising her voice. 'This whole bloody mess is a cliché. Do you expect me to be impressed that you fancy you've found your great love? It's happened before. And even if it's different this time, what's that to me? I'm going to be stuck in a flat with a baby.'

We walked on in silence again. At the station we learned that we had twenty-five minutes to wait for the last train to Charing Cross. To get out of the chill night air we went into the bar of the nearby Senlac Hotel. The place was crowded and noisy, but again Joan's obvious pregnancy got her a perch at the bar. While I was waiting to order drinks, she said in a low voice, 'She's over there.'

I felt a surge of relief, but though I looked all around the bar I couldn't see Sue.

'In the other bar,' Joan said.

The Public Bar had a separate entrance and was partitioned off from the Saloon, but the partition stopped at the bar. I saw Sue standing against the far wall with Malcolm Fraser and some other people. Among these others was a man I had met in a bar in the summer when I was alone. He was called Tony Pike and I understood he was a painter. He was about forty but dressed like a teen-ager, in tight trousers and a leather jerkin. When we met he had at first seemed friendly, but it turned out that he knew I was reputedly an 'angry young man', and he couldn't resist getting in some snide and mocking remarks. I had later learned that he had a reputation for sexual deviancy, and holding debauched parties at his house in a nearby village. It may have been baseless salacious gossip, but I had taken a dislike to him, which I'm sure was mutual, and I didn't like him being anywhere near Sue.

'Well, why don't you go to her?' Joan said.

'I'll see you on the train first.'

'Or we can both go round. Then you and Sue can both come and put me on the train, wave goodbye and live happily ever after.' She was smiling, in a way enjoying it, but she couldn't hide the hurt. It was in her eyes.

'Are you still going to take the flat?'

'Oh yes.' She expressed surprise. 'I'm going to take everything I can. I'm going to get for my baby, your baby, just the best start in life that's possible in the circumstances.'

'I'll help all I can.'

'You will,' she said. 'And you'd better start soon. There's all that decorating to be done. Perhaps you can get Sue to help you with it. It's mainly whitewashing, after all, and I should think you're quite practised at doing that together.'

I had been keeping an eye on the group in the other bar, and now they began to move towards the door. Joan noticed too. She said, 'You'd better go.'

I said, 'I'll be back,' and went out of the door and round to the other side of the building, where the entrance to the public bar was. The group were already half way across the car park. I hesitated a moment when I saw Sue at the rear of the group. Tony Pike was beside her. Suddenly he put his arm around her shoulder and bent his head down towards her. She tried to twist away and I heard her say, 'No!'

I had about twenty yards to cover. I called out, 'Don't touch her, you bastard,' which alerted him. He turned, crouched down, ready for me. His expression was amused and vicious. Crouching, weaving his body, arms held at the ready down by his knees, the palms of his hands turned towards me, the fingers beckoning all at once, he said, 'Come on, come, come on then.' My idea of a fight was a standing-up, man to man exchange of blows, and Pike's stance discomposed me. Nevertheless I flailed in and tried to land a blow on his face, but before I could get near enough I was doubled up by a kick in the crotch, which was followed by a rain of sharp blows on my head and face. I went down. I felt dizzy and for a second couldn't straighten up for the pain. People around were shouting. I heard Pike's voice saying, 'Fuck me if I know what it's about.'

Sue was kneeling beside me on the ground. She said, 'You shouldn't have done that. He fights dirty. Are you alright?'

The pain diminished and I was able to get to my feet again. I said, 'I could kill him, the degenerate slob.' I was shaking all over, but I was keyed up to launch myself at Pike again. But Sue was hanging on to me and Malcolm Fraser and two other young men were between us, remonstrating with Pike and trying to hustle him away.

Sue said, 'Stuart, for my sake, please! He didn't do anything.'

I said, 'He didn't get a chance, did he? But what if I hadn't been here?' The thought that my being there was so fortuitous, and of what might have happened otherwise, brought tears to my eyes and renewed my anger. I broke free and rushed towards the group surrounding Pike, but I couldn't get at him. There were more people around now, and some of them grabbed my arms and held me back.

Pike, among a group a few yards away, was laughing and saying, 'I'm prepared to forget it. In fact, I admire a man who stands up for his woman.'

Some idiot said, 'There, you see, why don't you shake hands on that and make it up?'

I said, 'An evil, degenerate slob like that shouldn't be walking about. I just want to kill him. Why do you all interfere?'

A voice said, 'He'd kill you, mate.' Then Malcolm Fraser and Sue hustled me back into the bar while some of the others made sure that Pike got off the scene.

Joan saw us as soon as we entered the public bar and hurried round from the saloon.

I said to Sue, 'You shouldn't have left us.'

She said, 'It was an impossible situation for me, seeing her so hurt and humiliated.'

Joan came in. She said, 'Whatever happened? There's blood on your shirt. Have you been in an accident?'

'No, in a fight,' I said. There was just a touch of bravura in it, which I saw Sue didn't miss and didn't like.

Malcolm Fraser handed me a large brandy. 'I do agree with you about Pike,' he said in his plummy voice. 'He's an unmitigated swine. I'm only sorry you didn't manage to lay one on him.'

'What was it about?' Joan said.

'Sue,' I said.

Sue frowned and shook her head slightly. She turned to speak to some of the group who had just come back into the bar. She was pointedly distancing herself.

'We must get down to the station,' I said. 'The train must be due.'

One of the people who had just come in overheard and said, 'London train was just pulling out as we came in. You've missed it.'

So Joan had to stay at the 'hateful cottage' after all. Before the fracas with Tony Pike they had all been about to leave to continue the party at someone's house in Robertsbridge. Malcolm Fraser suggested we join them. Sue said she couldn't because her mother was baby-sitting, so Malcolm offered to drop her off and to go to Robertsbridge himself by way of Brightling to save us having to wait in the cold for the last bus.

It was a bit of a squeeze to get into the back of the sports car, so Joan had to sit in the front while Sue and I climbed into the back. It was only a three or four minute drive up to the bungalow. I tried to take Sue's hand but she withdrew it.

I said, 'I'm sorry about this evening. I was a fool.'

She said, 'You trample all over everything and everyone.'

I thought of our 'tender shoot'.

I said, 'Shall I see you tomorrow?'

Sue said, 'I don't know. I need time to think.'

We had arrived. I got out of the car so that Sue could climb out. She thanked Malcolm for the lift and without so much as a 'good night' was gone into the darkness up the garden path. Malcolm drove off, and I was glad that the noise of the engine prevented conversation for the next quarter of an hour before he dropped us off on the road above the cottage.

After the crowds, the fireworks, the shouting and brawling, the hair-raising drive in Malcolm's sports car, the sudden silence of the fields by night was eerie. There was not much light and I had to take

Joan's arm to prevent her stumbling as we walked down the fields towards the cottage. We walked in silence. My mind kept running over the events of the evening, recalling Sue's words and expressions, trying to make sense of it all.

Joan must have been similarly preoccupied, for when we got near the cottage she said, 'You probably need someone like Sue.'

That could've been construed as a compliment to Sue or a veiled insult to me, but I didn't ask Joan to explain herself.

When we got into the cottage I put a match to the fire that I had laid that morning. Joan went into the kitchen and put a kettle on the stove.

'It's not a question of "someone like",' I said.

She came in from the kitchen and said, 'If this great love affair is all you say it is, you're probably going to be a father to another man's child. Ironical, isn't it?'

'You're looking further ahead than either of us has done,' I said. 'Nobody's mentioned marriage.'

Joan knelt down by the fire and stretched her hands out to the flames. 'Oh no, Sue wouldn't mention marriage. She's much too clever. That was one of my mistakes.' She smiled ruefully, not at me, but into the fire. 'And another was that I slept with you so soon. I didn't believe you when you said she wasn't your mistress, but I realise it could be true. It all adds up. That creepy mother is probably in on it as well. You're well and truly trapped, my lad.'

I said, 'I don't see how you can say that after what you've seen this evening. Not only the fact that she left us, but when we came together again, in the pub after the fight, she very obviously kept herself in the background, as if to say, "I don't want him, you can have him".'

Joan let out a tinkling laugh. 'Oh, it's incredible how a clever woman can run rings round a man. Is he worried, then, that the love of his life has jilted him? And does it fall to his pregnant ex-mistress to reassure him that she hasn't?' The ironies are coming thick and fast tonight, aren't they?'

'You don't know Sue,' I said. 'You don't know how her mind works.'

'It works like any other woman's,' Joan said. 'If I'd been in her position I'd have done exactly the same as she did tonight. I'd have thought: by backing down for this evening I can keep my dignity, avoid inflicting what you call unnecessary hurt and humiliation on the other woman, and at the same time give cocksure Stuart a bit of a jolt, which will keep his ardour on the boil.'

I shook my head. 'That's not the way she thinks,' I said. 'Throughout this she's been chiefly concerned to keep my ardour off the boil.'

Joan smiled. The fire was blazing now. She moved away from it and lowered herself heavily into an armchair. She sighed, laid her head back and closed her eyes. 'Well, at least I shall have picked up a few tips for when I want to catch me a father for my baby,' she said. 'Rule one: don't sleep with him. Rule two: never mention marriage. Rule three: keep him guessing and give him the occasional sharp jolt.'

'And rule four,' I said, 'is never to let your cynicism show through.'

'Ah!' She opened her eyes and looked at me. 'That, I think, will be the hardest rule to stick by.'

On the bus to Battle the next day we sat in silence for most of the journey, and towards the end of it Joan said, 'I've been thinking about the flat and I don't think I want to go there now.'

'You want to stay in London, in that flat without anyone to share the rent?'

'I don't know. Neither prospect is particularly exciting, but I came from a dreary seaside town, and I think that to end up back in one after just a year would be insufferably depressing.'

I could see her point, put like that. It brought to mind the bright, enthusiastic and ambitious girl, just up in London from Leigh-on-Sea, who I had once loved.

I said, 'You needn't think of it as ending up, but it could be preferable for a year or so while you get used to things.'

'Things? What things?'

This was getting awkward. The questions were shot out, barbed. I said, 'Well, you know, being a mother, having a baby to cope with.'

I knew it sounded lame and invited scorn, but she only said, rather wearily, 'I can't decide now, but don't confirm with Mrs Beavis or put any money down for a few days. I'll think it over. Phone me in a couple of days' time.'

Just before the train left, she leaned out of the window and said, 'Do something for me. Tell your mistress's creepy mother what she can do with her baby clothes.'

His Dear Time's Waste - Stuart Holroyd

9

After Joan had gone I immediately rang Sue. She had been expecting my call, she said, but she put me off going round to the bungalow, repeating her parting words of the previous night, 'I need time to think'. I protested that what we needed was to talk things over, but she was adamant that she didn't want to be, as she said, 'railroaded', any more, but needed time and space to get things in perspective, and begged me to respect that need if I still cared about our 'tender shoot'. She said, 'Give me a few days, at least, and maybe do a bit of thinking things over yourself.'

Back at the cottage, I was at a loss. I did some wood-gathering and chopping and had a desultory look through the script of *The Prophet* though I could work up no interest in getting involved with it. Sue had urged me to 'do a bit of thinking' about our situation. I did. I kept thinking about what both John and Joan had said about the 'conspiracy' of mother and daughter, and possibly father as well, to 'net' me, although only to still dismiss it as preposterous. In fact, after the bonfire night events I was no longer so confident of Sue's love. 'It was an impossible situation for me,' she had said in the Senlac Hotel bar, and later in the car, 'You trample all over everything and everyone.' Her distancing herself then, and this morning on the phone, was worrying.

My experience was that love was not something that could be given or withdrawn at will, that it was indeed something that possessed you irrespective of your will, but though it could not be withdrawn it might be withdrawn from, and what I had apprehensions about was not whether I had been conspired against but that Sue's standing back on that night and on the phone might have indicated on her part a decision to stand further back and for longer.

She had talked of 'getting things into perspective' and not wanting to be 'railroaded', which were ominous words. 'Railroaded', I thought, was an appropriate term for how I had been involuntarily, though foolishly, driven along by circumstances to bring Joan and Sue together at the bonfire night. Before that, all had seemingly been going well, Joan was going to take the flat, I had my job and income lined up, and Sue and I had developed through our lovemaking a depth of joyous intimacy that I felt established a basis for a long term bond, surely one that couldn't be fractured by a single act of thoughtless stupidity. She must feel the same, she couldn't feel otherwise if the experience had been for her anything like as overwhelming and significant as it had been for me. It was ridiculous for her to ask me to wait a few days while she mulled things over. What did she expect me to do during those days? There was nothing I could do except sink into a state of gloomy and resentful mulling myself. It was intolerable. Whatever the consequences, I resolved to go and see her the next day. I wouldn't phone in advance, I would just turn up and insist on talking things over.

However, by the next morning I had had further thoughts and decided that I would not fall into the role of the abject and contrite lover. I would call her bluff, if such it was, give her a few days to think it over, go to London and start to look for the room or flat that I would soon have to move into. After a snack breakfast I walked across the fields to the phone near the village store and arranged to spend a couple of nights at Michael and Anne's. I resisted an impulse to phone Sue, judging it best to do so when I was already in London.

Michael and Anne had had several homes in the couple of years they had been together, and I hadn't previously visited their current one, a ground floor flat in a quiet road in St John's Wood. Anne answered the door to my ring and welcomed me with a hug and a kiss on the cheek. Scruff the lurcher also greeted me, as if he remembered his visit to the house in the summer, with a couple of barks and a vigorous nuzzling of my crutch. Anne looked pretty, in a long blue polka-dot dress tightly gathered at the waist, and when she embraced me there was a distinct whiff of her familiar *Mitsouko* perfume. Michael was out at a lunch with some film people, she explained, but should be back soon. The flat was a very modern open-plan space with long bold-patterned curtains, a glass-topped dining table with chrome-framed dining chairs around it, a big basketweave sofa with matching armchairs and a large fitted kitchen with bright orange walls and matching formica work-tops. They had sub-let it, Anne explained, from friends of Michael's, the actor couple David McCallum and Jill Ireland. It was quite expensive, at six pounds a week, and they had had to come up with a two hundred pound premium, but they needed a place where they could receive and entertain people in some style.

'Michael must be doing well,' I said. 'So what about the marriage plans you were talking about in the summer?'

Anne made a little gesture of exasperation. 'He wants to make a big splash of it, with two hundred guests and a reception at the Café Royal, would you believe? And he's talking about buying me a two hundred pound engagement ring, which is all very exciting and lovely, but between you and me at present we're pretty well broke. He's got projects and promises galore, but right now we're really cash-strapped. We're hoping these film people will come up with an advance.'

'It must be very worrying.'

She shrugged it off. 'It's been the story of our life, hasn't it? Things work out. Michael is a sweetie, but he can be very impulsive and extravagant. I suppose in that way we're not very good for one another. You were always so careful and sensible, and kept me in check.'

'It wasn't a matter of being careful,' I said. 'There was never anything to be extravagant with.'

'I know, but you did keep me in check. Now I'm up to my ears in debt, with over a hundred pounds overdraft, and Pemberthys and Dickins and Jones both threatening to take me court if I don't pay them off pronto. So don't be surprised if before long I'm banged up in Holloway. Michael doesn't know how much I'm in the red. I don't suppose you could help out with a hundred or so, sweetie, now you've got the BBC job?'

'I wish I could,' I said, 'but I've already got an overdraft on the strength of the job, and I have to set up a flat or something for Joan.'

'I know, darling, I shouldn't have asked. Anyway, I wouldn't really mind going to jail because the dresses the women have to wear have become quite fashionable. The "sack look" is all the rage and they're frightfully expensive. Shall we have tea?'

'I was wondering when you'd ask,' I laughed. 'Let me come and help you in your space age kitchen.'

'So how's your love life?' she asked in the kitchen as we waited for the kettle to boil. 'Still crazy about the Colonel's daughter?'

'Still crazy,' I nodded.

'Oh dear! Marriage prospects?'

'Maybe.'

'My strange, solitary Stuart,' she said, with an unusually direct and rueful look, 'are you sure you're cut out for it? In those letters you wrote me from Germany, after you'd left knowing that I'd get involved with Michael, you very clearly said that the married state didn't suit you – those were your exact words – and that you didn't want to get what you called 'entangled' again.'

From flippancy to searching earnestness in the space of a minute. Typical Anne. 'That was over two years ago,' I said.

'Which isn't long, is it? You know, I still think about you a lot, and I've often regretted that we got divorced. Marriage isn't easy, I know, and I do have qualms about marrying Michael, though I love him, but I've sometimes thought that that you and I might have worked it out. And now I worry about what you've got yourself into, and think I should never have let you go.'

'Much as I love you,' I said, I don't think it could have worked out between us. When you came to Battle in the summer you asked me to give you and Mike my blessing. Now I have to ask the same of you.'

'Of course, for what it's worth.'

'It's worth a lot. Everyone else, with the exception of Tom, seems to disapprove of my involvement with the Colonel's daughter, as you call her, and some have even warned me of the dastardly machinations of the family to snare me.'

I was pleased that Anne laughed at the very idea.

Michael's boisterous homecoming, augmented by Scruff the lurcher's welcome, announced his good news before he said a word, and when he did speak it was to welcome me with a vigorous handshake and the greeting, 'Great to see you, daddy-o, and congrats about the job.' Then, turning to Anne, 'They liked the synopsis, they bought it.' She embraced him jubilantly, so jubilantly in fact that he had to qualify his enthusiasm with: 'There's no immediate cash, but that'll come when we get to contract stage, probably in a couple of weeks'

'I suppose we can manage on a diet of spaghetti and boiled eggs for a couple more weeks,' Anne said.

The project that Michael had been negotiating was a film version of a French novel, *The Blockhouse*. He talked enthusiastically about it later, over our spaghetti bolognaise dinner. It had something in common with *The Tenth Chance*, he said, being about a group of men trapped in a German prison camp blockhouse by a bombardment in which all exits were destroyed. 'They have stocks of food and drink and candles,' Mike explained, 'and the drama focuses on their arguments and passions and the psychological states they go through in their virtual entombment. The hero, Rouquet, is quite like your Peter Moen, the way he's always asking himself questions, but with the difference that he doesn't doubt, he sees doubt as a weakness that would drag him down to the level of the others, the level of animal existence, and he sees his responsibility to bring the others round to his way of thinking and believing. But as time goes by the original seven men are reduced to Rouquet and one other before they are eventually rescued by an incredible stroke of luck.'

'Sounds a pretty grim tale for a movie,' I said, 'without any women's parts.'

'It's true there's no part for Marilyn Monroe or Doris Day,' Mike laughed, 'but these aren't Hollywood types, and they think there's enough drama and enough fun – especially when the guys find an old bicycle and start having races – to get the bums on seats. I haven't done it justice in the telling. I'll send you a copy of the synopsis, and you'll see.'

'I'm sure it will be great,' I said. 'I'll look forward to reading it.'

Before dinner we had talked about the reason for my visit and Michael had said that he knew someone who he thought would have a room to rent, if I didn't mind being in the Belsize Park area.

'I know it well, and with fond memories,' I said, and Anne giggled, knowing that I was referring to the couple of years when we had lived in Belsize Crescent. So an appointment was made to go and see the room the next day.

Susan was agitated when I phoned. 'Where are you? I've been expecting you to call all day.'

'You asked me to give you time to think things over.'

'I took the bus out to the cottage this morning, and you weren't there.'

'I'm in London, came up to look for a room or a flat. We're seeing a place in Belsize tomorrow morning.'

'We?' Did she sound a little perturbed? her tone made me wonder. Could she perhaps imagine I might be going back to Joan?

'I'm staying with Michael and Anne. He's just sold a film option. We've been celebrating with spaghetti bolognaise and a bottle of red wine.'

'Oh, come back soon. I'm sorry.'

'I'm the one who should be sorry. I really was an idiot. It was unforgivable of me. So have you thought things over?'

'I've thought of nothing else. I was so worried when you weren't at the cottage. When will you come back?'

'Tomorrow.'

'Make it soon. Phone and tell me when.'

'I will. I love you.

'Oh yes, do.'

When I came out of the bedroom, where I had gone to phone, Anne said 'What are you looking so pleased about?'

I didn't answer her then, but I did the next morning. Over breakfast I told her and Michael about the whole bonfire night brouhaha, the visit to the bungalow, the march down the High Street with two women in tow, Sue's disappearance, the bonfire lighting scene and the fireworks, the ruckus in the car park, my being spurned by both women and Sue telling me I trampled all over everything and everyone. Michael thought the story very funny and hooted with laughter, particularly at the fight scene, and Anne was amused too but at the end she said, 'You did very well to come up here. She wanted to keep you guessing and you turned the tables.'

I said, 'I didn't intend it that way, but I was relieved last night when she said she'd been to the cottage.'

'So you did the right thing but for the wrong reason,' Michael commented.

Anne said, 'You never did understand women's ways, but now you may have snared yourself one by practising them.'

Mike too was surprised at the epigrammatic turn from scatty Annie. 'I could use that in a play,' he said.

The Belsize Park flat was perfect, quite small but with separate sitting room, a kitchen and a bedroom with a large double bed, which was the feature that pleased me above all. I paid a retainer and arranged to move in at the end of the month.

I prevaricated quite a bit before calling Joan. She'd asked me to give her a couple of days to think about the flat, and that was only yesterday, but as I was in London it seemed sensible to see if we could get the matter settled.

She sounded quite cheery and positive when she answered the phone. I said, 'I know it may be a bit soon, but as I'm in London I thought I'd ring to see if you have decided about the flat.'

She was more curious about what I was doing in London than concerned to answer my question immediately, but when she did so it was to say that she had decided to go to the flat, or at least give it a try for a few months. In that case, I said, I would start the work as soon as I got back to the country. 'And there are two things you may not have thought of,' she said. 'I won't be going out much, so I'd like to have television. And of course a telephone line.'

'I'll see to it,' I said.

'It's the least you can do,' she said in that by now quite innocuous mocking tone.

The 'Pilgrims' Rest', on the Green just opposite the tall Norman gateway to the Abbey, was not the sort of place that we normally went to, but as my train from Charing Cross arrived mid-afternoon and before the pubs opened Sue had suggested that we should meet there. It was an olde-worlde tea-house, 14th Century large barn of a place with high ceilings, massive oak beams, carefully laid tables with lace doilies, and elderly shuffling waitresses. It smelt of hot scones and cool propriety.

I was already seated at a corner table when Sue came in. I rose to greet her with an embrace constrained by awareness of the gaze of the idle waitress who had already asked for my order, but the eyes that mine engaged were quite unconstrained in their joyous and passionate expression.

'I was so worried when I went to the cottage,' she said. 'I couldn't imagine what had happened.'

The waitress returned, and I impatiently ordered tea and scones.

'Earl Grey, Lapsong Souchong, Darjeeling, or Typhoo?'

I deferred to Sue and was pleased when she chose Typhoo, no doubt the management's concessionary option for the hoi polloi.

'I should have phoned you earlier,' I said, 'but you were emphatic about needing time to think, and I too was worried. I couldn't just sit around at the cottage.'

'It was a horrible evening. I was so distraught at the end.'

'We all were. And it was my fault. I'm sorry. But in a way I'm not so sorry, because you went to the cottage, and that tells me something I really needed to know.'

'You must have known already how much I care, after those times we spent together.'

'Care?'

'Alright, love you,' she conceded. 'In fact I hate not to be with you now, all the time. But one thing I have been brooding on since the bonfire night is that we can't consider ourselves as the central figures in all this.'

'I know, and I understand how you feel about Joan, and I'm going to do all I can for her,' I said. I told her about Joan's going off to London undecided about the flat after the bonfire night events, and how she had now decided to go ahead with it, which meant that I was going to have my work cut out in the next couple of weeks preparing the place. I also told her about the Belsize Park flat, and particularly about the large bed and my anticipation of her sharing it with me.

'But that's going to be weeks away,' I said. 'I don't know that I can wait so long.'

'Is it so desperate?' It was a surprising question. By 'it' she clearly meant the need for sex. Maybe there was in it the implication that the need should not be allowed to subvert love, as perhaps was a risk in the present situation.

But I answered frankly, 'Yes, it is desperate. It has been the more so since we first made love. I can't help thinking about it.'

She smiled, reached across the table and took my hands. 'Me too. It becomes like an obsession, doesn't it? I wasn't only worried when you weren't at the cottage. I was disappointed too.'

The Heathfield bus would be along soon. I begged Susan to come back to the cottage with me. She said she couldn't at such short notice, but promised to arrange to come the next day.

Before we left that most incongruous venue for a lovers' meeting since the station waiting room in *Brief Encounter*, Susan asked the waitress sweetly for a 'granny bag' to take our uneaten scones home for Daphina. I loved her the more for that.

It was getting dark by the time I arrived at the cottage, and the place was as cold as a tomb. It would have been rather an unwelcoming place to bring Susan back to. However, there was plenty of wood in, and paraffin for the bedroom stove, so I would be able to make it cosy for her visit the next day. That night I kept thinking about the implication of her saying she had been disappointed not to find me at the cottage, and her talk about being desperate. Those were feelings I shared and could understand, and they were, I thought, utterly inconsistent with Joan's image of Sue as the cool schemer. 'She'll forgive you, everyone always does,' had been another of her sour aspersions, and clearly Sue had forgiven me, even after accusing me of 'trampling all over everyone and everything', but it was just daft, if not malicious, to suggest that her forgiveness was cynical. It could no more be so than my going to London had been, although Anne had figured that as 'turning the tables' on Sue, and a resort to 'women's ways'. Then there had been John, with his fictional analogy and crazy speculation about familial plotting. Did all these people live in a world where deviousness and manipulation were the norm, where so many Iagos and Becky Sharps strolled at their ease? Well, that was certainly not my and Susan's world, nor would it ever be.

After what was to be our last day together at the cottage, though I was not aware of the fact at the time, I went into Hastings daily and worked on the flat. I had been doing that for just a few days when the first snow fell. Brightling Needle, a landmark not far from the cottage, is the highest point in Sussex, so the snow fell heavier and thicker up there, and although it turned the woods and hills into an entrancing winter wonderland, it made getting to and from the cottage and all the chores of living there increasingly difficult and time-consuming. I would obviously save time and money and get more work done quickly by staying at the flat. I had already paid Mrs. Beavis a month's rent, so only had to buy in the bedding, and some heaters to augment the fixed gas fire in the sitting room, to make the flat habitable. Decorating was not so onerous a task as I had feared; in fact I quite enjoyed transforming the dingy and rather forbidding interior into a warm and welcoming one. Susan did not help me, as Joan had cattily proposed, in 'whitewashing', but she did help with the choice of such things as colours and curtains. She said she felt awkward being there, however, particularly after we had met Mrs Beavis in the hall and I had introduced her as a friend of Joan's, and she was adamant about not staying the night, or even making love there in the daytime, a suggestion I put only tentatively and didn't press, considering that any pressure would be construed as another 'trample'. The snow didn't melt, so the cottage remained inhospitable, and it seemed that our love life too was being driven into hibernation. Sue had said that we mustn't think of ourselves as the central figures in our present situation, which was of course a morally commendable attitude, but it didn't allay the nagging need that thinking of her and being with her aroused.

I had given the BBC people Susan's phone number as an interim way of contacting me while I was getting settled in London, and one morning she came to the flat to tell me they had called and asked me to ring back. I did so immediately. The number they had given was the direct line to Donald Wilson at the BBC, who asked if I might be available some time the following week for a meeting to discuss the job in general and in particular the project I would be working on. We arranged a date and time, and afterwards I told Sue and proposed that we should go to London together for a couple of days and stay at Belsize Park. I could probably bring forward the start of my tenancy by a couple of weeks, and it would be an opportunity buy some of the few things that didn't come with the flat, such as the bedding, and generally to get settled in.

'You mean an opportunity to initiate the lovely big bed?' she laughed. I said the thought had occurred to me, though there were other things we could do, maybe visit Tom in his new place, or Mike and Anne.

'Tom, yes,' Sue said, 'but spare me from meeting another of your ex-amours for a while.'

Daphina readily agreed to look after Christopher for a couple of days, a fact which Joan no doubt would have regarded as typically 'creepy', and I arranged with the landlord to take the keys to the flat early. By the evening of the day before my meeting we had moved in, kitted the place out and gloriously initiated the double bed. In the evening we had a curry at an Indian restaurant on Haverstock Hill and went to a showing of *Room at the Top* at the nearby cinema. Sue was close to tears at the end, with the death of Alice in a car crash after Joe has left her. I told her that John had asked me if she was my Alice and I had replied that she was much more, and that I was no Joe Lampton, willing to marry for convenience and turning his back on love.

She either didn't register or chose not to acknowledge my indirect avowal, for she asked: 'Why should John have asked you about me?'

The implication was that the question had been intrusive or inappropriate. I replied: 'Because he's a friend. We were just chatting. It was the last time I was at Chepstow Road, after the broadcast.'

'Doesn't he approve? Does he think you should marry Joan?'

'You've just seen the film. Do you think he approved of Joe? John is a novelist. He tells stories.'

'He's also a friend of yours.'

'And as such he just wants the best for me,' I said, 'and he now knows without doubt that that means being with you.'

Well, obviously I couldn't tell her about his wildly speculative scenario with the *Pride and Prejudice* analogy. That was just another idea for a novel.

My second meeting with Donald Wilson at the BBC was for the purpose of familiarising me with the details of the job. I was introduced to colleagues in the department, including the writer I would be sharing an office with, Troy Kennedy Martin, later the creator of the police drama series, *Z-Cars*. I was shown around a studio where a rehearsal was in progress, and over lunch we discussed the project that Donald proposed I might undertake as part of my job, which was to read through the stories of H.G. Wells with a view to selecting those that might be suitable for adaptation as TV plays, and write up one of them as a complete playscript, bearing in mind that it would be for live studio production, so location changes were limited. I would have the services of a secretary/typist if required, but attendance at the office was not obligatory, though I would be expected to participate in the script department's weekly conference on Thursdays. Sometimes at these meetings I might be assigned as script editor to plays in the planning or rehearsal stage, a job which generally didn't involve any writing or editing but was intended to enable writers to have studio and production experience.

That was about it, he said. Did I have any questions? I said I had none for the present, but things would no doubt turn up that I needed to consult about, and I was looking forward to taking up the job in a couple of weeks' time.

In the evening Sue and I had arranged to call on Tom. Following his directions, we found the chapel located on the Kensington/Earl's Court border. Entering from the street into a hall, we were confronted by a notice with arrows announcing: 'Heaven's Above' and 'Lucifer's Below', so we knew at once that we had come to the right place. There was even the 'Beware of the Doggerel' notice on Tom's door, which was accessed from the hall by a short staircase. The flat was not exactly a basement, but was sunk a metre or so below street level, so that you saw the legs of passers-by through the windows. All the familiar furnishings and kitsch devilish accessories from Chepstow Road were there, but as the space was bigger and had a separate kitchen there were some new items, notably a television set, a big sofa and a rather grand knee-hole desk. Tom explained that he had undertaken more work at the *Evening Standard* and in addition to contributing to the gossip column was now writing some of the leaders, so he had had a pay rise. To the news of my job he said:

'Good old Auntie BBC, always can be depended on for a juicy hand-out. Not much call for Existentialist dramas there, though, eh?'

'I suppose not,' I said. 'My assignment is to trawl through the works of Wells for stories and adapt one of them for TV.'

'Could do worse,' Tom said. 'If it was ITV you'd be assigned to the kitchen sink.' He was referring, I knew, to ITV's successful social-realist *Armchair Theatre* series. 'But right now,' he continued, 'we must assign ourselves to a little serious drinking by way of celebration and house-warming.' He poured three large glasses of brandy and we sipped the proposed toasts, plus one, he added, to Sue and me and our future.

'So how did the unveiling go?' I asked, aware that the blue plaque stunt was to have taken place the previous week.

'Like a damp squib,' Tom said. 'You could say it rained on Bill's parade, and with a vengeance. No TV news crew turned up, and from the papers there was just a gaggle of cub reporters.' He chuckled at the memory. 'One of them called out, "Who's Tom Greenwell?" and Bill answered "The Devil incarnate" and the next day his rag carried a paragraph with some lame quip about the angry young men recruiting Aleister Crowley. It was, my dears, a total non-event.'

'And how about Bill's other project, the Spartacans?' Sue asked.

'Ah, that was another. My, you have been out of touch, down there in the sticks, haven't you? At the time of the election somebody put it about – we suspected it was Chris Logue – that the Spartacans were going to support the Oswald Mosley candidate in the North Kensington constituency. The press took it up, Oliver Moxon and others, including the publisher, dissociated themselves, and as the membership dwindled Bill declared that the country wasn't ready for the revolution yet and meanwhile he would devote himself to writing.'

'Time of Totality', I said, recalling Bill's proposed title for his novel. 'So how is the magnum opus going?'

Tom waved a finger. 'We don't ask,' he said. 'If we did, he'd no doubt say "Like a bomb", though I suspect it's a bomb with a very long time fuse. Meanwhile I hear he's short of the readies and is dabbling a bit in the antiques trade.'

'It seems that for all of us it's the end of an era,' I said.

'I've seen eras come and go for centuries,' Tom said, 'and every ending is a new beginning. Depends on how you look at it, like seeing whether the glass is half full or half empty. Speaking of which, I see you could both do with a top-up.'

He poured more brandy, proposing that we drink to the new decade. 'To the nineteen-sixties, and all the marvels and madness they're going to bring for our diversion.'

And that was just the beginning of an evening that ended with our being in such a merrily tipsy state that when Sue bade Tom farewell she did so with a kiss and an inclination of the body such as she had bestowed on me on her visits to Chepstow Road, an act of coquetry that aroused in me, later when we got back to the flat and I made love to the most desirable woman in the world, an unprecedented fury and violence of possession.

It was early in the morning when the call came. I was a couple of weeks into the BBC job and preparing to go to the office at the TV centre when Sheila rang with the news that Joan had just been taken into Paddington hospital. Sheila had been with her through the night at the flat, having gone over from Putney when Joan started to have contractions, as they had previously arranged. It was a bit premature, but Joan seemed fine, and if I wanted up to date information or to arrange to visit I should ring the maternity ward. She gave me the number and I rang straight away. I had to identify myself as the father-to-be before the nurse told me that *Miss* Levers – the emphasis conveyed flinty disapproval –

was in labour and I should ring again in the afternoon. I did so at about three o'clock and was told that Joan had just had a boy and they were both doing well. I would be able to visit between seven and eight in the evening.

Bearing a tribute of chocolates and flowers I went to the hospital promptly at seven o'clock. A nurse showed me into a ward of about thirty beds and pointed out Joan's in the far corner. She was lying face down and didn't see me approach. I touched her shoulder and said, 'Joan'. She turned over, smiled and sat up. I kissed her on the cheek, and said she looked well.

'I feel marvellous,' she said. 'You can't imagine what a luxury it is to be able to lie on your stomach.' She had had a bad time, a long labour and a lot of pain, but it was over now and it had been worth it. The baby was perfect, and so sweet, such a blind helpless thing with little wavy arms. I should see him, but I couldn't at present because they took the new-borns away between feeds to let the mothers get some rest.

'I'm so glad I went through with it,' she said. 'We did the right thing, didn't we?' I said I didn't know about the 'we'. She was the one who had gone through all the suffering. 'No,' she said, 'you went through it too, but in a different way. And I promise that we won't be a burden to you.'

She looked radiant and lovely and I wondered whether, if I hadn't met Sue... But I suppressed the thought. I told her about the flat, how I had decorated and furnished it, and that it would be ready to move into whenever she liked. She would be out of hospital, she said, in five days' time, and would at first go back to her flat as the rent was paid up to the end of the month. Sheila had invited her to Putney for Christmas, so perhaps we could make the move to Hastings during the week between Christmas and New Year. I said that would be fine and that I would try to arrange for a car, but that wouldn't be necessary, she said, because Peter had a car and he and Sheila would take them to Hastings, so we could plan to meet down there.

'One thing you can do, though,' she said as I was preparing to leave, 'is help me decide what to call the baby. I'd like it to be something a bit different, unusual.'

'Like Aloysius?' I suggested.

She grimaced. 'A bit pretentious, and people wouldn't know how to spell it. No, something simple, but different.'

'Bruce?' I said.

Joan liked it. She clapped and said, 'Yes, Bruce Levers. It sounds good. Bruce Holroyd might have sounded better, but it's good.' She smiled to say that no reproach was intended.

And so it came about that our son acquired the name of Susan's erstwhile suitor. It certainly wasn't the case, as someone suggested later, that I proposed the name by way of linking the two losers in the situation. It was quite spontaneous, an instant response to an unanticipated question, carrying no subconscious baggage. In retrospect, the very idea of there being winners and losers seems inapposite. It would be truer to say that for all concerned there were both losses and gains. Young Bruce was certainly a winner, for at one time his very existence had been in the balance. That was something I realised to my shame when I met him eventually, some twenty years later. He had written to me and I had invited him to lunch in a West End restaurant. Meeting him was like confronting myself at the time of this narrative. He was studying medicine at Guys Hospital at the time, and would later pursue a career as a doctor and consultant psychiatrist. I knew that Joan had left Hastings and gone back to London after a couple of years and that she had subsequently married someone called Adamson. They had moved to Surrey, had eventually divorced, and Joan had become, Bruce said, a stalwart of the local synagogue. He later met his half-brother and half-sisters, for the year after Bruce was born Susan gave birth to twin girls, and fifteen months later to a boy. Existence, rather than Existentialism, became the thing that preoccupied me. I worked at a school of English, later set up my own school in St Leonards-on-Sea, and later still a second one in Eastbourne. But all that is another story. With the 1960s came another age, and quite other life challenges and experiences, the quotidian ordinariness that does not so readily resolve itself into a narrative, and where romantic love is hard pressed to retain its foothold.

It was romantic love that had narrowed down life for me from a prospect of infinite possibilities to one of very finite realities, and that made me accept gladly the dissolution of the sense of the unique importance of myself and my work. It was romantic love, too, that had endowed me within three years with a family of four: an aptly ironical turn-out for one who had so determinedly eschewed marriage and fatherhood.

I never really knew whether the imperatives of romantic love had driven Susan as compulsively as they had me. Several times over the ensuing years John and Pat Braine and their family came to stay with us in St Leonards, but of course John never again alluded to his conspiracy theory. I occasionally recalled it, though, particularly on occasions when Sue expressed her discontent with the reproach, 'I thought I was marrying a writer, not a bloody teacher.' Well, we had had our midsummer dream, with its magical moon and golden cornfield, its balmy days and nights and its deliciously pervasive eroticism, and if my Queen Titania eventually awoke to the real nature of her paramour, so equally did her ass.

www.ingramcontent.com/pod-product-compliance
Lightning Source LLC
Chambersburg PA
CBHW031312160426
43196CB00007B/502

9 780992 869694